Dialectical Approaches
to
Studying
Personal Relationships

Dialectical Approaches to Studying Personal Relationships

Edited by

Barbara M. Montgomery
Millersville University

Leslie A. Baxter
University of Iowa

IEA LAWRENCE ERLBAUM ASSOCIATES, PUBLISHERS
1998 Mahwah, New Jersey   London

Copyright © 1998 by Lawrence Erlbaum Associates, Inc.
All rights reserved. No part of this book may be repro-
duced in any form, by photostat, microfilm, retrieval
system, or any other means, without the prior written
permission of the publisher.

Lawrence Erlbaum Associates, Inc., Publishers
10 Industrial Avenue
Mahwah, New Jersey 07430

Cover Design by Kathryn Houghtaling Lacey

Library of Congress Cataloging-in-Publication Data

Dialectical approaches to studying personal relationships /
edited by Barbara M. Montgomery, Leslie A. Baxter.
      p. cm.
  Includes bibliographical references and index.
  ISBN 0-8058-2112-0 (hardcover : alk. paper). — ISBN
0-8058-2113-9 (pbk. : alk. paper)
    1. Interpersonal communication. 2. Interpersonal rela-
tions. 3. Dialectic. I. Montgomery, Barbara M. II. Baxter, Leslie A.
P94.7.S53 1997
158—dc21   97–37789
                                                CIP

Books published by Lawrence Erlbaum Associates are printed
on acid-free paper, and their bindings are chosen for strength
and durability.

Printed in the United States of America
10 9 8 7 6 5 4 3 2

For our daughters,
Angela and Emma,
with whom we dialogue in delight.

Contents

Preface   **vii**

1   A Guide to Dialectical Approaches to Studying   **1**
Personal Relationships
Leslie A. Baxter and Barbara M. Montgomery

2   Telling Stories: Dialectics of Relational Transition   **17**
Richard L. Conville

3   Mucking Around Looking for Truth   **41**
Arthur P. Bochner, Carolyn Ellis, and Lisa
Tillmann-Healy

4   Writing About *Friendship Matters*: A Case Study in   **63**
Dialectical and Dialogical Inquiry
William K. Rawlins

5   "Going Into and Coming Out of the Closet": The   **83**
Dialectics of Stigma Disclosure
Kathryn Dindia

6   Dialectic Empiricism: Science and Relationship   **109**
Metaphors
C. Arthur VanLear

7   Choice Points for Dialecticians: A Dialectical–   **137**
Transactional Perspective on Close Relationships
Barbara B. Brown, Carol M. Werner, and Irwin Altman

8   Dialogism and Relational Dialectics   155
    Barbara M. Montgomery and Leslie A. Baxter

Author Index   185

Subject Index   191

Preface

Over many years, we have been exploring ideas about relational dialectics in conference papers, journal articles, book chapters, and a book. We have not been alone. We have had the good fortune to share these scholarly adventures with a number of others charting their own courses in dialectical thinking. We summarized the perspectives of many of these fellow adventurers in our book, *Relating: Dialogues and Dialectics* (1996). We realized, as we summarized their work, the irony of our action. At the same time that we were embracing Mikhail Bakhtin's notion of multivocality, we were speaking for our dialectical colleagues, using our authorial voice to represent their ideas. In that moment of irony, the idea for this edited volume was born. We decided that it would be more consistent with our Bakhtinian perspective if these other dialectical theorists spoke for themselves. Many of the authors we spoke for are authors of chapters in this edited text. We invited them to join us in this project because each has something unique to say about social dialectics and because what they have to say is intriguing to us.

We also invited them to author chapters because they were willing to construct their works within the guiding framework we set for the project. We asked authors to emphasize the characteristics of their dialectical view that set them apart from other dialectical scholars and to describe their methods of studying relationships from a dialectical perspective. We also asked authors to honor the values of dialogism, which we learned from Bakhtin's writings. Essentially, these included showing respect for different and sometimes contradictory views, assuming that different and even contradictory views can be valid, joining in a dialogue with us and the other contributors about their emerging ideas, and allowing the dialogue that occurs within this frame the freedom to express creative, unique ideas.

The authors represented here struggled successfully, we believe, to be true to these commitments. From our first group dinner conversation about the book project (involving 10 of us) to the final exchange of editors' observations and authors' reactions, the flow of ideas was exquisitely informed, passionately engaged, creatively complicated, and respectfully articulated. In these chapters, readers will see the authors' convictions of the worth of their own views and, at the same time, their acknowledgment of the worth of others' views. Readers also will see the dialectic of similarity and difference play out within each chapter.

This book, then, describes many different and useful ways of understanding personal relationships from a dialectical perspective. For this purpose, it is written for scholars in higher education, both faculty and students, across the many fields in the social sciences and the humanities that seek answers to questions about how people relate to one another. Just as important, a second purpose of this book is to model a form of scholarly communication in which multiple voices can be acknowledged as valid, the worth of one perspective is not measured by the denigration of another, and difference is celebrated as conducive to learning, not threatening to it. For this purpose, this volume is written for all scholars who pursue new ideas. We invite you, the reader, to accept the guidelines and join in the dialogue.

We would like to thank all of those who worked behind the scenes to produce this book. Our special thanks go to Angela E. Montgomery for her editing and indexing help.

Barbara M. Montgomery
Leslie A. Baxter

1

A Guide to Dialectical Approaches to Studying Personal Relationships

LESLIE A. BAXTER
University of Iowa

BARBARA M. MONTGOMERY
Millersville University

Recall the last time you were introduced to a family. We'll refer to the family as the Smiths. If your experience was like ours, you probably sought out information that would enable you both to differentiate the Smiths from other families and to differentiate one Smith family member from another. That is, you were engaged in a process of locating unifying features common to all members of the Smith family while at the same time locating differences among family members. The Smiths all share the same last name. The Smiths all have thick, dark hair. The Smiths have shared "insider" stories, jokes, and idiomatic expressions. The Smiths all speak with an ever so slight hint of Kentucky roots. At the same time, two of the children appear to share their mother's nose, whereas the third child's nose does not appear to resemble anybody else's in the immediate family. Two of the family members share an interest in televised sports, an interest decidedly not shared by other family members. Some family members want water with their meal, and others do not. And so it goes as you come to know the Smith family.

Dialectical theory in the study of personal relationships is like the Smith family, and we invite you to come to know it in the same manner you come to know the Smiths. The contributions to this volume have a relationship of family resemblance; they share some features yet differ with respect to other features. As a reader, you undoubtedly form your own impressions about the pattern of similarities and differences that capture the dialectics family of theorists who study personal relationships. However, in this chapter we provide our own introduction, highlighting the similarities and differences that are apparent to us, the editors of the volume.

As you read this volume, we encourage you to frame the various chapters in a second metaphorical image in addition to the image of a family. Dialectical theory can be thought of as an intertextual dialogue, in the dialogic sense envisioned by Bakhtin (1984). The essence of dialogue, according to Bakhtin, is simultaneous differentiation from and fusion with another. To enact dialogue, the parties form a unity through conversation but only through two (or more) differentiated voices. Dialogue, unlike monologue, is multivocal. Similarly, dialectical theory is simultaneous unity and difference. The various contributors have unique perspectives on dialectics in the study of personal relationships, yet commonalities across contributors are apparent as well. However, the analogy to Bakhtinian dialogue is intended to invoke more than the interplay of similarity and difference.

Dialogue is unfinalizable, as is dialectical theory. Like other scholars in these postmodern times, we have abandoned the myth of a unified theory consisting of a set of deductively rendered axiomatic statements to which all users of the theory agree. Unified consensus is not a goal we hold for dialectical theory building. To be sure, the absence of such a goal is frustrating to some, perhaps including some contributors to this volume (see, e.g., Brown, Werner, & Altman, chap. 7). Also, some readers might argue that we should not even employ the word *theory* in the absence of total consensus among dialectical theorists on a tightly woven system of concepts, categories, and propositions. However, we think of dialectical theory as an example of what Turner (1986) referred to as *descriptive/sensitizing theories,* that is, "loosely assembled congeries of concepts intended only to sensitize and orient researchers to certain critical processes" (p. 11). In contrast to traditional social scientific theoretical perspectives, in which consistency and stability are valued and contradictions are abhorred, dialectical theory embraces the ongoing contradictory tensions between consistency and inconsistency and between stability and instability. Although all dialectical theorists focus on the contradictory and contingent nature of social life, the particular theoretical approach to which each gives voice affords us with unique insights.

The differences among dialectical theorists nicely illustrate what Bakhtin (1986) calls the *extralocality,* which characterizes dialogue between two or more persons. According to Bakhtin, each person in dialogue is located in a concrete temporal–spatial position that affords him or her a unique perspective. Each interlocutor has unique perceptions and insights unavailable to the other. For example, we have access to the other's facial expressions while he or she talks, which the other does not see, and vice versa. Each person has a "surplus of seeing" that comes from his or her unique location. Like extralocality in dialogue, the variety of perspectives on dialectics provides us with a surplus of seeing in our capacity to understand contradiction and contingency in everyday relating. Each contribution to this volume gives us a slightly different lens through which to understand the dynamics of dialectical opposition.

A dialogue consists of utterances, and we think of each chapter in this volume as a textual utterance in the dialogue of this book. Bakhtin uses the term *utterance* in a very particular way, as do we. Although spoken by a single person (or, in the case of a written utterance, an author or group of co-authors), an utterance can be viewed as a link in a dialogic chain. A given utterance does not stand by itself, but is inseparably linked to other utterances: the already spoken utterances of the past, the already spoken utterances that immediately precede it in a given conversation, the anticipated utterances that will follow from fellow speakers or writers in the conversation, and the anticipated responses that will follow from generalized others. Many utterances transpired to bring this volume to the reader, including utterances embedded in dialogues between the editors and each contributor, dialogues between and among contributors as they wrote their chapters, the intertextual dialogues between first and subsequent versions of each chapter, and intertextual dialogues between a contributor's current position and his or her prior work. To this list of utterances overlaid on top of one another, we draw your attention to one additional chain of utterances that we see in the volume. Although the chapters were not written in direct response to one another, they seem to have been written in this manner, and we encourage the reader to engage them as a dialogue in which each chapter's utterance is linked to all of the others.

When we originally conceived this book, we envisioned a volume that focused on issues of method, and, in fact, all of the contributing authors address in varying detail the particular methods they use in studying contradictions in personal relationships. However, methods never stand in isolation from underlying theoretical issues (Duck & Montgomery, 1991). Thus, this volume not only reveals similarities and differences in the methods employed by dialectical scholars, but also reveals commonalities and uniquenesses in interpretations of what dialectical theory is and should be.

SIMILARITIES AND DIFFERENCES
AT THE THEORETICAL LEVEL

Dialectical scholarship, in general, tends to cohere around four core concepts: *contradiction, change, praxis,* and *totality* (Altman, Vinsel, & Brown, 1981; Baxter, 1988; Baxter & Montgomery, 1996; Benson, 1977; Buss, 1979; Cornforth, 1968; Murphy, 1971; Rawlins, 1989; Rychlak, 1976). Although these core concepts are commonly referenced by dialectical scholarship on personal relationships, they also serve as the sites of difference.

CONTRADICTION

Contradiction refers to the dynamic interplay between unified opposites. In general, phenomena are opposites if they are actively incompatible and mutually negate one another definitionally, logically, or functionally. At the same time, dialectical opposites are interdependent with one another, and it is this interplay or unity between opposites that creates a relational system characterized by contingency, fluidity, and change. Beyond this basic conceptual level, dialectical scholars differ on several issues.

Binary and Multivocal Contradictions

The majority of contributing authors frame contradictions in terms of binary oppositions, whereas other contributors argue that contradictions are not represented well with simple, binary oppositions and might be better conceived as constellations of "complex, overlapping domains of *centripetal* or dominant forces juxtaposed with *centrifugal* or countervailing forces" (Montgomery & Baxter, chap. 8, p. 157). For example, in contrast to a binary opposition of independence versus connection, VanLear invites us to consider the multivocal web or constellation of "desires for autonomy versus commitment, attraction versus repulsion, self-concern versus concern for other, . . . identification versus differentiation . . . approach versus avoidance, association versus privacy, sharing versus possessiveness" (chap. 6, p. 120). A binary conception of contradiction most likely seems to follow an Aristotelian logic base, that is, a logic in which the opposite of "X" is "not X." By contrast, a multivocal conception seems more likely with a functional logic in which any number of phenomena can constitute a contradictory knot so long as they function to negate one another.

The Location of Contradictions

Where are contradictions located? The contributors to this volume answer this question differently, but a basic fault line can be identified with individual-level versus relationship-level analyses. Dindia (chap. 5), for example, emphasizes contradiction as an internal struggle in the mind of the individual as he or she decides whether to disclose a stigmatized identity; according to Dindia, the dialectical dilemma of openness and closedness transcends any particular relationship and resides in the individual. Grounding his argument in social evolution, VanLear (chap. 6) similarly argues that individual emotions, motivations, and cognitions often contradict one another and thus comprise individual-level dialectics. He continues on, however, to posit relationship-level dialectics, which largely reflect the parties' negotiations based on their respective individual-level dialectics. From VanLear's perspective, each individual grapples with the dialectical tension between expression and restraint; the similarity or difference in how the individuals grapple with expression and restraint would constitute a relationship-level dialectic from this perspective. Societal-level contradictions, VanLear argues, exist in the collective negotiations surrounding the interplay of persons and relationships. Like VanLear, Brown and her colleagues recognize that contradictions can be located in a variety of social units, including the individual, the relationship, the family, the social group, and the culture. However, unlike VanLear, Brown, Werner, and Altman (chap. 7) appear more interested in the contradictory interplay between and among these social units, rather than the study of contradictions that may exist within a given social unit in isolation.

Other contributors eschew a distinction between individual-level and relationship-level contradictions. Conville (chap. 7), for instance, argues that such a distinction is unnecessary because one cannot act on one's own in a relationship without affecting the relationship. Montgomery and Baxter (chap. 8) also reject traditional notions of an individual–relationship distinction, arguing from a dialogic perspective that the individual does not exist as an autonomous entity, but instead becomes only in and through relating. In contrast to Dindia and VanLear, in which the individual precedes the relationship, Montgomery and Baxter locate contradiction as a fundamentally social, not cognitive, phenomenon. Although both Rawlins (chap. 4) and Bochner, Ellis, and Tillmann-Healy (chap. 3) rely on narratives of individuals as a source of data, neither locates contradiction as an individual-level, cognitive phenomenon. Instead, narratives are stories about persons-in-relation as they interact with others.

Particular and General Contradictions

Should dialectical theorists be in the business of identifying basic contradictions with widespread generalizability across relationships and contexts? The contributors differ substantially in their answer to this question. Brown and her colleagues, for example, see too much chaos in existing dialectical research because insufficient attention has been given to the identification of a core set of generalizable contradictions. These authors assume that oppositional forces "arise from pervasive aspects of human behavior and society" (chap. 7, p. 138) and posit three basic dialectics at play across a wide variety of social units ranging from the individual to culture: dialectics of engagement, affect, and regulation. These contradictions may vary contextually in how they are manifested and managed, however. Similarly, VanLear argues for a small set of universal-like contradictions that result from social evolutionary processes: independence versus connection, expression versus restraint, and dominance versus deference. These show remarkable similarity to those posited by Brown et al. Although Dindia deals exclusively with the dialectic of openness and closedness among stigmatized persons, it is clear that she regards this dialectic as a general one relevant to both stigmatized and nonstigmatized alike.

In contrast, Bochner and his colleagues argue for the particular over the general, urging methods that provide an evocative rendering of persons' unique lived experiences. They opine that it "seem[s] unfaithful" to the essence of dialectics to abstract typologies or categories of generalized contradictions.

Remaining contributors are somewhere in the middle on the particular versus general issue. Rawlins refers to general interactional and contextual contradictions, using narrative accounts from friends at various life-course stages to illuminate the contradicting process with respect to these basic contradictions. Montgomery and Baxter argue that contradictions may be common across relationships that occupy the same sociohistorical milieu, but they urge attention to the particularities of a given relationship as well. Conville emphasizes a similar position in his call for the study of what he calls "indigenous" contradictions in conjunction with "conventional" contradictions. Some contradictions, he argues, are likely to be specific to the narrative history of a given relationship, but he recognizes the issue is not an either–or one and appreciates, as well, the general or conventional contradictions that may be widespread across relationships.

The Possibility of Different Types of Contradiction

Several of the contributing authors argue that not all contradictions are of the same order. Conville, for example, distinguishes *metadialectics* from *dialectics,* the former consisting of two dialectical pairs (security–alienation and disintegration–resynthesis) that, taken jointly, speak to how change occurs in relationships. Other authors do not invoke the label of metadialectics, but they too suggest that stability–change is a contradiction fundamentally unlike other contradictory pairs such as autonomy–connection, expression–restraint, and so forth. VanLear joins Brown and her colleagues in arguing that stability–change is not a substantively distinct dialectic, but rather a feature of all dialectical oppositions. Stability–change is a metadialectic, thus, because it is a contradiction about contradictions. Although Rawlins does not invoke the vocabulary of metadialectics, stability–change is a process that weaves throughout all of the interactional and contextual dialectics that he lists.

By contrast, Montgomery and Baxter take a different position from that of other contributors with respect to the stability–change dialectic. Although they see stability–change as a fluidity that characterizes all contradictions, they argue that the dialectic of certainty–uncertainty has integrity in its own right as a substantive contradiction.

CHANGE

A second core assumption common to dialectical theorists is the concept of change, motion, or process. It is not useful conceptually to separate change from contradiction because it is the interplay or tension of opposites that results in ongoing fluidity for any relationship. The contributors to this volume differ substantially on several issues related to change, however.

The Patterning of Change

Change refers to a difference in some phenomenon over time. Several dialectical theorists see the change process as patterned in predictable ways, in contrast to other theorists who emphasize contingency and motion instead of pattern. Common to all of the contributors who envision order in dialectical change is the notion of change as a spiral (Brown et al.; Conville; Dindia; Montgomery & Baxter; VanLear; this volume). Spiraling change combines both directional change (movement to somewhere different) with cyclical change (patterned repetition). Two contributors, Conville and VanLear, provide quite detailed models of spiraling change, the former through qualitative interpretive analysis and the latter through mathematical modeling. According to Conville, relationships spiral through four phases of relational transition based on these two metadialectics of change: security to disintegration, disintegration to alienation, alienation to resynthesis, and resynthesis to security. Thus, from Conville's perspective, dialectical change is an orderly, patterned process. VanLear sees orderly patterning, as well, in his mathematical modeling of relationship emergence; from his perspective, dialectical change consists of both a predictable component ("a scheduled trajectory") and an unpredictable component ("an unscheduled trajectory").

In contrast to those who see order in change, Bochner and his colleagues emphasize the uncertainty of dialectical motion: "The vocabulary of dialectic shifts attention away from certainty, control, and destiny toward epiphany, contingency, and chance" (chap. 3, p. 47). These authors choose to emphasize the process of feeling, understanding, and living with contradiction from firsthand, autobiographical experience. Rawlins similarly seeks to understand the process of dialectical motion in the lives of friends, eschewing "demonstrable certainty about some social patterns."

Dialectical change is an interplay of stability with instability. Some dialectical theorists clearly privilege the search for stable pattern in their work, whereas other theorists emphasize the instability of contingency. Presumably, everyone recognizes the unity of these oppositions.

Change and Resolution

With one exception, the contributors to this volume take a nonteleological view of dialectical change. That is, they do not subscribe to a view that relationships are moving toward some idealized state of resolution, synthesis, or transformation, as typified in the popularized notion of change as thesis–antithesis–synthesis. The dialectical interplay of opposites is an ongoing feature of relating, a feature of sociality that is not resolvable. Conville stands alone in giving us a view of dialectical change as teleological. According to Conville, dialectical movement through the four phases of relational transition results in relationship transformation in which relationships are propelled from one traditional stage of relationship development to the next. The thesis–antithesis interplay of security–alienation and disintegration–resynthesis transforms relationships into their next developmental stage. In contrast to the majority of contributors who see dialectical tension as omnipresent and ongoing, Conville appears to conceive dialectical tension as periods of instability that punctuate more or less stable stages of relationship development.

Dialectical Change and Relationship Development

What are the implications of dialectical change for how one conceptualizes relationship development? Some dialectical theorists weave dialectical thinking into traditional developmental models of relationship development, that is, models of incremental progression in, or stages of, interdependence, certainty, and closeness (Brown et al.; Conville; Dindia; VanLear; this volume). Other theorists find the implications of dialectical change so profound that traditional conceptions of relationship development are rejected (Bochner et al.; Montgomery & Baxter; Rawlins; this volume). In general terms, those who merge traditional developmental models with dialectics suggest that relationship development is directional; dialectical interplay captures back-and-forth motion embedded in a broader trend toward directional development. By contrast, Montgomery and Baxter argue that traditional conceptions of relationship development are monologic in their "presumption of unidirectional, linear, usually quantitative and cumulative change toward some idealized or preferred end state." They reject the concept of *development* and substitute the concept of *dialogic complexity* to capture relational change. Dialogic complexity gives us a view of relationship change as multidirectional, polysemic, and unfinalized. Bochner and his colleagues similarly challenge the simplicity of traditional conceptions of relationship development, urging an alternative conception that captures the ambiguities and nuances of the ebb and flow of lived relational experience.

PRAXIS

The concept of praxis focuses on the simultaneous subject-and-object nature of the human experience. Individuals both act and are acted on; their actions in the present are constrained and enabled by prior actions and function to create the conditions to which they will respond in the future. As Marx (1963) so eloquently stated, "Men [sic] make their own history, but they do not make it just as they please" (p. 15). However, unlike Marx, who positioned praxis in the economic realm of material production, the contributors to this volume are interested exclusively in the social realm of meaning making. Because most of the contributors are based in the communication studies discipline, it is hardly surprising that the actions of primary interest are communicative, not economic. Perhaps the most microlevel orientation to praxical actions is provided by VanLear, whose work involves the coding of verbalized utterances between interlocutors. At a more macrolevel, several authors emphasize a single communicative form or genre. Bochner et al., Conville, and Rawlins, for example, emphasize the narrative or story. To these dialectical scholars, stories do more than provide representational accounts of parties' relationships. As Bochner and his colleagues express it, "stories are not only the way we tell ourselves to others, but also the very instrument of our being—our way of becoming who we are." Dindia also focuses on a single communicative form—self-disclosure—in her examination of stigmatized identity management. Brown and her colleagues expand their focus to include the role of the physical environment rather than limiting their analysis simply to verbal and nonverbal messages between interlocutors. However, we see their project as one that still emphasizes the meaning-making process; for example, their work in physical objects and physical spaces emphasizes the meanings these hold for individuals and groups as they create and manage various dialectical tensions. Montgomery and Baxter also focus broadly on a full range of communicative forms, including all actions that "figure in interpretations of meanings." Although meaning making is common to the perspectives found in the volume's chapters, the contributors differ in their treatment of time and in their focus on general versus particular praxical action.

Treatment of Time

A focus on praxis obligates dialectical researchers to address temporality: past, present, and future are inextricably linked, as Bakhtin's utterance chain, discussed earlier, makes apparent. However, the contributors address time in different ways. Rawlins' work, for example, emphasizes time by examining the dialectical experience of friendship for various life-cycle stages. By contrast, several authors (Conville; Dindia; VanLear; Bochner et al.) address contradiction in and through time. Conville's structural analysis method is based on the sequenced episodes that comprise a relationship's history. Similarly, Bochner et al. are attracted to the narrative form because it depicts in episodic form the "motion of connected lives across the curve of time." Dindia's focus on the disclosure of stigmatized identities underscores the on-goingness of the disclosure process, both within the history of a given relationship and across the life span of the stigmatized person. VanLear's chapter emphasizes that longitudinal data are necessary to discern how parties punctuate their process of relating; for example, what looks like a linear change over a short span of time may look like part of a periodic cycle if extended over a longer time period. Montgomery and Baxter and Brown et al. also recognize the importance of studying contradiction in and through time. However, they also urge researchers to adopt a more social approach to temporality. As Montgomery and Baxter express it, "Temporality is addressed by attending not only to processes in and through time, but also to processes by which actors jointly construct meaningful continuities and discontinuities among the past, present, and future." For example, Brown and her colleagues argue that how parties enact the rhythm and pacing of their relating is an important component of praxis.

General and Particular Praxis

The contributors differ in their commitment to identifying generalizable patterns of praxis. Some authors (Bochner et al.; Rawlins) appear to emphasize the local and the particular in how parties react to dialectical exigencies. Other authors (Brown et al.; Conville; Montgomery & Baxter) appear to take an intermediate position, arguing that indigenous reactions and conventional responses both merit scholarly attention. By contrast, other authors (Dindia; VanLear) appear to emphasize the identification of more abstract, generalizable patterns of praxis. In one way or another, these latter authors build on Baxter's (1988) typology of praxis responses. In general, the positions that authors take on the generality versus the particularity of praxis responses parallel their respective positions on the generality versus the particularity of contradictions.

TOTALITY

By *totality*, dialectical theorists mean the inseparability of phenomena. At least two different senses of totality are subsumed under the general umbrella term. Dialectical theorists refer to the inseparability of contradictions;

one contradiction cannot be considered in isolation of other contradictions with which it is integrally linked. A second sense of totality is the contextual embeddedness of the dialectical experience; contradiction cannot be separated from its temporal, spatial, and sociocultural settings. The contributors to the volume differ in how they use the totality concept.

The Knot of Contradictions

Some authors (Brown et al.; Montgomery & Baxter) emphasize the inseparability of contradictions and thus urge researchers not to limit their study of contradictions to one at a time. Montgomery and Baxter refer to this as the "knot" of contradictions that characterize the dialectical experience. Brown and her colleagues provide an extended discussion of this knot, as it implicates dialectics of engagement, affect, and regulation. The richly textured narratives studied by Conville, Bochner et al., and Rawlins nicely illuminate the notion of interdependence among contradictions. Although VanLear's general model of relationship emergence appears to allow for a set of substantive dialectical oppositions, his illustrative example emphasizes but a single contradiction. Similarly, Dindia's emphasis is on the single contradiction of openness and closedness.

The Relationship–Context Boundary

Because phenomena are not separable from one another, a dialectical perspective emphasizes a relational perspective; that is, the focus of attention is on the relationships between and among phenomena. Phenomena are constantly becoming through their interplay with other phenomena. From this perspective, it is somewhat arbitrary to demarcate a clear boundary where the relationship ends and the context begins; the relationship and its context bleed into one another in a dynamic way. However, dialectical scholars make an analytical distinction between the relationship and its context in order to focus attention on certain aspects of the dialectical experience of relating. Furthermore, the contributors to this volume differ in their approach to the relationship–context boundary.

Some of the authors emphasize that relationships do not exist in isolation of other social groupings and focus their attention on possible dialectical tensions that exist between different social units. Brown and her colleagues, for instance, acknowledge the "simultaneous interdependence of social units." They argue that understanding of the dialectical processes of dyads is enriched by the recognition of the pair's intricate connection to kin, friends, and the broader culture. Other contributors (Montgomery & Baxter; Rawlins) similarly acknowledge the social embeddedness of relationships in the distinction between internal dialectics and external dialectics, the former taking place within the boundaries of the dyadic relationship and the latter situated at the borders of the dyad and other social units.

Several contributors adopt a more or less traditional conception of "context," that is, the set of individual, relationship, physical, social, historical, and cultural factors that can influence, and be influenced by, the dialectics of relating. Rawlins, for example, refers to his book, *Friendship Matters* (1992), in which the individual's gender and life-cycle stage were featured prominently as contextual factors that were related to the dialectical experience of friendship. Conville emphasizes the relationship's developmental stage as an important contextual backdrop. For Conville, the presumption is that as a relationship moves between any two adjacent stages or phases, it will move through the four phases of his metadialectical helical model. Brown and her colleagues, reflecting their grounding in the transactional world view, emphasize physical environmental factors in their analysis of the dialectics of relating. Montgomery and Baxter, adapting Bakhtin's notion of the chronotope, argue for the importance of temporal, spatial, and sociohistorical contextual factors in understanding fully the dialectical experience. Dindia reviews the literature on disclosure of stigmatized identities, pointing to a variety of contextual factors that are related to the openness–closedness dialectic in stigma identity work.

A somewhat different sense of context comes in the narrative focus of Bochner and his colleagues. In their emphasis on the lived experience, Bochner et al. take a holistic approach to context, but theirs is an approach whose goal is not to analyze which factors relate in a systematic manner to the dialectical experience. Instead, their goal is "to create the effect of reality, a convincing likeness to life as it is sensed, felt, and lived" in the life experience of the person whose story is being told. Bochner and colleagues strive to place the reader in the context of the person's lived experience.

In sum, the members of the dialectics family share a commitment to core concepts of contradiction, change, praxis, and totality. However, within the boundaries of these four concepts, distinctions can be made that enable us to appreciate differences among the various dialectical approaches represented in this volume.

SIMILARITIES AND DIFFERENCES AT THE METHODOLOGICAL LEVEL

A second point of distinction among authors is method. All have had to grapple with the question, "What methods are suitable for studying the dialectics of relating?" Our contributing authors answer this question differently, depending on their particular dialectical perspective. In general, four basic methodological positions can be identified in these chapters: (a) dialectical empiricism; (b) the study of narratives; (c) the method of intertextuality; and (c) principled eclecticism.

VanLear's dialectical empiricism comes closer to traditional, quantitative social scientific methods than the approaches taken by other dialectical scholars in the text. However, VanLear cautions readers not to mistake his approach with positivistic science. VanLear does not believe in a single, objectifiable reality. Furthermore, his goal is the description of complex patterns, not causal explanation. According to VanLear, both qualitative and quantitative data are compatible with dialectical empiricism. However, VanLear favors the symbol system of numbers instead of the symbol system of words, "sacrific[ing] 'thick description,' subtlety of meaning, and the sense of having been there, for analytic precision, generality, and prediction." Acknowledging the inappropriateness of most linear models to dialectical analysis, VanLear advocates statistical time-series models as a better mathematical fit to dialectical processes.

Two of the chapters in this volume commit to narrative as the method of choice in understanding the dialectics of relating. Bochner et al. and Conville argue that narratives simultaneously represent a relationship and create one. As Conville expresses, "Like the moving tree branches that indicate the presence of wind, stories proclaim the presence of relationships." Both chapters display an interest in the case study, seeking to understand the dialectical process for a particular individual or relationship. Beyond this common commitment to the narrative case study, however, Bochner et al. and Conville markedly differ on a number of methodological issues. Conville provides us with a detailed, step-by-step method of interpretive analysis based on Lévi-Strauss' structural analysis. This method allows researchers to identify underlying dialectical and metadialectical tensions in the episodic sequences recounted in a party's relationship story. Conville's focus on a technique or procedure of analysis is motivated by his concern that dialectical studies may languish in the absence of procedures to teach others how to conduct dialectical analyses. He seeks a method or technique that makes studies "repeatable and therefore teachable." In contrast, Bochner et al. advocate autobiographical narrative in which the researcher's relationship experiences are captured through the literary power of the story. This narrative approach emphasizes subjectivity, self-reflexivity, and firsthand experience, in contrast to the distanced third-person perspective of Conville's researcher. Simply put, the method of autobiographical narrative is the capacity to write a good relational story. In contrast to Conville, Bochner et al. focus not on repeatability, but believability as a criterion for good narrative study.

Two chapters display what we are calling the *method of intertextuality*. Well-articulated in Rawlins' chapter, intertextuality is based on the juxtaposition of different discourses. Consistent with the dialectical notion that discourses come to mean only in relation to one another, Rawlins describes the intertextuality he achieved in his 1992 book by pairing reviews of traditional social scientific research on friendship with his own interpretive work based on open-ended interviews with friends across the life cycle. Bakhtin (1981) reminds us that any dialogue consists of *centripetal,* or dominant, voices in conversation with *centrifugal,* or subordinate, voices. Thus, it is not surprising that in the intertextual dialogues described by Rawlins, the discourse he favors is the interpretive and the hermeneutic. Nonetheless, Rawlins declares the importance of the juxtaposition, which is privileged over any single discursive voice. Dindia's chapter on the self-disclosure of stigmatized identities similarly illustrates the method of intertextuality. She brings traditional social scientific research on stigmas into conversation with a dialectical perspective, providing us with an alternative way to read that body of literature. She also brings that work into conversation with her own work on the disclosure of sexual orientation. The method of intertextuality is not to be mistaken with a traditional review of literature that typically precedes one's own research findings from a study. Rather, the goal of intertextuality is the juxtapositioning of different scholarly discourses so that new insights emerge.

The remaining two chapters (Brown et al.; Montgomery & Baxter) commit to a position we call *principled eclecticism.* The word *principled* is an important qualifier, for we wish to differentiate the methodological eclecticism endorsed by Brown et al. and by Montgomery and Baxter from a general anything goes perspective. Brown and her colleagues are interested in complex dialectical patterning that is fully contextualized and multivocal. They recognize that there are multiple observers, and thus truths, in a given dialectical process. Methods that are compatible with these assumptions are embraced by Brown and her colleagues, and over the past 15 years or so, the research programs of these scholars have drawn on a variety of different methods of data collection and analysis. Similarly, Montgomery and Baxter endorse what they call *dialogic principles* for research, legitimating any and all methods that are compatible with these principles: sensitivity to contextualized, contradictory interplay; sensitivity to temporality; sensitivity to the dialogue between and among different sets of data (what we just referred to as *intertextuality*); and sensitivity to researcher involvement.

CONCLUSION

Buss (1979) insightfully observed that the word *dialectic* has "through the centuries . . . taken on different meanings so that today it is neither possible, nor desirable, to attempt to stipulate *the* meaning of dialectic" (p. 75). We concur with this assessment. Although the dialectical approaches in this volume share a certain family resemblance in their shared assumptions of contradiction, change, praxis, and totality, many differences are also apparent on closer inspection. Like Buss, we and the contributing authors choose to celebrate this dialogue or interplay of unity and difference. To some who subscribe to traditional scientific canons of hypothetico–deductive research, dialectical theory appears hopelessly incomplete and riddled with internal inconsistencies. Such a view, however, is predicated on a distinctly non-dialectical world view, a view in which consistency, certainty, and closure are regarded as both possible and desirable. Dialectical theory is a sensitizing tool, a prism that contains multiple, related perspectives on the process of relating. We invite you to join the dialectical conversation contained in the several chapters that follow. The contributors to this volume have accumulated a substantial body of dialectically oriented research over the past 15 years. These chapters do not pretend to summarize this work in depth, but rather suggest underlying similarities and differences in orientation and approach.

REFERENCES

Altman, I., Vinsel, A., & Brown, B. (1981). Dialectic conceptions in social psychology: An application to social penetration and privacy regulation. In L. Berkowitz (Ed.), *Advances in experimental social psychology* (Vol. 14, pp. 107–160). New York: Academic Press.

Bakhtin, M. M. (1981). *The dialogic imagination: Four essays by M. M. Bakhtin* (M. Holquist, Ed.; C. Emerson & M. Holquist, Trans.). Austin: University of Texas Press.

Bakhtin, M. M. (1984). *Problems of Dostoevsky's poetics* (C. Emerson, Ed., Trans.). Minneapolis: University of Minnesota Press. (Original work published in 1929)

Bakhtin, M. M. (1986). *Speech genres and other late essays* (C. Emerson & M. Holquist, Eds.; V. McGee, Trans.). Austin: University of Texas Press.

Baxter, L. A. (1988). A dialectical perspective on communication strategies in relationship development. In S. Duck (Ed.), *Handbook of personal relationships* (pp. 257–273). New York: Wiley.

Baxter, L. A., & Montgomery, B. M. (1996). *Relating: Dialogues and dialectics.* New York: Guilford.

Benson, J. K. (1977). Organizations: A dialectical view. *Administrative Science Quarterly, 22,* 1–21.

Buss, A. (1979). *A dialectical psychology.* New York: Irvington Publishers.

Cornforth, M. (1968). *Materialism and the dialectical method.* New York: International Publishers.

Duck, S., & Montgomery, B. M. (1991). The interdependence among interaction substance, theory, and methods. In B. M. Montgomery & S. Duck (Eds.), *Studying interpersonal interaction* (pp. 3–15). New York: Guilford.

Marx, K. (1963). *The eighteenth brumaire of Louis Bonaparte.* New York: International Publishers. (Original work published in 1869)

Murphy, R. (1971). *The dialectics of social life.* New York: Basic Books.

Rawlins, W. K. (1989). A dialectical analysis of the tensions, functions, and strategic challenges of communication in young adult friendships. *Communication Yearbook, 12,* 157–189.

Rawlins, W. K. (1992). *Friendship matters: Communication, dialectics, and the life course.* New York: Aldine de Gruyter.

Rychlak, J. F. (Ed.). (1976). *Dialectic: Humanistic rationale for behavior and development.* New York: S. Karger.

Turner, J. H. (1986). *The structure of sociological theory* (4th ed.). Chicago: The Dorsey Press.

2

Telling Stories:
Dialectics of Relational Transition

RICHARD L. CONVILLE
University of Southern Mississippi

Many believe personal stories provide a window onto the world of relationships, and it is no wonder. Baxter's (1992) experience of collecting relationship stories through in-depth interviews is shared by many of us: "I was
struck by the contradictions, contingencies, nonrationalities, and multiple
realities to which people gave voice in their narrative sense-making" (p. 330).
I believe that personal narratives hold the lived experience of personal relationships, structural methods unveil their formal qualities and dialectical interpretations tell of their dynamics.

In this chapter, my aim is fourfold: (a) to outline an approach to the study
of relationships, The Dialectics of Relational Transition; (b) to demonstrate
the approach in a case study; (c) based on the case, to make some observations on the interpersonal communication occurring at the interface of relational culture and professional culture; and (d) to extend current thinking on
dialectical studies of relationships.

THE DIALECTICS OF RELATIONAL TRANSITION:
CONCEPTUAL CONSIDERATIONS

Certain presumptions — one could even call them beliefs — furnish the under-
carriage for the approach outlined here. Taken as the basis of a nascent theory, *relational transition* refers to a process that is recursive, evolutionary,
and indigenous to interpersonal communication. I use *process* to refer to a
repeated pattern of episodes of a particular type. Thus, we may speak of the

political process, the process of extracting minerals from the ground, or the process of recovery. In each case, observers may agree that certain predictable persons are engaged in certain expected actions in approximately the same order with similar outcomes. By analogy, a conversation is a process: Although I do not know the next sentence my speaking partner will utter, I do know that it will contain words, that they will be of a certain kind (e.g., nouns, verbs), in a recognizable order, and that it will soon be my turn.

I use *recursive* to refer to actions that are repetitive without repeating. Thus, I may speak with my friend who is recovering from a divorce and learn of his uncertainties about his self-worth, then months later, during which time he seems to have been doing quite well, have a similar conversation and know that those uncertainties have returned. Our second exchange is not identical to the first one, but it is similar enough to the first one that I, and perhaps he too, recognize it as one of the same type. The conversations were recursive. They had the quality of repetitiveness without being duplicative.

By *evolutionary*, it is meant that relational transition is not a random, whimsical happening. Rather, it reflects the unfolding into the future of what was latent in the past. For example, knowledge of the administration of 20th-century European colonialism and of the peoples thus managed may lead one to observe that the revolutions throwing off that absentee landlordship were quite natural outcomes, given the incipient and contrary goals of rulers and ruled. One is applying this attribute of relational transition—evolutionary—in a quite normal way when he or she admits to not being surprised at hearing about a certain divorce, "They never did have much in common."

Indigenous is a different matter, however. Relational transition is found naturally in and confined to human relationships. Just as manatees are indigenous to the tropical waters off the Florida peninsula, relational transitions have a kind of natural habitat—human relationships—in which, left to their own devices, they flourish, and apart from which, they are not found.

Besides these narrative descriptors—process, recursive, evolutionary, indigenous—relational transition can be depicted in a helical model. The Dialectics of Relational Transition employs two metadialectics to account for the inherent relational change that occurs as a result of relational partners' struggling with dialectical contradictions. They are security–alienation and disintegration–resynthesis. Imagine these two dialectical dimensions positioned orthogonally with respect to each other and lying in a plane perpendicular to the central core of a helix. Further, imagine the dialectical oppositions to be displayed on the perimeter of the helix as regions that stand in opposing positions (as depicted in Fig. 2.1).

The four poles of the two metadialectical dimensions are taken as the four phases of relational transition. The presumption of the Dialectics of Relational Transition is that all relationships, over time and regardless of the par-

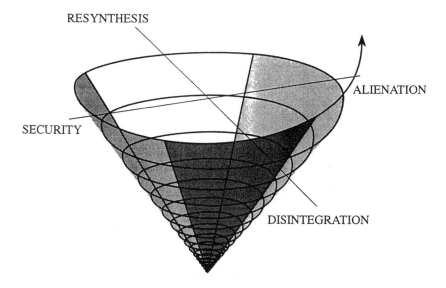

RESYNTHESIS

ALIENATION

SECURITY

DISINTEGRATION

FIG. 2.1. A structural-helical model of relational transition. Reprinted, with permission, from *Relational Transitions* (p. 77), by R. L. Conville, © 1991, Westport, CT: Praeger, an imprint of Greenwood Publishing Group.

ticular relational dialectics they experience (e.g., autonomy–connectedness, oblique–direct, etc.), go through these four general phases many times.

The first phase of relational transition is *security*, "a state of affairs in which the persons involved feel comfortable, share complementary roles, and act in coordinated fashion" (Conville, 1991, p. 80). At such times, relationships, according to Levinger (1983), are "accompanied by familiarity, predictability, and the reduction of cognitive and emotional tension" (p. 336).

Then there is the *disintegration* phase, entered when relational partners "begin noticing their relationship, noticing it instead of simply being in it. Something is askew, out of kilter" (Conville, 1991, p. 93). Their differences are becoming problematic. They become uncertain of their relationship as it has been defined. The prevalence of such relationship experience is attested to in research on relationship uncertainty and its co-occurence with relationship change (Planalp & Honeycutt, 1985; Planalp, Rutherford, & Honeycutt, 1988).

Next is the *alienation* phase in which "one or both partners reject the relationship-as-presently-constituted, become alienated from it" (Conville, 1991, p. 114). A closely related concept is found in Bolton's (1961) pioneering work on relational *turning points*. He took that key term to stand for "transformations in actors' definition of themselves and their relations to others . . . a reformulation . . . a shift from one perspective to another" (pp. 236–237). In the phase of alienation we have the dialectical opposite of security, and the pair, security–alienation, exhibits the expected dialectical attributes of contradiction, dynamism, and interdependence.

Finally, there is the resynthesis phase. Here, one regains the certainty lost in the disintegration phase.

> The origins of Resynthesis are found in a flight from uncertainty, in a playing out of instinctive proclivities [for sociation], in a search for security, in an imitation of nurturing actions, or in a desire for existential meaningfulness. (Conville, 1991, p. 135).

In the phase of resynthesis, we have the dialectical opposite of disintegration and as with security–alienation, disintegration–resynthesis exhibits the dialectical attributes of contradiction, dynamism, and interdependence.

The helical model is taken to be the context in which relationships are conducted. By *context* is meant something like site or location. A relationship is presumed to lie somewhere on the curve of the helix, and, lying about that relationship are phases it has already passed through and phases it will pass through. Moreover, change is imminent as well, for by virtue of passing about the helix, the relationship moves into new regions, driven as it is by the opposing forces of the two metadialectical dimensions.

In addition, the helix itself may be taken to rest in a particular context — the interstage — that is, the in-between of relationship stages. The helix was designed to help explain what was occurring as a relationship moved from, for example, Knapp's (1984) experimenting stage to his intensifying stage; or from Duck's (1982) dyadic phase to his social phase; or from Levinger's (1980) buildup phase to his continuation phase. Consider, for example, that line of ink on a page dividing, in Knapp's model, experimenting from intensifying, and enlarge it 100 times. That now enlarged space is where the helix comes into play. The presumption is that as a relationship moves between experimenting and intensifying (or between any two adjacent stages or phases), it moves through the four phases of the helical model by virtue of experiencing the opposing forces of the the two metadialectics — security–alienation and disintegration–resynthesis.

Finally, the Dialectics of Relational Transition, as an approach to relationship studies, includes the assumption that dialectical movement, whether in the form of conventional dialectics, such as autonomy–connection, or as metadialectics, such as disintegration–resynthesis, results in relationship transformation. The model thus weds dialectical movement to relationship evolution by presuming that dialectical movement, itself, inherently results in relational change. In this manner, the approach differs from other current approaches that employ dialectics mainly to describe interpersonal communication (Baxter, 1988) or the relationships engendered by it (Rawlins, 1992). Rather, the presence of dialectical movement, from this point of view, is evidence that the relationship is in the process of changing. The conceptual considerations just discussed, as well as the methodological issues to be outlined, may be found in fuller form in my book, *Relational Transitions* (Conville, 1991).

THE DIALECTICS OF RELATIONAL TRANSITION: METHODOLOGICAL CONSIDERATIONS

Certain presumptions or beliefs about method also furnish the underpinnings of the approach. The Dialectics of Relational Transition is to be considered a narrative–structural–dialectical approach to knowledge about personal relationships: narrative in that relationships endure as narratives in our speaking and our writing; structural in that the analytical procedures are based on Lévi-Strauss's (1963) essay, "The Structural Study of Myth" in his *Structural Anthropology;* and dialectical in that relationships are seen as the ongoing interplay of opposing, yet interdependent forces that move persons.

Narrative

Investigators often find that their best access to personal relationships is found in participants' narratives about those relationships (whether direct access to human action is possible at all is a relevant question but well beyond the reach of this inquiry). A narrative methodology entails discourse itself as site for the observation of personal relationships and as data for the application of appropriate interpretive methods (Conville, 1997).

Like the moving tree branches that indicate the presence of wind, stories proclaim the presence of relationships. If I want to study the relationships among members of an extended family, the stories that they tell about each other would signal for me the place I should pause and look carefully, and the characters in their stories would furnish the objects of my attention. Their accounts preserve their relationships in oral or written discourse so that I and others may have access to them.

> Stories and relationships are thus inextricably intertwined . . . in the sense that people come to define themselves and others through the stories they tell. (LaRossa, 1995, p. 555)

There are several advantages to this narrative approach. First, relationships are transient and evanescent, but once captured as discourse in stories, they are stored away in memory or in text and can be brought out again and again for worry or analysis or interpretation. What we lose in up-to-date accuracy when we capture a relationship in discourse, we gain in ability to examine it closely and repeatedly.

Conversely, looking into stories for relationships is also advantageous in dealing with the problem of change. Relationships change, and stories about relationships can change with them. The rhetorical dimension of our stories allows them to reflect our present conditions and social roles as well as project our futures (LaRossa, 1995). Thus, relationship stories change over time as told by the same person; at a given time, relationship stories differ depending on the person telling them. Thus the flexibility of stories gives them the potential for being accurate indicators of relationships.

If stories point to relationships, portray relationships, and preserve relationships as I am suggesting, then a reasonable question is, "How does the investigator use stories to elucidate relationships and make theory?" The upshot of the procedure to be described is what Barthes (1972) called a *simulacrum* or analytical model of the story. In this case, it is one that highlights the interaction of the relational partners, and that would have otherwise "remained invisible, or . . . unintelligible in the natural [unanalyzed] object [story]" (p. 149). Moreover, rather than feigning detachment, the investigator produces an "interested *simulacrum*" (Barthes, 1972, p. 149)—one constructed with a view toward a certain end, the creation of dialectical dimensions along which relational partners are said to move in the story, thus constituting their relationship.

Structural

That interested *simulacrum* of the relationship narrative is constructed by employing the method devised by Lévi-Strauss (1963) for the analysis of myths. A brief outline of the procedure involves two steps and is demonstrated in the following section. Step one requires the researcher to compile a chronological list of the significant episodes in the narrative. A significant episode is taken to be an instance of human interaction, depicted or implied, in which an actor defines self or the relationship and that directs the course of the story.

Step two involves classifying the episodes and displaying them in a rows-and-columns grid in which the classes or groups of like episodes comprise the columns. This is accomplished by considering each succeeding pair of episodes in turn and asking the question, "Are they the same or nearly so, or are they different?" If the answer is "different," they go into different columns; if it is "same," they go into the same column. After the first two groups or columns are formed, new episodes that are encountered may, of course, repeat prior formed groups. Thus, the same-or-different question must also be posed for each new episode vis-à-vis the already established columns (episode types). The resulting grid may then be read left to right and top to bottom (as one would read a page) in order to follow the order of episodes in the narrative and see the distribution of episode types among the columns. Typically, the columns or episode types suggest particular dialectical oppositions that the investigator can employ in an interpretation of the relationship under consideration.

Dialectical

The Dialectics of Relational Transition is an approach that is qualitative and interpretive. Neither statistical inference nor prediction is the goal of this research. As Cissna, Cox, and Bochner (1990) stated, "interpretive studies seek intelligibility, rather than predictability" (p. 49). The goal of an interpretive study is to articulate an argument for a certain understanding of phenomena. Interpretive studies do not seek to mathematize the phenomena under consideration or to reduce those phenomena to psychometric scales and ultimately to statistical analysis. Scholarship conducted as an interpretive enterprise takes the form of a lively and engaging conversation sustained by different perspectives (O'Neill, 1974; Rorty, 1979) rather than a predictable monologue of measurements seeking validity. What Gallie (cited in Geertz, 1973) said of ethnography seems to be appropriate for interpretive studies in communication: They are "essentially contestable" (p. 29).

Dialectical studies are conducted on the belief that the social world is constituted by persons who move along imaginary dimensions between opposing forces. Two forces stand in dialectical relationship with each other when one is defined in terms of the absence of the other, yet they form a coherent unit or whole. Thus, the polar oppositions are interdependent both definitionally and experientially. The resulting tension of a person being drawn to (or merely preferring) first one pole then the other introduces a certain dynamism to a relationship. So, a dialectical relationship entails the attributes of dynamism, interdependence, and opposition (Baxter, 1988, 1994; Conville, 1991; Montgomery, 1993; Rawlins, 1983). The researcher who believes that important aspects of relationships can be understood in dialectical terms enters upon a study looking for (expecting to find) dialectical dimensions evidenced in the relationship narratives under consideration (Conville, in press).

THE NARRATIVE DATA

The relationship story I have chosen to use as a case to demonstrate the approach just outlined is found in an article in the November, 1988 *Quarterly Journal of Speech* by Michael Pacanowsky. It is not your typical journal article, for it is presented as a short story, a piece of fiction. I chose it because some already are familiar with it and for those who are not, it is easily accessed. The tone in which the story is written, the journal in which it was published, and the subject matter (one's personal and professional choice between superficial success and substantive significance) suggest that the story's omniscient narrator is the voice of the author himself, drawing on years of academic convention experience. Thus, it seems very much a personal relationship story.

The narrative recounts the struggle of a youngish faculty member, Jack, to make his professional work meaningful. As the story opens, he is torn between, on the one hand, sticking singlemindedly with the long-term book project he is working on, which expresses his most basic professional (and perhaps personal) commitments and, on the other hand, agreeing to the hard sell of a friend who cajoles him to be on a panel at the next (presumably Speech Communication Association, SCA) convention.

In the end, Jack agrees to go because it is a strong panel; besides, he sees it as a platform for espousing his view that fiction is a great untapped resource for theorizing about human communication. However, conventions (which lately, he finds boring) and panels (which now, he finds banal)—despite the laudatory attention they have begun to bring him and the enjoyment of keeping up with old graduate school chums—stand in direct competition for the time he could be devoting to doing something he believes is truly meaningful—the book.

The story is about many things, but one of them is Jack and Penny's relationship, and that is my focus. They are married and have a 3-year-old son, Joshua. There are three other characters in the story with whom Jack has some relationship: Radner, his pushy, conventioneering colleague and grad school buddy who called about the panel; Kauffmann, the elder statesman-respondent on the panel, who (Jack finds out just before the convention) plans to ignore Jack's paper in his response; and Other Members Of The Profession, none of whom Jack seems to like.

The story is made up of 11 episodes interspersed with 6 excerpts from Jack's notebooks—excursions into theory that furnish commentary on the story as it progresses. Three of the episodes involve Penny. These are the ones I have chosen for this case study, and I will refer to them as *Penny One, Penny Two* and *Penny Three*.

RELATIONAL CULTURE AND PROFESSIONAL CULTURE

The story is about Jack and Penny's relationship, but their relationship can also be seen as a case study of a current social issue that is reflected in the personal relationships literature: the interface of relational culture and what I have chosen to call "professional culture." "Relational culture," Wood (1982) explained:

> refers to a privately transacted system of definitions, values and meanings that establish for partners in a relationship a consensual order of interpretation and

action. Relational culture is highly dynamic and dialectical; through discourse partners create their relational culture and amend it. (p. 77)

Professional culture then, by analogy, would be a publicly transacted system of definitions, values and meanings established in the workplace that results in a consensual order of interpretation and action meant for the workplace. Like its private counterpart, it is highly dynamic and dialectical as well as created and amended by discourse.

Close friends, members of long-term romantic relationships, and married couples all create relational cultures that mark their particular dyads as unique. Likewise, the discourse of their workplaces (whether inside or outside the home) creates a professional culture for relational partners.

However, the issues and problems encountered in the one culture can hardly be isolated from the other. The two cultures, relational and professional, intermingle and influence each other in important ways. Issues originating on the job often spill over into relational partners' private lives—their relational culture—and inhibit or boost their effectiveness as friends, parents, or marital partners. Likewise, issues from the relational culture often spill over into the workplace and facilitate or interfere with job performance (Bridge & Baxter, 1992).

Quite often, then, a stress point for personal relationships lies at the interface of relational culture and professional culture. Higgins and Duxbury (1992) have pointed out that the influence of work conflict on family conflict is well-documented. In their own study of 748 managers and professionals across 19 large public and private sector organizations, they found work conflict to be a strong and significant predictor of family conflict (p. 67).

The particular kinds of work stressors experienced are important as well as the direction of their influence. Williams and Alliger (1994) investigated the effects of three types of task, or work, characteristics on mood—task demands, feelings of personal control, and perceived progress toward goals. Greater task demand was positively related to distress and negatively related to calmness; greater task control was negatively related to distress and positively related to calmness; greater goal progress was negatively related to distress and positively related to elation (p. 852). Presumably, distress originating in the workplace will affect mood and therefore relationships at home. Indeed, these same researchers found significant spill over of both distress and fatigue from work to home and from home to work (p. 856).

Finally, the mood and fatigue level of one spouse influences the other spouse's mood and fatigue level, home to work, as well as work to home. Such crossover effects from one spouse to another are also well-documented (Chan & Margolin, 1994).

While the main purpose of this chapter is to present and demonstrate a dialectical approach to relationship studies, an ancillary purpose is to shed further light, from a qualitative perspective, onto the common problem of the interpenetration of workplace-related stress and home-related stress: what I call the interface of professional culture and relational culture.

A CASE STUDY

Structural analysis of relationship narratives amounts to a discovery procedure for ferreting out the dialectical oppositions that may be operating there. Details of the procedure are given in my book, *Relational Transitions* (Conville, 1991). Step one is to produce a chronological list of the most important episodes in the story. Here is the list I propose from Penny and Jack's story.

1. Jack announces he is going to the convention in Chicago.
2. Penny is not impressed.
3. Jack overexplains.
4. Penny calls the convention trivial.
5. Penny alleges disaffection with traditional approaches as well as problems with new (i.e., interpretive) approaches.
6. Penny questions, "What beast will be born in Chicago?" (in her rewrite of Yeats' "Slouching Towards Bethlehem").
7. Penny advises Jack to keep his Chicago paper in perspective.
8. Jack sees himself as caught between slouching and posturing in Chicago.
9. Jack asks Penny to read his paper.
10. Penny sees the main character in Jack's story as "struggling between careerism and cynicism."
11. Jack says that was not what he intended in the story.
12. Penny asks, "What are you then?"
13. Jack answers, "I'm not sure."

Step two is to arrange the episodes into a rows-and-columns grid with similar episodes comprising the columns, and the rows, read left to right and top to bottom, preserving the chronology. Figure 2.2 is the grid that reflects my reading of the story. Numbers in the grid refer to the order of episodes in the previous chronological list of episodes.

Inspection of the grid ideally leads the analyst to detect one or more dialectical oppositions that are at work in the story. I suggest three for our consideration. The first involves Column I and Column V. The episodes in Column I (1, 3, and 9) portray Jack as confident. He accepted the invitation to appear on the panel and wrote the paper that he later asked Penny to read. In dynamic opposition to Column I are the episodes in Column V (11 and 13), in which Jack admits serious uncertainties about the paper and about himself. The first indigenous dialectic I call certainty–uncertainty.

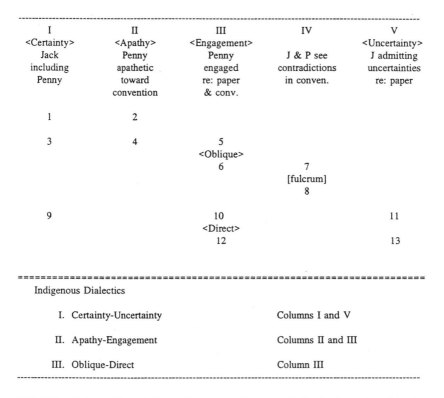

FIG. 2.2.   Jack and Penny's Story: Rows-and-columns grid of episodes and resulting indigenous dialectics.

Keep in mind that, as with most of our relationships, except when we are engaging in metacommunication, these episodes are enacted under the auspices of something other than the relationship. Here, the "something other than" are the convention paper and the social occasion of the convention. In other words, there is very little explicit relationship talk in this story. Rather, the relationship is enacted by Jack and Penny. The explicit content of Jack and Penny's conversations is about the convention paper, whereas they play out their relationship implicitly for the most part. Therefore, although a dialectic of certainty–uncertainty is suggested by the analysis, and those degrees of certainty seem to be about things in the professional culture, I am contending that the dialectic is, nevertheless, also and simultaneously a dialectic of their relational culture.

The second dialectic indigenous to this particular relationship story involves the opposition between episodes in Column II (2 and 4) and Column III (5, 6, 10, and 12). In Column II, Penny is depicted as uninterested in the convention, but in Column III, she is fully engaged with both the convention paper and the convention itself. The second indigenous dialectic is called apathy–engagement.

As with the first proposed indigenous dialectic, the dialectic of apathy–engagement seems to be enacted obliquely. Although Penny and Jack are ostensibly focused on the convention paper and its implications, they are, by the by, also and simultaneously doing relationship work, for they are, unavoidably, creating an ongoing conversation, in which they present themselves to each other. This observation is one basis for the efficacy of the helical model just introduced (Fig. 2.1), for movement about a helix effectively depicts this inherent attribute of relationships. That is, as one moves about the coil of a helix, one is moving on a particular trajectory (imagine a near horizontal one), but at the same time one is moving up or down the center pole of the helix in a direction virtually perpendicular to the apparent direction of movement. Thus, the convention paper is the task at hand, the movement about the coil, while the ascending movement around the center pole of the helix is the relationship work. The former is explicit, in the foreground and in the forefront of relational partners' consciousness; the latter is implicit, in the background and generally, out of mind. The latter movement (relationship) happens automatically as the former movement (content) occurs (Conville, 1978, 1983; Watzlawick, Bavelas, & Jackson, 1967).

The third indigenous dialectic lies along a vertical axis within Column III. Episodes 5 and 6 constitute Penny's oblique advice regarding Jack's dilemma. There, she playfully reads aloud for him her altered version of William Butler Yeats's (1983) poem, "The Second Coming," in which the last line is "Slouches towards Bethlehem to be born" (from which Pacanowsky derived the title of his story, "Slouching Towards Chicago"). The title of Penny's version, adapted to provide commentary on Jack's struggle, is "A Kuhnian Paradigm Shift" and speaks of the center not holding and anarchy being loosed on the world; of a beast (Jack?) coming out of the desert; and the time being right for The Second Coming (is it Jack? Does he think he is God?). In contrast, Episodes 10 and 12 present Penny as quite direct in giving Jack her interpretation of his story and further pressing Jack on what he is really trying to get at in the story. Therefore, I call this third indigenous dialectic oblique–direct.

An interesting sidenote to the dialectics that seem to be at work in this personal story concerns the episode class, Column IV (Episodes 7 and 8). It seems to furnish a fulcrum for all three dialectics, certainty–uncertainty, apathy–engagement, and oblique–direct. Only after Penny advised Jack in Episode 7 to keep his Chicago paper in perspective (do not confuse important with unimportant) and after Jack admitted to himself in Episode 8 that he was not sure whether he would be slouching or posturing toward Chicago, Penny moved to direct engagement with Jack in his struggle (Dialectics two and three), and Jack admitted his deep uncertainties (Dialectic one).

TABLE 2.1
Conventional Dialectics in Penny's Episodes

Conventional Dialectics	Penny One	Penny Two	Penny Three
I	Autonomy	Connectedness	(reframed) as Interdependence
II	Openness	Openness	Openness (selection)
III	Novelty	Predictability	Novelty (cyclic alternation)

The structural analysis serves not only as a discovery procedure for indigenous dialectics, but also it helps locate significant pivotal episodes that provide a catalyst for the movement of the three dialectics to their opposite poles, movement that constituted the relationship as it was depicted in the narrative.

INDIGENOUS AND CONVENTIONAL DIALECTICS

Indigenous dialectics, those home grown in a given unique relationship, serve to balance the temptation to treat existing dialectical systems as a "one-size-fits-all" analytical recipe. However, one can fit Jack and Penny's story into such a conventional scheme to some extent, and to do so is instructive (see Table 2.1 and Appendix). Although a number of such schemes appear in the literature, consensus seems to hold that autonomy–connection is fundamental (Montgomery, 1993). I will employ that dimension plus two more from Baxter (1988), openness–closedness and novelty–predictability, as exemplars of conventional dialectics.

From the perspective of conventional dialectics, Penny and Jack's relationship is marked by autonomy, openness, and novelty in Episode Penny One, by connectedness, openness, and predictability in Penny Two, and by interdependence, openness, and novelty in Penny Three. Strategies that Jack and Penny employed for coping with these three sets of dialectical contradictions were reframing for Dialectic I (autonomy–connectedness); selection for Dialectic II (openness–closedness), and cyclic alternation for Dialectic III (novelty–predictability; see Baxter, 1990).

The three indigenous dialectics—certainty–uncertainty, apathy–engagement, and oblique–direct—cannot be derived from these three conventional dialectics. Neither conventional nor indigenous dialectics is superior, but rather, both are needed to guard against premature orthodoxy on the one hand and "mere anarchy loosed upon the world" (Yeats, 1983, p. 187, l. 4) on the other.

Moreover, there is some overlap and thus, mutual confirmation between the conventional and the indigenous in the case of Jack and Penny. The first indigenous dialectic—certainty–uncertainty—can be seen as the other's perspective on novelty–predictability: When the other is uncertain, she is likely to be unpredictable, and when she is certain, is likely to be predictable. The second indigenous dialectic—apathy–engagement—can be seen as a species of autonomy–connectedness. In addition, engagement would probably entail a kind of openness and apathy, a kind of closedness. Thus, Jack and Penny's personal relationship, not surprisingly, shares with many others a basic dynamic. However, Jack and Penny's relationship remains just that, theirs, unique, not just another of a type and thus, also displays its own dialectical oppositions in their own unique configuration: certainty–uncertainty, apathy–engagement, and oblique–direct.

RELATIONAL AND PROFESSIONAL CULTURE

Here are some observations on Jack and Penny's relationship narrative that follow from the foregoing analysis and expose the interface of relational culture and professional culture. First, the dialectic of certainty–uncertainty occurred over several episodes. Uncertainty was, from the beginning, part and parcel of Jack and Penny's coping with the intrusion of the professional into the relational. The uncertainty did not come as a result of a single event, as is implied in several landmark studies (Baxter & Bullis, 1986; Planalp & Honeycutt, 1985; and Planalp, Rutherford & Honeycutt, 1988). Useful as these studies have been, they unnecessarily limit our understanding of relationship development by conceiving of changes in relational uncertainty in the narrow terms of *events* and *information* gains.

By contrast, the uncertainty experienced by Penny and Jack had a history, its outcome was unclear, and it was connected with a variety of issues and relationships—a characterization that more clearly reflects the common experience of relational partners. This broadened perspective on the natural history of uncertainty in personal relationships was foreshadowed by Planalp, Rutherford, and Honeycutt (1988) when they extended their investigations to include antecedents of the event, as well as the types of talk about the event (and other coping strategies) that occurred afterward (pp. 535–538).

Second, in this story, relational culture and professional culture were brought together, rather than isolated from each other. This process is indicated in the indigenous dialectics of apathy–engagement and oblique–direct. The professional struggle became the conversational content around which Jack and Penny wove their relationship in the story. For example, Penny gives Jack advice in Episode 7 and Jack asks Penny to read his paper in Episode 9. Although the convention paper—an artifact of professional culture—is at issue in both cases, giving advice and asking for feedback simultaneously portray both Jack and Penny as playing out a part of their relational culture. One could even say that the professional culture was brought into the relational culture and was subsumed by it. Jack did not do what many commentators on male–female communication have reported is normal for males—keep his problem to himself and shut out Penny (Tannen, 1990). Moreover, Jack's professional struggle became an occasion for Penny and Jack to collaborate on their relationship work.

METADIALECTICS OF RELATIONAL TRANSITION

The final kind of analysis I want to do is at the metadialectical level and concerns the evolution of Jack and Penny's relationship. In the Dialectics of Relational Transition, dialectical studies are always set in a developmental context. The perspective affirms that dialectical movement always takes a relationship somewhere. Dialectical theory holds that relational partners are in constant motion along certain dimensions. Yet, this movement is not merely casual or periodic or even necessary motion; it has developmental consequences. After relational partners experience their relationship's differing dialectical moments, they are not the same: Time has passed and they see each other in a different light. Our dialectical theorizing should take into account this natural evolution of relationships, and the helical model permits us to portray this process.

In other words, Jack and Penny's relationship changed as a result of their being pulled between the poles of the indigenous dialectics—apathy and engagement, certainty and uncertainty, oblique and direct—and between the poles of the conventional dialectics—autonomy–connectedness, openness–closedness, and novelty–predictability. This kind of change is clearly illustrated by the shape of the helix, for one turn of 360° about the helix results in a relationship being placed in a different location. It is not back where it started, for the incline of the coil has placed it above or below its starting point.

From this point of view, there are no repeats in the history of a relationship. One member of a relationship saying, "We've been through all this before," or "Here we go again!" is prima facie evidence that the episode and the relationship are not the same as before. Rather, the episode is recognized. Relational partners now have expectations of the outcomes for the currrent episode they did not have before, and by now they have formed explanations for why it occurred. In short, the episode wears a patina of familiarity and presumption gathered from the intervening time and interactions.

How then does Jack and Penny's relationship fit this model of relationship evolution? Episodes 1 through 4 (see Fig. 2.3), that comprise certainty on

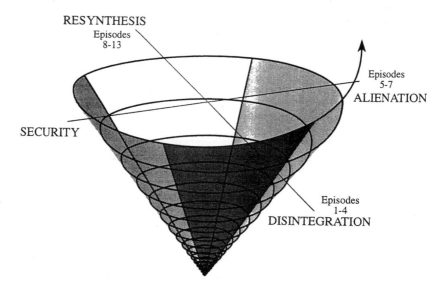

FIG. 2.3.   A structural-helical model of relational transition. Reprinted, with permission, from *Relational Transitions* (p. 77), by R. L. Conville, © 1991, Westport, CT: Praeger, an imprint of Greenwood Publishing Group.

Jack's part and apathy on Penny's, fall at the disintegration pole of the disintegration–resynthesis metadialectic. After two negative reactions from Penny in Episodes 2 and 4, Jack had reason to call into question their relationship as it is evidenced in the particular issues of the convention and the panel and conventions in general. For her part, Penny overtly questioned the value of conventions and the use of Jack's time for them. Their relationship is clearly out of kilter regarding this issue.

Episodes 5 through 7 seem to fall at the alienation pole of the security–alienation metadialectic. Here, Penny is warning Jack, albeit indirectly through her adapted rendition of Yeats' poem, about the danger of straying from his priorities and his possible arrogance in doing so. She is clearly alienated from their relationship, as it is playing itself out around the issue of the convention at this point in the story. Also at this point, Jack does not seem to be buying her assessment of the situation, so he does not have the relationship with her that he would like to have. That is, he too is alienated from the relationship that seems to be forming around the convention issue.

Finally, Episodes 8 through 13 are characteristic of the resynthesis pole of the disintegration–resynthesis metadialectic. They signal the beginning of the two forms of resynthesis—redefinition and transformation. In Episode 8, Jack, for the first time, admits to himself the possibility that he may be guilty of posturing in his anticipation of the convention panel. After that, he asks

Penny to read his paper (Episode 9), which gives her the opportunity to offer her interpretation of the story's main character (Episode 10) and ask Jack how he sees himself as the writer of the story (Episode 12). After such questions, which Jack is willing to engage honestly, he is open to the possibility of a transformation in his view of conventions in general, of this panel, and of himself as a professional. In terms of the model, such a state is preparatory to entering a new security phase, in which case Jack and Penny's relationship would have gone around the helix one full turn.

METADIALECTICS, STORY, AND COMMUNICATION

How do those indigenous and conventional dialectics previously developed fit into these metadialectics and ultimately enhance our understanding of Jack and Penny's relationship evolution? What dialectical movements contributed to Penny and Jack's movement about the helix and their apparently successful negotiation of a relational transition? Two of the conventional dialectical dimensions seem particularly relevant. Throughout the story Jack and Penny selected the openness pole of the openness–closedness dialectic. Using a variety of means, they let each other know their feelings and positions on the issues they were discussing. At strategic points in the story, they had a choice whether to speak or remain silent, and they chose to be open. For example, Penny read Jack her version of Yeats' poem parodying his trip to Chicago, and Jack told Penny that he did not intend what she saw in the story.

In addition, Jack and Penny are depicted in the story as alternating between autonomy and connectedness, which in the end they reframed as interdependence. Their openness led to both disintegration and alienation, but these phases were necessary to reach resynthesis—a place where redefinition and transformation were possible. Their coming together in a reframed interdependence also made possible Jack and Penny's working together instead of separately or competitively as they coped with the stresses inherent at the interface of their relational and professional cultures.

Two of the indigenous dialectics also seem particularly associated with Jack and Penny's movement about the helix of relational transition. Jack's movement from certainty to uncertainty opened to him the possibility of rethinking his motives for going to the convention as well as gaining a degree of self-conscious reflection on his professional identity. This movement led the relationship out of security, through disintegration and alienation and to the threshold of the resynthesis phase. In addition, Jack had the advantage of another person, Penny, who moved from apathy to engagement with him. Her apathetic style first landed them squarely in disintegration, but then her persistent inquiry (engagement) pushed the relationship through alienation and into resynthesis. In particular, Penny's direct questioning of Jack, even to the point of, "What are you then?" (in the context of mutual affection they had established earlier) cleared the ground for Jack's self-reflection, as well as for the possiblity of relational transition, necessary, I would argue, for dealing with the stresses found at the interface of the relational and professional.

What more can we note from this close look at a relationship story using a narrative–structural–dialectical approach? First, it is a story that demonstrates the interpenetration of relational culture and professional culture and the workings of interpersonal communication as both cause and effect. Second, the story is presented as fiction, but Jack made a telling point in that regard when he commented on his own convention paper that was to be a piece of fiction: "The issue with my piece . . . is not so much 'did this happen?' but, presuming it did happen or could happen, 'what does it mean?' " (Pacanowsky, 1988, p. 462). Moreover, what the story means, in particular, Jack and Penny's portion of the story, is in part explicated by the narrative–structural–dialectical analysis that I have presented.

Finally, no distinction between individual dialectics and relational dialectics was made because I do not believe such a distinction is necessary. Personal relationships entail mutual responsiveness and adaptation. For example, Penny's apathetic style evoked different actions on Jack's part as compared to her later engagement. In a personal relationship, one cannot act on one's own without affecting the relationship. At any given time, one partner's actions are evoked by the other's actions.

CONCLUSION

I want to use these remaining paragraphs to address two final issues. The first is to briefly enumerate the unique contributions of the dialectical approach just outlined to the ongoing dialogue on dialectical studies of personal relationships, and the second is to point out potential problems I see with those unique contributions.

The Dialectics of Relational Transition brings four unique perspectives to the table: (a) it employs a technique for coming up with dialectical dimensions that may be at work in a relationship; (b) its focus is on discourse, accounts, stories, and narratives of relationships; (c) the approach hypothesizes two metadialectics that subsume all others and directly address the evolution of personal relationships; and (d) it introduces two new concepts into the conversation on dialectical approaches—indigenous dialectical dimensions (in contrast to conventional ones repeated in the literature) and the notion of the fulcrum, which enables us to think about relational shifts from one pole of a dialectical dimension to the other.

Technique or procedure is important to dialectical studies; without procedures to teach others who might be interested in alternatives to current practice in the field, the approach would languish the private possession of a few, rather than be freed to be employed by those students who might want to work with it. One reason statistical, quantitative, laboratory approaches have gained the currency they enjoy is that there exists a common practice that is easily passed down to succeeding generations of students.

A good example of this need for procedural common practice appears in the methods section of a recent dialectical study. When it comes time to find (or create) dialectical dimensions in the subjects' stories of four critical incidents, we are simply told that "the coding categories of identified problems, difficulties and challenges were grouped into more fundamental dialectical tensions based on friend-work negations explicitly mentioned in participant answers" (Bridge & Baxter, 1992, p. 212). Yet, how was this grouping accomplished? Given the subjects' raw data—the narratives of critical incidents—and left to one's own devices to do the grouping, what exactly is the inquisitive student to do? I believe that some procedure or technique is needed in order to make dialectical studies repeatable and teachable.

The technique of structural analysis as demonstrated, is applied to narratives, stories about relationships. Relationship narratives are presumed to depict relationships in important and insightful ways. The rich, multilayered meaningfulness of personal stories preserves, intact, the relationship's natural habitat and avoids the reductive finality of assigning numbers to summarize their meaning.

A third contribution of the approach is that it assigns to dialectical studies the office of explaining relationship evolution. Dialectical dimensions are no longer limited to the important-but-quite-typical role of describing a particular population or relationship type or stage. Rather, the Dialectics of Relational Transition suggests that dialectial movement causes relationships to change. Moreover, the role of the helical model (Fig. 2.1), with its metadialectics of security–alienation and disintegration–resynthesis, is to summarize this unique function of dialectical movement. All dialectical dimensions are to be seen in the service of pushing a relationship around the helix and through the four phases of relationship evolution, which are the poles of the two metadialectical dimensions.

Finally, two ideas have emerged in my own work since the publication of *Relational Transitions* (Conville, 1991). One is the notion of a fulcrum that appears in Fig. 2.2. Because dialectical studies are about the movement of relationships between the poles of a dialectic, it seems useful to be able to point to a time in the relationship when it could be said to have moved from one pole to the other. Such a time appeared in Penny and Jack's story, in Episodes 7 and 8, both depicting pensive moments in the story. Those episodes stood between oblique and direct, certainty and uncertainty, and apathy and part of engagement. This is not a perfect fit, but it is close enough that I believe dialectical fulcrums warrant study in future investigations.

The second new development is the distinction between indigenous and conventional dialectical dimensions. The presumptions here are that orthodoxy is never good (for it means creative thinking has been tamed) and that investigators should remain as close as they can to the real people whose lives they are studying (so their theorizing can be informed by that exposure). So, to keep dialectical thinking alive, investigators should always look for dialectical dimensions not found on the standard list, the conventional ones. Indigenous dialectics are those that seem to be peculiar to the particular relationships under study. They may be just that, unique to those specific persons, and that would be all right. Yet, those indigenous dialectics, on closer examination, may also be found in many other relationships and thus be conventional. Either way, the research is enriched.

Now, of course, each of these unique aspects of the Dialectics of Relational Transition is liable to be problematic. The secret to preventing this is to keep our collective balance. First, we should give technique its due attention. Yet, to go to the other extreme of letting technical virtuosity become an end in itself or degenerate to mere technique would be just as impoverishing as I believe the current extreme is. Second, if our concern is with relationship narratives, the pressing question, "Which ones shall we study?" will occupy many often dreary pages and hours of conversation—as it should. Third, a commitment to dialectical movement as the engine of relationship evolution should not blind us to other possible functions that may be served by such movement. Finally, an overemphasis on indigenous dialectics to the exclusion of conventional ones would severely curtail our ability to produce useful understandings about personal relationships.

To examine the dialectical dimensions of personal relationships is not to shun the "contradictions, contingencies, nonrationalities, and multiple realities" (Baxter, 1992, p. 330) that are the stock in trade of our daily narratives. Rather, it is to plunge headlong into those ordinary stories, affirm their insights and bring their wisdom into the conversation.

REFERENCES

Barthes, R. (1972). The structuralist activity. In R. T. DeGeorge & F. M. DeGeorge (Eds.), *The structuralists from Marx to Lévi-Strauss* (pp. 148–154). Garden City, NY: Doubleday.

Baxter, L. A. (1988). A dialectical perspective on communication strategies in relationship development. In S. Duck (Ed.), *Handbook of personal relationships* (pp. 257–273). Chichester, UK: Wiley.

Baxter, L. A. (1990). Dialectical contradictions in relationship development. *Journal of Social and Personal Relationships, 7,* 69–88.

Baxter, L. A. (1992). Interpersonal communication as dialogue: A response to the "Social Approaches" forum. *Communication Theory, 2,* 330–336.

Baxter, L. A. (1994). Thinking dialogically about communication in personal relationships. In R. L. Conville (Ed.), *Uses of "structure" in communication studies* (pp. 23–38). Westport, CT: Praeger.

Baxter, L. A., & Bullis, C. (1986). Turning points in developing romantic relationships. *Human Communication Research, 12*, 469–493.

Bolton, C. D. (1961). Mate selection as the development of a relationship. *Marriage and Family Living, 23*, 234–240.

Bridge, K., & Baxter, L. A. (1992). Blended friendships: Friends as work associates. *Western Journal of Communication, 56*, 200–225.

Chan, C., & Margolin, G. (1994). The relationship between dual-earner couples' daily work mood and home affect. *Journal of Social and Personal Relationships, 11*, 573–586.

Cissna, K. N., Cox, D. E., & Bochner, A. P. (1990). The dialectic of marital and parental relationships within the stepfamily. *Communication Monographs, 57*, 44–61.

Conville, R. L. (1978). Change, process, and the future of communication education. *Southern Communication Journal, 43*, 265–282.

Conville, R. L. (1983). Second-order development in interpersonal communication. *Human Communication Research, 9*, 195–207.

Conville, R. L. (1991). *Relational transitions.* Westport, CT: Praeger.

Conville, R. L. (1997). Between spearheads: *Bricolage* and relationships. *Journal of Social and Personal Relationships, 14*, 373–386.

Conville, R. L. (in press). Narrative, dialectic, and relationships. In R. L. Conville & L. E. Rogers (Eds.), *The meaning of "relationship" in interpersonal communication.* Westport, CT: Praeger.

Duck, S. (1982). A topography of relationship disengagement and dissolution. In S. Duck (Ed.), *Personal relationships 4: Dissolving personal relationships* (pp. 1–29). London: Academic Press.

Geertz, C. (1973). *The interpretation of cultures.* New York: Basic Books.

Higgins, C. A., & Duxbury, L. E. (1992). Work–family conflict in the dual-career family. *Organizational Behavior and Human Decision Processes, 51*, 51–75.

Knapp, M. L. (1984). *Interpersonal communication and human relationships.* Boston: Allyn & Bacon.

LaRossa, R. (1995). Stories and relationships. *Journal of Social and Personal Relationships, 12*, 553–556.

Levinger, G. (1980). Toward the analysis of close relationships. *Journal of Experimental Social Psychology, 16*, 510–544.

Levinger, G. (1983). Development and change. In H. H. Kelley, E. Berscheid, A. Christensen, J. H. Harvey, T. L. Huston, G. Levinger, E. McClintock, L. A. Peplau, & D. R. Peterson (Eds.), *Close relationships* (pp. 315–359). New York: Freeman.

Lévi-Strauss, C. (1963). The structural study of myth. In C. Jacobson & B. G. Schoepf (Trans.), *Structural anthropology* (pp. 206–231). New York: Basic Books.

Montgomery, B. M. (1993). Relationship maintenance versus relationship change: A dialectical dilemma. *Journal of Social and Personal Relationships, 10*, 205–223.

O'Neill, J. (1974). *Making sense together.* New York: HarperCollins.

Pacanowsky, M. (1988). Slouching towards Chicago. *Quarterly Journal of Speech, 74*, 453–467.

Planalp, S., & Honeycutt, J. M. (1985). Events that increase uncertainty in personal relationships. *Human Communication Research, 11*, 593–604.

Planalp, S., Rutherford, D. K., & Honeycutt, J. M. (1988). Events that increase uncertainty in personal relationships II, replication and extension. *Human Communication Research, 14*, 516–547.

Rawlins, W. K. (1983). Negotiating close friendship: The dialectic of conjunctive freedoms. *Human Communication Research, 9*, 255–266.

Rawlins, W. K. (1992). *Friendship matters: Communication, dialectics, and the life course.* Hawthorne, NY: de Gruyter.

Rorty, R. (1979). *Philosophy and the mirror of nature.* Princeton, NJ: Princeton University Press.

Tannen, D. (1990). *You just don't understand.* New York: Ballantine.

Watzlawick, P., Bavelas, J. H., & Jackson, D. D. (1967). *Pragmatics of human communication.* New York: Norton.

Williams, K. J., & Alliger, G. M. (1994). Role stressors, mood spillover, and perceptions of work–family conflict in employed parents. *Academy of Management Journal, 37,* 837–868.

Wood, J. T. (1982). Communication and relational culture: Bases for the study of human relationships. *Communication Quarterly, 30,* 75–83.

Yeats, W. B. (1983). *W. B. Yeats, the poems.* (R. J. Finneran, Ed., new ed.). New York: Macmillan.

APPENDIX*

Penny One

"Well, looks like I'll be going to Chicago in November." It was at dinner time. Jack managed to squeeze it into the ongoing patter that mealtimes with a three-year-old inevitably involved. He thought it might go unheard.

"Oh?" said Penny, catching it.

"Can I go with you?" asked Joshua, who caught it too.

"No, Josh, I'm afraid not. It's for a convention, and Chicago is very far away."

"A convention?" said Penny, a bit sharply. "I thought you had sworn off on them."

"I want to go with you," said Joshua.

"It'll only be a couple of days, Josh. I have to present a paper."

"A paper? From your book?"

"No," Jack confessed. "It's another project."

"Oh," said Penny, disappointed.

"I don't want you to go," said Josh.

"It's kind of an interesting thing, though. Jim Radner asked me to be on a panel. He put it together. New directions for communication research. I'm doing something about using fiction as a form of scholarly discourse. I'll be able to pound it out in a weekend. It won't interfere with my book. Well, maybe just a little. But it's something I want to do." He felt he was blabbering. Penny hadn't accused him of anything, so why was he over-explaining? He tried to make light of it. "I'm toying with the idea of writing the paper itself in fiction. I mean, a fictionalized argument about using fiction as a form of — "

---

*From M. Pacanowsky (1988). "Slouching toward Chicago." *Quarterly Journal of Speech, 74,* 453–467. Used by permission.

"Oh," said Penny, dismissing him.

"I don't want you to go," said Joshua.

Penny Two

"I found it," said Penny, impishly. She was carrying a dusty copy of the *Norton Anthology* in her hand. "I had to dig up in the attic to find it."

Jack swiveled from his desk in the study. "Whatcha got?"

"I am going to oral interp a poem for you. The poem is entitled 'A Kuhnian Paradigm Shift' by William Butler Yeats."

"I thought that Yeats considerably predated Kuhn."

"Hush," said Penny, pretending to be stern. She opened the book melodramatically. "This poem is about quantitative versus qualitative research. It is about yelling and screaming at academic conventions. It is about men who interrupt important work for trivial pursuits." She began reading Yeats's "Slouching Toward Bethlehem."

" 'Things fall apart; the center cannot hold.' See, that's about the disaffections that people have with traditional approaches. 'Mere anarchy is loosed upon the world, / The blood-dimmed tide is loosed, and everywhere / The ceremony of innocence is drowned.' See, this refers to the moaning and groaning going on about there being no standards by which interpretive work can be evaluated, and how everybody comes to see that the standards are less important than the academic-political system that supports them. 'The best lack all conviction, while the worst / Are full of passionate intensity.' That's the part about academic conventions."

She stepped back, feigning a startled, cringing posture. "Here comes the part about the paradigm shift. 'Surely some revelation is at hand. / Surely the Second Coming is at hand. / The Second Coming!' " She raised her arms in alleluia praise. Then quickly she slumped, as "out of the desert" the "shape" comes. Her "gaze" was "blank," and scornfully "witless." She moved her thighs slowly, crouching toward him, hands at the ready to clutch his throat. " 'And what rough beast, its hour come round at last, / Slouches towards Chicago, to be born?' " She leaped on him and playfully choked him, laughing in good spirit.

"I thought the last line was 'slouches towards Bethlehem'?" said Jack.

"That was a different paradigm shift, a considerably more important one," said Penny, changing her chokehold into a hug. "The switch from Bethlehem to Chicago is just my little way of reminding you to keep some perspective on the ultimate significance of all this stuff you're getting so worked up about."

When she left the room, Jack went back immediately to his work. But later that night, he bothered to write in his notebook: To Slouch—to stand 'not like a man,' to slump when one should stand tall. To Posture—to stand tall, when one oughtn't. Am I slouching, or posturing, towards Chicago?

Penny Three

"So, what did you think?"

Jack would frequently give his papers to Penny to read. He respected her as a reader. She was seldom given to "I like it" or "I don't like it" responses. She treated his work with more seriousness than that.

Penny sat herself in the rocker, and dropped the manuscript onto her lap. "You show your age."

"Too autobiographical?"

"No, though it will be read that way. But what I meant about you showing your age has to do with theme. An academic neophyte would be more idealistic than your narrator. An emeritus-to-be would have resolved, successfully or otherwise, the tension in the issue that your narrator attempts to negotiate."

"And just what do you see his issue to be?"

"He's struggling between careerism and cynicism. He's far enough along to see the choices, but still young enough to think he can opt out, overcome really. He still believes in the possibility of the redeeming grace of accomplishment."

"Interesting, I didn't intend that."

"I also am not sure you intend what you think you intend."

"Huh?"

"Well, this is supposed to extol fiction, but I'm not sure that's what you're really interested in. At first I thought you were interested in particularity, not fiction, and you are to an extent. But it's not an empiricist's interest in particularity. You don't care so much if you describe a real reality. So what then is the purpose of this particularity?"

"It's just where I operate best. I'm not a theoretician."

"But what are you then?"

Jack was silent for a moment, "I'm not sure."

"See, that's what I mean. I think you want to be a moralist."

3

Mucking Around
Looking for Truth

Arthur P. Bochner
Carolyn Ellis
Lisa Tillmann-Healy
University of South Florida

> *You and Joy always said, while growing up, "Well, if I had a*
> *normal mother . . . !" meaning the apron and the cookies*
> *and none of this typewriting stuff that was shocking the*
> *hell out of friends' mothers, . . . But I say to myself*
> *better I was mucking around looking for truth.*
> —letter from Anne Sexton to Linda Gray Sexton (1994)

In *Searching For Mercy Street*, Sexton (1994) tells the riveting story of her troubled relationship with her mother, poet Anne Sexton, who committed suicide in 1974 at the age of 45. She begins with the event that defined both her childhood and Anne's motherhood—being sent away for 2 years to live in the home of relatives while her mother recuperated from a psychotic episode. Expressing complex feelings of abandonment and confusion, isolation and yearning, and disgust and admiration, Linda describes her lifelong struggle to free herself from the grip of her powerful, dependent mother without relinquishing the love and empathy she felt for her. She recounts details of her mother's extramarital affairs with both women and men, her sexual abuse of her children, her cruelty toward her husband, and her disturbed reversal of the mother–child bond. Accounting for her mother's destructive behavior as "the price and reward of madness . . . and . . . genius" (p. 276), Linda refuses to demonize her mother as a monster or exempt her as a victim; nor is she willing to oversimplify her complicated feelings of love and rage:

> I loved my mother when she was alive; I love her still—despite anger, despite
> her mental illness and the things it allowed her to do. I never wanted her to
> seem like "a monster" to anyone. She was loving and kind, but she was also
> sick and destructive. She tried to be "a good mother," but in truth, she was
> not. Mother was simply human, subject to all sorts of frailties and problems.
> (p. 281)

Sexton (1994) challenges her readers to question the usefulness of applying simplistic labels, such as "abused child" or "vengeful daughter," to
summarize terribly complicated family relationships. Her narrative is a grace-
ful exposition of the concrete lived circumstances in which a person struggles to deal with the dialectics of attachment–loss, separation–integration,
vulnerability–cruelty, and expression–protection. Moreover, *Searching For
Mercy Street* is uniquely self-reflexive. The text bends back on itself and its
author, as Sexton puts words to her memories in order to mourn her losses
and to better understand the meaning of a rich and agitated bond between
daughter and mother. As her mother once said, "I write to master experience," so Sexton writes to "take control of the demons inside and let them
know who was boss"—to earn "the reward of a mind clearer for the effort,
a soul cleansed and released" (p. 296). Inevitably, her insistence on telling the
whole painful truth as she remembers it leads her to confront not only the
demons of a disturbed relationship, but also the taboos that silence writing
from the heart:

> Though I am no longer a child, to write of these things feels forbidden, to give
> voice to memories such as these, taboo. Family matters: dark and secret. I re-
> member the snake who comes in the dark, the taste of fear sour in my mouth,
> the blackness of a bedroom not my own, and worst of all the voice whispering:
> *If you tell they will not love you anymore. If you tell they will send you away
> again.* (p. 21)

PERSONAL NARRATIVE

Searching For Mercy Street is an exemplar of the kind of narrative inquiry
that fuses social science and literature by creating texts in which the language
of science merges with the aesthetics of art (Benson, 1993). The products of
what Brady (1991) calls "artful science" are narratives that simulate reality,
applying the imaginative power of literary, dramatic, and poetic forms to
create the effect of reality, a convincing likeness to life as it is sensed, felt, and
lived.

In recent years, numerous writers have advocated a turn toward narrative
modes of scholarship in the social sciences (Bochner, 1994; Bruner, 1986,
1990a; Crites, 1986; Polkinghorne, 1988; Richardson, 1990; Rosenwald &

Ochberg, 1992; Sarbin, 1986). Emphasizing the stories people tell about their lives, these writers construe narrative as both a means of knowing and a way of telling about the social world. As Richardson (1990) suggests, "narrative is the best way to understand the human experience because it is the way humans understand their own lives" (p. 183). This call for stories (Coles, 1989; Frank, 1995) is echoed by Schafer (1980) who observes that stories are not only the way we tell ourselves to others, but also the very instrument of our being—our way of becoming who we are. Generally, narrative inquiry focuses on the functions of stories and storytelling in creating and managing identity in a social world, the expressive forms for making sense of lived experience and communicating it to others, the entanglements that permeate how interpersonal life is lived and how it is told to others, the reflexive dimensions of the relationship between storytellers and their audiences, and the canonical narratives that circulate through society and culture, offering scripted ways of acting (Bochner, 1994).

Using what she calls a "dialectical lens" grounded in Bakhtin's (1981) concept of dialogue, Baxter (1992) identifies narrative inquiry as an alternative to the dominant psychological approaches to the study of interpersonal communication. Looking toward the future, Baxter (1992) predicts that "personal narratives are likely to emerge as the distinguishing method of social approaches to personal relationships" (p. 333).

Since 1990, we and our colleagues at the University of South Florida have been engaged in a project on personal narrative that emphasizes subjectivity, self-reflexivity, emotionality, dialogue, autobiographical experience, and the goal of connecting social sciences to humanities (Bochner, 1994; Bochner & Ellis, 1992, 1995, 1996; Bochner, Ellis, & Tillmann-Healy, 1996; Bochner & Waugh, 1995; Ellis, 1991, 1993, 1995a, 1995b, 1995c; 1996; Ellis & Bochner, 1992, 1996a, 1996b; Ellis & Flaherty, 1992; Kiesinger, 1995; Tillmann-Healy, 1996). These narratives are presented in forms of writing that radically depart from the conventions of rational–analytic social science reporting. In many respects, the personal narratives we write and the research practices we promote are more similar to the texts and methods of works like Sexton's *Searching For Mercy Street* (1994) and Hamill's *A Drinking Life* (1994) than to the monographs of traditional academic journals such as *Communication Monographs* or *The Journal of Personal and Social Relationships*.

We can identify five distinguishing features of this narrative project. First, the author usually writes in the first person, making herself or himself the object of research (Tedlock, 1991), thus breaching the conventional separation of researcher and subject (Jackson, 1989). Second, the narrative text normally breaches the traditional focus on generalization across cases by focusing on generalization within a single case extended over time (Geertz, 1973). Third, the text is presented as a story replete with a narrator, characterization, and plotline, akin to forms of writing associated with the novel or biography, and thus fractures the boundaries that traditionally separate social science from literature. Fourth, the story often discloses hidden details of private life and highlights emotional experience, and thus challenges the rational actor model of social performance that dominates social science. Fifth, the ebb and flow of relationship experience is depicted in an episodic form that dramatizes the motion of connected lives across the curve of time (Weinstein, 1988) and thus resists the standard practice of portraying a relationship as a snapshot (Ellis, 1994).

These features are also present in narratives such as Sexton's *Searching For Mercy Street*. Sexton writes her story as a first-person account in which she is both the narrator and the main character. She observes and interprets the meanings of her own actions as well as those of her mother and other family members. Thus, she acts as both a researcher and a participant.

Second, Sexton's story covers events that took place in her family over a period of nearly 40 years. She does not try to extend the meanings and conclusions she draws about her family to other families, although readers certainly can locate some of their own experience in that of the Sextons. Rather, she focuses on the patterns of interaction that recurred over time in the case of her particular family (across the span of three generations). In the process, she shows how reality was constituted in this family culture, within this time frame, and at this place.

Third, Sexton presents her family history as a story. She uses many of the storytelling techniques associated with fiction to animate the drama of her experience and to heighten interest in the story. Yet, she relies on a core of empirical "facts" that give her story credibility as a "true" account. As a reader, you are aware that Sexton is negotiating the meaning of these events as she goes along, using what Bruner (1990) called the "shadowy epistemology of the story" to try on different interpretations (p. 54). She keeps you open to the multiple and uncertain meanings of a good story. Thus, her narrative falls between fiction and fact, between the imaginary and the real. As Berger (1983) observes, "life outstrips our vocabulary" (p. 77), so Sexton (1994) recognizes the complex connection between words and reality: "Words can capture truth or promulgate lies. Words can clarify or disguise . . . what I seek is only the truth of how I *felt,* a truth far more revelatory *about me* than any exact history" (p. 39).

Fourth, by articulating her feelings within an intelligible frame of family relationships—one that centers on painful, hidden family secrets—Sexton openly confronts the moral predicament of what constitutes a good life *for her.* She has to come to grips with what really matters—her children, her husband, and her career as a writer—and what she gives to and takes from other people. Thus, by making sense of her past, she clears a path for her future.

Finally, the story of life in the Sexton family is revealed in concrete episodes of interaction. Sexton recreates scenes from her history in which the members of her family enact the patterns that bind them. Readers witness family members interacting with each other, feel their moods, and sense their entrapment. These scenes include both the commonplaces of everyday life— cooking, cleaning, transporting, and celebrating holidays—and the exceptional events that characterized the family's particularity—sexual abuse, family violence, corruption of normal family roles. We learn that the Sextons are like most families much of the time, but they also endure extreme episodes of deviance and disturbance. If we witnessed only one or two of these episodes, our capacity to grasp the larger configuration of imbalance between ordinary and extraordinary events would be greatly inhibited.

NARRATIVE AND INQUIRY ON DIALECTIC

As social scientists, how do we write about human experiences? This is a question that every social scientist who uses the print medium of expression inevitably confronts. The issue of writing is particularly important to our project because we seek to legitimate a space for composing texts that coincide with the variety, ambiguity, and contingency of lived experience (Jackson, 1995). As we see it, social scientists need to understand the goal of their writing not as representation but as *communication* (Bochner & Waugh, 1995; Tyler, 1986).

We begin with the assumption that writing is a process of turning life into language. Written reality, as Jackson (1995) says, is always a second-order reality. Whether we use qualitative or quantitative methods, or call our work empiricist, interpretivist, or critical makes little difference. All of us rework and reshape the way the events we are representing or expressing are seen when we render them as language. As Rorty (1989) states, "where there are no sentences there is no truth" (p. 5). When we fit language to the world, all of us are "mucking around looking for truth" (Sexton, 1994, p. 93).

Nevertheless, traditional social science writing differs in important ways from the styles of evocative narrative writing associated with our project. Traditional social science writing privileges the types of events and data that are amenable to conceptual analysis and theoretical explanation. Ambiguous, vague, and contingent experiences that cannot easily be covered by concepts or organized into a coherent system of thought are bypassed in favor of experiences that can be controlled and explained. Immediate experience becomes grist for the theoretical mill. Moreover, distancing oneself from the subject matter (like a spectator at a sporting event) is taken as an appropriate and normative model of research and writing practices. Thus, the text is written in a neutral, authoritative, and scientific voice.

Bruner (1986) regards narrative and traditional scientific (logico–scientific) ways of knowing as two distinctively different, but complementary means of organizing experience and constructing reality. According to Bruner, the logico–scientific, or *paradigmatic,* mode emphasizes general causes and uses standardized procedures to assure public verifiability and reach empirical truths. The paradigmatic mode tests logically derived possibilities (hypotheses) against observables to reach formal conclusions about general causes, however tentative, that are warranted by empirical observations. Truthfulness is established by marshalling empirical evidence.

Like paradigmatic arguments, narratives also function as a means of persuasion. However, as Bruner (1986) observes, they are "fundamentally different: arguments convince one of their truth, stories of their lifelikeness" (p. 11). The storyteller is preoccupied with showing how lived experience is endowed with meaning. The result is not so much conclusive as it is believable. Stories invite readers to enter horizons of the human condition where lived life is shown as comic, tragic, and absurd, and where opportunities exist to mold a reality and live in it. "How to encompass in our minds the complexity of some lived moments in life?" asks Coles (1989, p. 128). "You don't do that with theories. You don't do that with a system of ideas. You do it with a story" (p. 128).

We believe that narrative inquiry is consonant with a dialectical world view and should be more widely encouraged and appreciated as a legitimate form of inquiry. Because only a few evocative narrative texts have been published in mainstream social science journals or by academic presses, we are compelled to ask some hard questions about why data tend to be privileged over stories, variables over episodes, and categories or typologies over concrete details of lived experience. It is not our purpose to argue that narrative should replace conventional social science writing. We are merely trying to say that there are goals we can achieve with a story that we cannot achieve with a theory; these goals are crucially important to the moral and ethical calling of the social sciences and we should try to create an atmosphere of harmonious tolerance in which we understand the differences between these modes of inquiry and nurture attempts to place narrative on an equal footing with logico–scientific inquiry. After considering the fit between dialectic and narrative, we will try to explain why narrative has assumed a marginal existence in social science inquiry on close personal relationships.

Dialectic begins with the view that every idea is based on relationship; we can think of something only by connecting it to something else. In traditional philosophy, dialectic was considered a unique method for discovering truth, constructing arguments, and elucidating ideas. Dialectic was a verbal art, a search for truth through dialogue (Maranhao, 1990). Speakers used dialogue to ameliorate differences between two or more related ideas or arguments, showing that each position is ultimately incomplete unless integrated to reach a higher truth. Gradually, dialectic became not only a method of analysis and reasoning, but also a way of understanding how people and things evolve and change. The dialectical principle of a fusion of opposites was appropriated from the realm of argument and logic to the realm of human development. Dialectical movement explained how relations between people irresistibly move toward contradictions that ultimately evolve toward more complex wholes, that is, toward a unity of opposites.

Terms such as *dialectical movement, dialectical process,* and *dialectical development* emphasize active, dynamic, and evolving qualities of relations lived over time. The vocabulary of dialectic shifts attention away from certainty, control, and destiny toward epiphany, contingency, and chance. Change becomes the prime condition of relationship. Nothing stays the same; every stage of life unfolds as an oppositional conflict in need of reconciliation. In this sense, dialectic can be understood as a philosophy of strife. Struggle is the law of progress.

Our project treats dialectic as a tool for dealing with the world. Contradictions are not issues to be resolved, but rather circumstances to be felt, understood, and lived with (Rorty, 1989). Dialectical knowledge gains significance by being put to use. By offering stories that show the struggles of ordinary people coping with contingencies of relationship life, dialectical research can help people put themselves in the place of others (Jackson, 1995) and consider important aspects of their own lives in the terms offered by the contexts of other peoples' stories. These stories express lived experience as riddled with contingencies that concede the incomplete and unfinished qualities of human relationships. Ideally, dialectical research authenticates the novelty, creativity, and complexity of human relationships.

Research associated with a dialectical perspective, however, rarely shows people actively struggling with predicaments of personal relationships (see reviews by Baxter, 1988; Bochner, 1984; Werner & Baxter, 1994). Indeed, most published research omits concrete details of connected lives, eclipsing lived experiences with concepts, categories and typologies.[1] Readers are not encouraged to see and feel the struggles and emotions of participants. Normally, readers are deprived of an opportunity to care about the particular people whose struggles nourish the author's hunger for dialectical truth.

---

[1] For exceptions that promote a narrative or interpretive view of dialectic, see Ellis (1995a), Ellis and Bochner (1992), Rawlins (1991), and Yerby and Gourd (1994). Although Rawlins' (1991) work shows more respect for maintaining the integrity of lived experience, it preserves many of the conventions of social science writing that we seek to change (see Ellis, 1994). Conville's (1991, 1997) research expresses a narrative sensibility that is sensitive to the emotional struggles of relationship partners over time, but his work is composed within an orthodox conceptual framework that privileges narrative analysis. Altman and his colleagues (i.e., Altman, Brown, Staples, & Werner, 1992) apply an ethnographic and cultural approach to studying dialectics of close relationships, but their work is written within the realist tradition associated with the spectator or distanced model of social science we are calling "orthodox" and "mainstream."

Instead, taking a dialectical perspective has largely become a cognitive activity in which investigators present themselves as disinterested spectators — surveying, watching, analyzing, and reporting on other people's marriages, families, or friendships. Although contradictions are recognized in most dialectical perspectives as concrete lived experiences (Werner & Baxter, 1994), they are usually expressed in forms of writing that dissolve concrete events in solutions of abstract analysis. The reader is left to look through a stained glass window (to use Turner's apt analogy), seeing only murky and featureless profiles (Turner, 1993). The concrete details of sensual, emotional, and embodied experience are replaced by typologies and abstractions that remove events from their context, distancing readers from the actions and feelings of particular human beings engaged in the joint action of evolving relationships. Although writers repeatedly emphasize the importance of dynamic and developmental processes, their research usually abstracts themes, typologies, or categories of dialectical contradiction that seem unfaithful to the sense of movement, process, and change over time on which dialectic is predicated.

Of course, many researchers working within a dialectical framework recognize the importance of concentrating on the particularities of their subjects' accounts and the potentially rich descriptions offered by using qualitative or textual data. As a result, they have turned to in-depth interviewing as a strategy for recovering and representing lived experiences (Baxter, 1990; Conville, 1991; Rawlins, 1983a, 1983b, 1991; Stamp, 1994; Stamp & Banski, 1992). Whereas interview studies usually attempt to preserve the integrity of subjects' accounts, the narratives presented in these studies tend to reproduce research and writing conventions associated with realist social science. Thus, when represented in research articles, lengthy interviews are reduced to what we call *snippets*—textual fragments presented in the native voice for the express purpose of illustrating concepts and showing their interpretive significance (Ellis, 1994). The focus is on the concept being illustrated (not on developing empathy for the person having the experience), the universality of the experience (not on its particularity), and analysis abstracted from experience (not on transporting readers into an experience in which they must feel as well as think). Consequently, the reader usually does not know enough about the subjects from these excerpted snippets to feel for them or empathize with their particular plights. Moreover, in these studies, subjects talk to each other or to the interviewer under conditions controlled by the interviewer. Then, the influence of the researcher over the subjects' accounts is downplayed as the researcher writes herself out of the report, maintaining the appearance of a spectator at the research event who speaks in a neutral, scientific voice.

In this approach to research, narrative is an instrumental means to an analytical end. Used primarily to illustrate concepts, stories give way to the authoritative analytical voice of the author. The author's voice overshadows stories of the subjects, who never get to share authority or negotiate the meaning of their remarks. To their credit, these researchers emphasize interpretive meanings and native voices, but the shadow of a modernist empiricism hovers over their written documents.

We are belaboring a curious circumstance in which a gap exists between the premises of dialectical inquiry and the forms of writing normally used to represent dialectical knowledge. We do not mean to imply that the body of work that exists on relational dialectics is without merit. Indeed, we are impressed by the growing interest in dialectical approaches to communication and the substantial influence of dialectics on how scholars think about relationship life (Baxter & Montgomery, 1996; Rawlins, 1991). We are not trying to draw a line between ourselves and everyone else studying relationships from a dialectical perspective; we are not insisting that there is only one acceptable or proper approach to dialectical inquiry. Many of the studies discussed were not attempting to produce the kind of effects we seek in our work, and we do not feel at loggerheads with scholars who are struggling to understand and use dialectical inquiry for other purposes. However, we question whether the promise of dialectical research can be realized without a strong commitment to a narrative approach that emphasizes modes of writing that show the situated concrete details of lived experience. As Yerby (1995) points out, a dialectical perspective directs us to explore "what people do in the process of generating meaning—and what they do is to construct and co-construct narratives" (p. 338). It is important to understand why a narrative approach that coincides so well with the premises of relational dialectics (Baxter & Montgomery, 1996) continues to experience a marginal legitimacy.

HOW WE LEARN TO WRITE AS SOCIAL SCIENTISTS

Why have experiences like strife, struggle, opposition, and epiphany been represented so often in the cool and detached terms of abstract concepts and categories—a language that robs the lived reality that gives dialectic significance? We think it is because dialectical perspectives have gained currency by becoming a scientific inquiry that treats contradiction mainly as something to be grasped conceptually, controlled rationally, and consumed as knowledge (Jackson, 1995). To a large extent, the process orientation associated with dialectics has been obliged to fit the goals of orthodox social science, which typically wrestles abstract systems of knowledge from the flux of lived experience. It is this sense of obligation, duty, or allegiance to a monolithic standard for conducting, writing, and judging research that we believe needs to be understood and altered. To do so, it is necessary to understand how much our careers as academics depend on how successfully we learn to craft our research texts.

The literature referred to as "dialectical perspectives on communication" is situated mainly within the corporate institutional framework of academic social science, namely departments of communication, sociology, and social psychology. As academics, writers working within the boundaries of these disciplines learn to conform to the research practices and conventions of writing that are taken for granted by their disciplines. Success as a scholar is largely determined by how well one masters and conforms to these practices.

Academic life involves reading, observing, and writing. We learn to conduct research and write monographs by reading and studying the work of our predecessors and mentors (Rose, 1993). Thus, the norms of what will count as legitimate research and publishable writing are carefully controlled by our disciplines through instrumental contacts with peers, professors, articles, monographs, and books. Methods of gathering and accumulating documentation are formulated within the constraints of accepted practices of inquiry and recognized modes of representation. Regardless of the subject matter, these conventionalized practices confine inquiry to a limited range of researchable experiences represented in a narrow domain of recognizable texts (Rose, 1993). We are groomed to engage in certain types of research experiences and compose texts that satisfy the expectations of our discipline's norms (Richardson, 1996). If our professional socialization takes, we learn to write effectively in the largely standardized genres that are accepted as legitimate in our discipline (Rose, 1993). In short, what we learn is a great deal of conformity (Krieger, 1991). As Rose (1990) points out, "If you write a nonconforming text, then the rewards of the discipline may be withheld because the book does not read as a legitimated contribution to knowledge" (p. 14). Although human experience may be abundantly diverse, the accepted canons of representing or expressing it within our disciplines are highly conventionalized and monolithic. As Richardson (1994) indicates, the conventions of mainstream social science marginalize and discourage experimental, poetic, or creative modes of writing.

As we write these words, we are reminded of Sexton's (1994) poignant remarks about the taboos against voicing family secrets and long hidden memories: "to write of these things feels forbidden . . . *If you tell they will not love you anymore. If you tell they will send you away again*" (p. 21). Often, we feel like we are anchored in a forbidden zone too, risking the loss of community and collegiality offered to those who conform without resistance. Is it too much to expect that the craving for certainty, control, and a distanced objectivity can be moderated by an appreciation for the moral, creative, and emotional aspects of social inquiry? If we take the risk of writing in ways that breach orthodox conventions, will we be sent away, cast out, exiled from our disciplines (Ellis & Bochner, in press)?

DIALECTIC AS REDESCRIPTION

Our goal is to make it possible to practice an artful, poetic, and empathic social science in which readers can keep in their minds and feel in their bodies the complexities of concrete moments of lived relationship life (Ellis & Bochner, 1996a). Dialectical experience can be expressed in forms of writing that position readers as active participants engaging in a wide horizon of contextualized meanings. We want readers to be able to put themselves in the place of others, within a culture of experience that enlarges their social awareness and empathy. Our research becomes a form of what Jackson (1989, 1995) calls "radical empiricism,"[2] in which the desired outcome is care not control: "Its field is experience undergone rather than gone beyond. Knowledge is seen as a form of worldly immanence, a being-with-others, an understanding" (Jackson, 1995, p. 164).

Werner and Baxter's (1994) review of the literature on dialectical approaches to interpersonal communication calls attention to the importance and distinctiveness of dialectical discourse by suggesting that dialectical (and other temporal) approaches "offer a richer vocabulary for describing relationship dynamics" (p. 323). Yet, the literature they review clearly shows that the vocabulary of dialectic is inscribed within the privileged terms of causal social science discourse. As we just suggested, much of the research associated with dialectical approaches begins with the premises of the old vocabulary of traditional social science. Thus, the vocabulary of dialectic, as represented by these studies, is not so much a radical redescription of relationship dynamics as it is a modest attempt to squeeze one way of talking into another.

Regrettably, Werner and Baxter's (1994) summary of the research literature reduces what dialectical contradiction offers the study of close relationships to a language of driving forces, and motors of change, a way of talking about dialectic that conforms to the language of orthodox causal social science. To their credit, Werner and Baxter (1994) emphasize that "contradictions are not reified abstractions but concrete, lived experiences" (p. 354), and they understand that "dialectics encourages a focus on how contradictions flow and unfold over and in time" (p. 351). Yet, the studies they review

---

[2]Jackson (1989) differentiates radical empiricism from traditional empiricism. *Radical empiricism* rejects the boundaries between observer and observed, and method and object, focusing instead on the interplay of these domains. In radical empiricism, the subject is necessarily a participant, and the observer is necessarily included in the field of the observed as primary data. Radical empiricism is nonreductive (to mathematical or mechanical models), focuses on the temporality of experience, and centers on the everyday world of lived experience in which the value of an idea is judged against the practical, ethical, and emotional demands of living. For a fuller treatment of radical empiricism, see Jackson's *Paths Toward a Clearing* (1989).

never try to show what it feels like to experience a dialectical contradiction in a lived bodily way; they do not provide detailed, concrete depictions of relational partners in the process of narrating or coconstructing their lived experiences in a fashion that would provide a temporal sweep or psychological depth germane to dialectical contradiction. In the final analysis, Werner and Baxter's (1994) reading of the literature offers little reason to deviate from the practices, conventions, and criteria of the orthodox canon of social science inquiry.

We share Werner and Baxter's desire to champion the cause of dialectical approaches. Our resistance to the ways in which they talk about dialectic stems from our different view of what vocabularies do. Whereas Werner and Baxter (1994) see dialectic as a better way of representing the world than other ways and thus a richer vocabulary, we see dialectic as a tool for dealing with the world for certain purposes (Rorty, 1989) and thus as a mode of redescription. For us, dialectic changes the way we talk, what we want to do, and what we think relationships are. Dialectic is an alternative tool, one that is not truer, but only more useful for certain purposes. By calling attention to the multiplicity of meanings in social actions, the oppositional and contradictory qualities of an engaged life lived in a world of others, the ambiguity and deniability of utterances, the incompleteness of joint action (Shotter, 1987), and the local and momentary contingencies out of which sense is coconstructed and co-enacted, dialectical discourse implies a relational world that is made or invented rather than found or discovered—not a very good language if one is seeking driving forces or motors of change.

For instance, a dialectical orientation tells us that the self is existentially hungry for alliance with others and, ironically, the famished self often becomes its own greatest barrier to the requisite mutuality of relationship. This is precisely the plot of many relationship disasters depicted in fictional literature and cinema and lived out in many of our own lives. It is one thing to worry about whether objective, scientific methods can be applied to plot in a generalizable form the spiraling of the hungry self charged, but unprepared for the perils of intimate connection. It is quite another thing to want to retain and communicate the sense of life and drama immured in such a tale, a sense that would create for the reader the effect of reality of what the original event felt like.

To exploit what dialectic has to offer as a vocabulary of relationship life and relationship study, we find it useful to view relationship as akin to fiction, as Weinstein (1988) suggests, something made rather than found, generated from beliefs not facts. Fiction has a double meaning here, insofar as we emphasize both the storied quality of relationship life associated with fiction and the idea that a relationship is endowed with fictitious qualities. A relationship is an often vague, jointly created, unfinished story built out of the fragile and fallible material of beliefs and meanings (Bochner, Ellis, &

Tillmann-Healy, 1996). It is a work of art co-created through joint action, a contingent fiction given shape and meaning by the stories that form and inform its enactments (Bochner, Ellis, & Tillmann-Healy, 1996). As Weinstein (1988) implies, fiction is a useful metaphor for the study of relationships because it has a temporal sweep, a psychological depth, and a narrative expansiveness that challenges and illuminates the vicissitudes and density of lived relationship experience.

Our project reconfigures dialectic as a narrative activity permeated by contradiction. Narrative is both a means of coping with contradiction and a way of communicating to others the concrete details associated with the experiencing of contradictions. As Bruner (1990b) says, "narrative, unlike logic, is not stopped dead by contradiction" (p. 350). Our model for writing such stories is akin to narrative ethnography (Tedlock, 1991), in which the curve of coupled lives unfolds over time in a layered story that encourages new ways of seeing and feeling the situational dramas of contingent relationship life (e.g., Ellis, 1995a).

If time is the medium of relationship, then narrative offers promise for showing how relationships are lived because narrative is an artful medium for depicting the continuous life of experience across time. Bakhtin (1981) argues that the special accomplishment of the novel is its layered consciousness, its immediacy, and its radical treatment of life lived and remembered over time. These same features characterize personal relationships. By self-consciously experimenting with forms of writing that characterize fiction, we can radically transform relationship study and make its modes of expression more congruent with the way people understand their own lives— through narrative (Richardson, 1990).

Thus, we are drawn to texts of relational life that make us feel something about the people they depict, texts with characters who are not anonymous. The stories we write and analyze show action unfolding over time in scenes that give context to the lives and actions they depict. Drawn from the events of everyday relational life, the plots of these stories are ideally expressed in multiple voices and enacted through dialogues and conversations that have the sound and feel of lived reality.

CASES

A narrative approach to dialectical research on personal relationships is intended to show how people breach canonical conventions and expectations; how they cope with exceptional, difficult, and transformative crises in their relationships; how they invent new ways of speaking when old ways fail them; how they make the absurd sensible and the disastrous manageable; and how they turn the calamities of fate into the gifts of humanity. Stories activate subjectivity and compel emotional response; stories long to be used rather than analyzed, to be told and retold rather than theorized and settled, to teach lessons for further conversation rather than truths that are unrivaled, and to offer the companionship of intimate detail as a substitute for the loneliness of abstracted facts. Stories not only breach ordinary and canonical inscriptions about living, but ideally, they challenge norms of writing and research. They force us to reconsider the goals of our work, the forms we use for expressing relationship experience, and the divisions we accept and enforce uncritically that separate literature from social science. Thus, a narrative approach to dialectic should encourage dialogue about the issues and values at stake in research on relationships and promote conversation about the purposes and legitimate forms of communicating this work.

 We regret that we do not have a sufficient opportunity here to provide a robust example of the narrative genre we are advocating in this chapter. Our space limitations preclude the kind of longitudinal depiction of events that a useful example from this genre would provide. In another publication (Bochner, Ellis, & Tillmann-Healy, 1996), we discussed several books and monographs that resist the standard practice of portraying a relationship as a snapshot and, instead, illustrate the motion of connected lives sustained across the curve of time and fate (Butler & Rosenblum, 1991; Ellis, 1995a; Ellis & Bochner, 1992; Franck, 1994; Kiesinger, 1995; Roth, 1991).

We do not think it is appropriate, however, to pitch our entire appeal to a narrative approach to dialectical research at a level of abstraction removed entirely from concrete examples. Thus, we offer two short examples that capture the spirit of our approach. These examples are episodes taken from longer texts representative of the work we embrace. Readers should consult the original sources for a more complete appreciation of a narrative approach to dialectic research (Ellis, 1995a; Tillmann-Healy, 1996).

The first two examples are taken from Lisa Tillmann-Healy's (1996) "A Secret Life in a Culture of Thinness," in which she illustrates the gradual development of her own bulimia and shows the dark, covert operations necessitated by living with an eating disorder (pp. 92–93, 97–98; copyright © 1996 by AltaMira Press, a division of Sage Publications, Inc.). Emphasizing how a bulimic woman lives and feels, Tillmann-Healy also portrays the dialectics of secrecy and candor (Bochner, 1984; Rawlins, 1991; Werner & Baxter, 1994), as she struggles with the guilt she feels about what she must hide from her parents and her need to tell her story to the man she loves. In the following scene, Lisa expresses her hidden desire to confess her secret life to her mother:

AN OPEN DOOR

A shadow unfolds across springtime floral wallpaper and hinges squeak as my bedroom door opens. My mother speaks in an unusually hesitant voice. "Honey?"

Lying in bed with my back to her, I glance at the alarm clock—ten after four. Quietly sucking air through my mouth, I hope that Mom will think me asleep and leave me alone.

"Lisa?" she calls out, more purposefully this time.

"Whaaaht?" I respond, as if just regaining consciousness.

"Something's wrong, isn't it?"

Oh, my god. She knows.

"What do you mean?" I say, trying to postpone the impact.

"Something's not right with you."

Maybe she doesn't.

"Like what?" I ask her.

"I just know it's something. Something's definitely wrong with you." She's trying not to cry.

She doesn't know.

"Go back to bed, Mom."

"You've always been able to talk to me," she says.

Jesus, maybe you should tell her.

"Lisa?"

Face it, it's no longer an experiment.

"Please tell me, Lisa."

The door's open. Just walk through it. Just walk through. She can help you. You need her to help you.

"There's nothing to tell," I hear myself say.

Damn you! Take that back. Take it back now!

She doesn't give up. "Nothing?"

Another chance. This is it, Lisa. Tell her about it. Please just tell her. Don't let her leave!

"Nothing, Mom."

Stupid girl!

The shadow recedes across springtime floral wallpaper and hinges squeak as my bedroom door closes behind her. It never opens in this way again.

I am 18 years old.

* * *

Five years later, Lisa falls in love and is faced with another choice between secrecy and disclosure:

MY FIRST CONFESSION

My cheek presses against his chest. His breathing shifts over from consciousness to sleep.

Do it, Lisa. Don't wait.

"Douglas?" my strained voice calls out.

"Umhmm . . ."

"There's something I need to tell you."

Probably not a good opening line.

"What's that?" he asks.

"I know I should have told you this before, and I hope you won't be upset that I didn't." Deep breath. Swallow.

It's okay. You're doing fine.

"What is it?" he asks, more insistent this time.

Loooong pause. "Lisa, what is it?"

He's getting nervous. Spit it out.

"Oh, god, Douglas. I don't—I . . . shit!"

You've come too far. Don't fall apart. Just say it, Lisa. Say the words.

"To one degree or another . . . I have been . . . bulimic . . .

Fuck! I hate the sound of that word.

. . . since I was 15."

It's out there. You said it.

He pulls me closer. "Who knows about this?"

"A few old friends and some people I go to school with."

"Your family?"

Oh god. Here we go.

"No . . . I haven't told them."

Boom!

"Jesus," he says.

No shit.

"Well, how bad is it now?"

"It's been much worse."

"That's not what I asked."

"It's not that bad."

Liar.

"Have you done it since you met me?"

If you only knew.

"A couple of times. But I don't want you to be concerned."

Oh, please. Please be concerned.

"You must know what that does to your body."

Believe me, I know. I know everything.

"I'm really glad you told me," he says as I start to cry. "I love you, Lisa. Tell me how I can help you. Please."

You just did. You can't imagine how much.

He pulls me close, stroking my hair until I go to sleep.

I am 22 years old.

* * *

In *Final Negotiations,* Ellis (1995a) narrates a personal account of a 9-year intimate relationship with Gene Weinstein, who died of emphysema in 1985. Her story takes the measure of a relationship caught in the relentless grip of the dialectics of attachment and loss, as she and her partner wage their insatiable appetite for life against the relentless progression of his disease. One evening, when they arrive at the movies, Gene discovers that his oxygen tank, which he needs in order to walk, is low. To Carolyn's dismay, he refuses to ride his battery-powered wheelchair into the theater. During the movie, Gene has difficulty breathing because of the low oxygen flow, but he refuses Carolyn's offer to get the wheelchair when the movie is over so he can get back to the car more easily. On the way out of the theater, Gene carries the oxygen tank and she carries his cane, which opens up to a chair. Readers enter the scene as Carolyn, struggling for some measure of independence from the weight of her caretaking role, walks away from Gene momentarily to greet some friends she sees in the lobby of the theater:

> I forget Gene as I say hello, but the conversation is interrupted by a loud voice yelling, "Carolyn, help!" Embarrassed and angry, I rush to Gene. "The chair. I need the chair," he gasps, pointing to the cane. I unfold it and he sits down quickly in the middle of the lobby. I narrow my shoulders and look to the floor, trying to make myself invisible as people walk around us.
>
> When he says between gasps in a loud voice filled with hatred, "You castrating bitch," I storm out of the theater, not waiting to see if he is OK. I don't care. I hate him.
>
> Determined to take control, I get into the driver's seat and let Gene struggle alone into the passenger's side. (Our friends get in the back.) No one talks. Driving faster than normal, I am out of control.
>
> I drop my friends off at their home, and immediately I explode. "You disgust me," I yell. "You make bad decisions and I suffer. I come to help after you yell in a public place. Then you scream complimentary terms like 'castrating bitch.' I've had it. I can't live like this anymore. I want out."
>
> Although I have had these thoughts before, and we've discussed the pros and cons of separating, I have never threatened in anger to leave him. Normally I could not get past his pain to say hurtful things.
>
> "You were angry at me the whole evening and then you punished me by not staying beside me with the cane like I asked you."
>
> "I wasn't punishing you," I interrupt. "I was being introduced to people. What was I supposed to do?"
>
> "Then when I yelled for you," he continues as though he hasn't heard me, "you still waited before you came to help. You are a castrating bitch."
>
> His words get me going again. "Go to hell," I say. "I've had it." I jerk the van to the side of the road and open the door to get out.
>
> The urgency of my action calms his anger, and he pleads, "Please don't leave me." I soften at his tone, which reveals how much he needs me. My god, I am caught, the voice inside screams as I clutch the steering wheel, trying to figure out what to do. It doesn't matter how irritable he is, I can't leave him.
>
> . . . As usual when we attempted to understand each other, our love drew us together. Yet I felt emotionally drained and knew these episodes did irreparable damage. I would never forget the words "castrating bitch"; Gene would never forget feeling alone and scared as he panicked in the lobby. (Ellis, 1995a, pp. 122–124)

* * *

These excerpts are intended to illustrate the craft and purpose of a narrative approach to relational dialectics. When using stories such as these, we ask readers to stay with the story, try to resonate with the dilemmas it poses, understand its ambiguities, and feel its nuances; in short, let yourself become part of the story. We also encourage readers to think with the story from the framework of their own lives. Who are you becoming as you take it in? How can you use it for your own purposes? In what directions does it lead you? Then, we stress the moral and ethical issues raised by the story. In the last account, Ellis (1995a) provokes readers to consider how you can live a good life while being ill or caring for a loved one who is ill. How much can we expect of ourselves? What moral commitments does illness call us to (Frank, 1995)? What is good to want for oneself and others? In Tillmann-Healy's (1996) narrative, readers are faced with an unfinished story about the past that is pointed toward the future. A bulimic woman must confront the question of what kind of person her story is shaping her into from each of her multiple identity positions which, in Lisa's case, involves the contradictory demands of woman, scholar, bulimic, daughter, and lover.

TOWARD NEW SOCIALIZING PRACTICES

As scholars approaching the next generation of work on relational dialectics, we face vexing questions about the inspiration, purposes, and significance of our work. We want people to read our work, to find it interesting, useful, and evocative. Yet, most social science writing is not widely read because it is inaccessible, dry, and overly abstract (Richardson, 1994). Left to the conventions of social science writing, ordinary experiences too often become more opaque than they were before researchers set their sights on them.

Our project breaks away from these conventions by refocusing attention on the concrete events and dynamic encounters on which knowledge of personal relationships is based (Stewart, 1995). These are the irreducible particulars of being with another (Stewart, 1995). Our approach calls for a broadening of the boundaries of research and writing practices that focus on personal relationships. Following Rorty (1996) and Jackson (1995), we think the goal of research on relationships should not only be to produce knowledge, but also to inspire hope and promote caring.

Students of personal relationships can be inspired to recontextualize their own experiences in the terms offered by the stories they encounter. By showing people actively engaged in the process of negotiating and co-constructing their relationships, we invite more direct contact with practices of communication. The connection between our research products and our readers becomes dialogic; the text is not meant to be received but rather to be engaged and used. Narrating these events becomes a way of inviting involvement and dialogue—our own and our readers'—with contingencies of relationship life. Readers are asked to connect their own experiences to those of the author (or other characters in the story).

How can we educate future generations of students of personal relationships to embrace the goals of narrative inquiry? The first step is to be more self-critical ourselves. We must be willing to engage in critical reflexivity—to question our own complicity in the self-interested research practices that sustain a narrow range of alternatives. We do not have a sufficient understanding of our own culture of inquiry (Rose, 1993). We need to understand the academic subculture in which we live and toil as a socially constructed form of life that may need to be remolded if we want to keep it alive and vital. Each of us needs to seriously ask, "What am I doing here? How is my work meaningful? How necessary are the conventions under which I labor? Whose interests do they serve?" These questions should give us pause to reflect on the silences in our work. What is absent and missing says a great deal about our values, our practices, and our goals.

Reform begins with education. Thus, any attempt to broaden the range of dialectical research must include revision of the graduate curriculum. If what we read sets the parameters for how and what we think, what we do, and what we write, then our students need exposure to different literature—to fiction, popular culture, cinema, music, art, and history—as well as to traditional social science (Rose, 1993). Also, they need to be guided to appreciate research as an activity of engagement and participation rather than as a spectator sport. When this happens, the boundaries that separate the social sciences and humanities will begin to dissolve. Then, we can recognize research as a mode of using experiences in other people's worlds to understand, reform, and cope with our own, and helping others use experiences in our worlds to understand, reform, and cope with theirs.

Of course, there are always colleagues who ask, "Why can't you just be normal social scientists?" To this, we reply, "Better to admit what all of us really know: we're just mucking around looking for truth."

REFERENCES

Altman, I., Brown, B. B., Staples, B., & Werner, C. M. (1992). A transactional approach to close relationships: Courtship, weddings and placemaking. In B. Walsh, K. Craik, & R. Price (Eds.), *Person–environment psychology* (pp. 193–241). Hillsdale, NJ: Lawrence Erlbaum Associates.

Bakhtin, M. M. (1981). *The dialogic imagination.* Austin: University of Texas Press.

Baxter, L. A. (1988). A dialectical perspective on communication strategies in relationship development. In S. W. Duck (Ed.), *Handbook of personal relationships: Theory, research, and interventions* (pp. 257–273). New York: Wiley.

Baxter, L. A. (1990). Dialectical contradictions in relationship development. *Journal of Social and Personal Relationships, 7,* 69–88.

Baxter, L. A. (1992). Interpersonal communication as dialogue: A response to the "Social Approaches" Forum. *Communication Theory, 2,* 330–337.

Baxter, L. A., & Montgomery, B. M. (1996). *Relating: Dialogues and dialectics.* New York: Guilford.

Benson, P. (Ed.). (1993). *Anthropology and literature.* Urbana: University of Illinois Press.

Berger, J. (1983). *Once in Europa.* New York: Pantheon.

Bochner, A. P. (1984). The functions of communication in interpersonal bonding. In C. Arnold & J. Bowers (Eds.), *Handbook of rhetorical and communication theory* (pp. 544–621). Boston: Allyn & Bacon.

Bochner, A. P. (1994). Perspectives on inquiry II: Theories and stories. In M. L. Knapp & G. R. Miller (Eds.), *Handbook of interpersonal communication* (pp. 21–41). Thousand Oaks, CA: Sage.

Bochner, A. P., & Ellis, C. (1992). Personal narrative as a social approach to interpersonal communication. *Communication Theory, 2,* 165–172.

Bochner, A. P., & Ellis, C. (1995). Telling and living: Narrative co-construction and the practices of interpersonal relationships. In W. Leeds-Hurwitz (Ed.), *Communication as social construction: Social approaches to the study of interpersonal interaction* (pp. 201–213). New York: Guilford.

Bochner, A. P., & Ellis, C. (1996). Talking over ethnography. In C. Ellis & A. P. Bochner (Eds.), *Composing ethnography: Alternative forms of qualitative writing* (pp. 13–45). Walnut Creek, CA: Altamira Press.

Bochner, A. P., Ellis, C., & Tillmann-Healy, L. M. (1996). Relationships as stories. In S. W. Duck (Ed.), *Handbook of personal relationships* (pp. 307–324). Chichester, UK: Wiley.

Bochner, A. P., & Waugh, J. (1995). Talking with as a model for writing about: Implications of Rortian pragmatism for communication theory. In L. Langsdorf & A. Smith (Eds.), *Recovering pragmatism's voice: The classical tradition and the philosophy of communication* (pp. 211–233). Albany: State University of New York Press.

Brady, I. (Ed.). (1991). *Anthropological poetics.* Lanham, MD: Rowman & Littlefield.

Bruner, J. (1986). *Actual minds, possible worlds.* Cambridge, MA: Harvard University Press.

Bruner, J. (1990a). *Acts of meaning.* Cambridge, MA: Harvard University Press.

Bruner, J. (1990b). Culture and human development: A new look. *Human Development, 33,* 354–355.

Butler, S., & Rosenblum, B. (1991). *Cancer in two voices.* San Francisco: Spinster's Press.

Coles, R. (1989). *The call of stories: Teaching and the moral imagination.* Boston: Houghton Mifflin.

Conville, R. L. (1991). *Relational transitions: The evolution of personal relationships.* New York: Praeger.

Crites, S. (1986). Storytime: Recollecting the past and projecting the future. In T. Sarbin (Ed.), *Narrative psychology: The storied nature of human conduct* (pp. 152–173). New York: Praeger.

Ellis, C. (1991). Sociological introspection and emotional experience. *Symbolic Interaction, 14,* 23–50.

Ellis, C. (1993). There are survivors: Telling a story of sudden death. *Sociological Quarterly, 34,* 711–730.

Ellis, C. (1994). Between science and literature: What are our options? Review essay of *Friendship matters: Communication, dialectics, and the life course* by W. K. Rawlins. *Symbolic Interaction, 17,* 325–330.

Ellis, C. (1995a). *Final negotiations: A story of love, loss, and chronic illness.* Philadelphia: Temple University Press.

Ellis, C. (1995b). The other side of the fence: Seeing black and white in a small, southern town. *Qualitative Inquiry, 1,* 147–167.

Ellis, C. (1995c). Speaking of dying: An ethnographic short story. *Symbolic Interaction, 18,* 73–81.

Ellis, C. (1996). Revealing a life: On the demands of truthfulness in writing personal loss narratives. *Journal of Personal and Interpersonal Loss, 1,* 151–177.

Ellis, C., & Bochner, A. P. (1992). Telling and performing personal stories: The constraints of choice in abortion. In C. Ellis & M. Flaherty (Eds.), *Investigating subjectivity: Research on lived experience* (pp. 79–101). Thousand Oaks, CA: Sage.

Ellis, C., & Bochner, A. P. (Eds.). (1996a). *Composing ethnography: Alternative forms of qualitative writing*. Walnut Creek, CA: Altamira Press.

Ellis, C., & Bochner, A. P. (Eds.). (1996b). Taking ethnography into the twenty-first century. *Journal of Contemporary Ethnography*.

Ellis, C. & Bochner, A. P. (in press). Writing from sociology's periphery. In S. Cole (Ed.), *What's wrong with sociology?* Princeton, N.J.: Princeton University Press.

Ellis, C., & Flaherty, M. (Eds.). (1992). *Investigating subjectivity: Research on lived experience*. Newbury Park, CA: Sage.

Franck, D. (1994). *Separation*. New York: Knopf.

Frank, A. W. (1995). *The wounded storyteller: Body, illness, and ethics*. Chicago: The University of Chicago Press.

Geertz, C. (1973). *The interpretation of cultures*. New York: Basic Books.

Hamill, P. (1994). *A drinking life: A memoir*. Boston: Little, Brown.

Jackson, M. (1989). *Paths toward a clearing: Radical empiricism and ethnographic inquiry*. Bloomington: Indiana University Press.

Jackson, M. (1995). *At home in the world*. Durham, NC: Duke University Press.

Kiesinger, C. E. (1995). *The anorexic and bulimic self: Making sense of food and eating*. Unpublished doctoral dissertation, University of South Florida.

Krieger, S. (1991). *Social science and the self: Personal essays on an art form*. New Brunswick, NJ: Rutgers University Press.

Maranhao, T. (Ed.). (1990). *The interpretation of dialogue*. Chicago: University of Chicago Press.

Polkinghorne, D. (1988). *Narrative knowing and the human sciences*. Albany: State University of New York Press.

Rawlins, W. K. (1983a). Negotiating close friendship: The dialectic of conjunctive freedoms. *Human Communication Research, 9, 255–266*.

Rawlins, W. K. (1983b). Openness as problematic in ongoing friendships: Two conversational dilemmas. *Communication Monographs, 50, 1–13*.

Rawlins, W. K. (1991). *Friendship matters: Communication, dialectics, and the life course*. New York: Aldine de Gruyter.

Richardson, L. (1990). Narrative and sociology. *Journal of Contemporary Ethnography, 19, 116–135*.

Richardson, L. (1994). Writing: A method of inquiry. In N. K. Denzin & Y. S. Lincoln (Eds.), *Handbook of qualitative research* (pp. 516–529). Thousand Oaks, CA: Sage.

Richardson, L. (1996). Educational birds. *Journal of Contemporary Ethnography, 25, 6–15*.

Rorty, R. (1989). *Contingency, irony, solidarity*. Cambridge, England: Cambridge University Press.

Rorty, R. (1996). The necessity of inspired reading. *The Chronicle of Higher Education, 22,* A48.

Rose, D. (1990). *Living the ethnographic life*. Newbury Park, CA: Sage.

Rose, D. (1993). Ethnography as a form of life: The written word and the work of the world. In P. Benson (Ed.), *Anthropology and literature* (pp. 192–224). Urbana: University of Illinois Press.

Rosenwald, G. C., & Ochberg, R. L. (Eds.). (1992). *Storied lives: The cultural politics of self-understanding*. New Haven, CT: Yale University Press.

Roth, P. (1991). *Patrimony: A true story*. New York: Simon & Schuster.

Sarbin, T. (Ed.). (1986). *Narrative psychology: The storied nature of human conduct*. New York: Praeger.

Schafer, R. (1980). Narration in the psychoanalytic dialogue. *Critical Inquiry, 7,* 29–53.

Sexton, L. G. (1994). *Searching for mercy street: My journey back to my mother, Anne Sexton.* Boston: Little, Brown.

Shotter, J. (1987). The social construction of an (us): Problems of accountability and narratology. In R. Burnett, P. McGee, & D. Clarke (Eds.), *Accounting for relationships: Explanation, representation, and knowledge* (pp. 225–247). London: Methuen.

Stamp, G. H. (1994). The appropriation of the parental role through communication during the transition to parenthood. *Communication Monographs, 61,* 89–112.

Stamp, G. H., & Banski, M. A. (1992). The communicative management of constrained autonomy during the transition to parenthood. *Western Journal of Communication, 56,* 281–300.

Stewart, J. (1995). Philosophical features of social approaches to interpersonal communication. In W. Leeds-Hurwitz (Ed.), *Social approaches to communication* (pp. 23–45). New York: Guilford.

Tedlock, B. (1991). From participant observation to the observation of participation: The emergence of narrative ethnography. *Journal of Anthropological Research, 47,* 69–94.

Tillmann-Healy, L. M. (1996). A secret life in a culture of thinness: Reflections on body, food, and bulimia. In C. Ellis & A. P. Bochner (Eds.), *Composing ethnography: Alternative forms of qualitative writing* (pp. 76–108). Walnut Creek, CA: Altamira Press.

Turner, E. (1993). Experience and poetics in anthropological writing. In P. Benson (Ed.), *Anthropology and literature* (pp. 27–47). Urbana: University of Illinois Press.

Tyler, S. (1986). Post-modern ethnography: From document of the occult to occult document. In J. Clifford & G. Marcus (Eds.), *Writing culture: The poetics and politics of culture* (pp. 122–140). Berkeley: University of California Press.

Weinstein, A. (1988). *The fiction of relationship.* Princeton, NJ: Princeton University Press.

Werner, C. M., & Baxter, L. A. (1994). Temporal qualities of relationships: Organismic, transactional, and dialectical views. In M. L. Knapp & G. M. Miller (Eds.), *Handbook of interpersonal communication,* second ed. (pp. 323–379). Thousand Oaks, CA: Sage.

Yerby, J. (1995). Family systems theory reconsidered: Integrating social construction theory and dialectical process. *Communication Theory, 5,* 339–365.

Yerby, J., & Gourd, W. (1994, April). Our marriage/their marriage: Performing reflexive fieldwork. Paper presented at the annual Gregory P. and Gladys Stone and Society for the Study of Symbolic Interaction Symposium, University of Illinois, Urbana-Champaign.

4

Writing About *Friendship Matters:* A Case Study in Dialectical and Dialogical Inquiry

WILLIAM K. RAWLINS
Purdue University

> *We long for intense engagement in a story,*
> *and we long for a coherent story of our own lives.*
> —Booth, 1988, p. 192

> *We all hanker after essence and share a taste for theory*
> *as opposed to narrative. If we did not, we should*
> *probably have gone into another line of work.*
> —Rorty, 1991, p. 71

Acknowledging the worth of Booth's and Rorty's observations, I grappled with and gave voice to my own desires for both stories and theories in a book about friendship—the book is entitled, *Friendship Matters: Communication, Dialectics, and the Life Course* (Rawlins, 1992). It seeks to analyze the varieties, tensions, functions, and dialectical challenges of communicating in friendships across the life course, pursuing this task through a series of paired chapters addressing five periods of life—childhood, adolescence, young adulthood, middle adulthood, and later adulthood. Two chapters discuss each period. The first in each pair synthesizes available orthodox social science research concerning friendships during that period, and the second provides an illustrative analysis of practices and predicaments of friendship suggested or sometimes overlooked by the first chapter. These illustrative analyses utilize excerpts from in-depth interviews with persons ranging from 14 to 100 years old, as well as from literary texts such as short stories and novels.

At the time, I wrote:

> I want to cultivate conversation and interplay among extant social scientific
> and humanistic research on friendship, people's verbal descriptions and the ac-
> tual discourse of friends, fictional representations of friends facing situated ex-
> igencies, my experiences and opinions as a person/writer/social investigator,
> and those of the reader(s) of this book. (Rawlins, 1992, p. 4)

In retrospect, I can now view what I was doing as orchestrating dialogical activity in some of Bakhtin's senses, although I did not know I was speaking
some of his language(s) at the time. As I emerged from the consuming project
of writing that book, I became aware of Bakhtin's *oeuvre* through Baxter's
recent writings (1992, 1994). What I want to do in this essay is dialogue with
a text that I once wrote about the dialectics of friendship. In doing so, I raise
and respond to questions about dialogical and dialectical outlooks and my
use of both in writing about friendship matters.

DIALECTICAL AND DIALOGICAL PERSPECTIVES
ON *FRIENDSHIP MATTERS*

In *Friendship Matters,* I describe the communicative accomplishment of
friendships throughout life using a dialectical perspective. From a dialectical
perspective, friendships are dynamic, ongoing social achievements involving
the constant interconnection and reciprocal influence of multiple individual,
interpersonal, and social factors. The interaction of friends continually gen-
erates and manages multiple contradictions and dialectical tensions that
arise over time in dyads and in light of how they are situated in enveloping
social contexts.

Dialectical conceptions of interpersonal life share several theoretical commitments (Altman, Vinsel, & Brown, 1981; Baxter, 1988; Bochner, 1984;
Rawlins, 1983a; 1989a). I thematized these basic elements as *totality, contradiction, motion,* and *praxis* (Rawlins, 1989a). Viewed as a *totality,* communicating in friendships involves the constant interconnection and reciprocal influence of numerous individual, interpersonal, and social factors. Discrete "things," actions, or events are inconceivable from a dialectical perspective; reality is composed of relations and relations among relations.
Moreover, dialectical totalities are not static or fixed, but are in constant
movement and alternation between contextualizing and being contextualized. Thus, I conceive any component or aspect of friendship as existing in
dynamic connection with all of the others in the friends' embracing life situations.

Contradictions are the antagonistic, yet interdependent aspects of communication between friends. Such dialectical tensions are considered inher-

ent features of ongoing friendships because friends' activities and experiences necessarily interweave personal biographies, dyadic practices, social collectivities, and cultural matrices, whose demands often oppose, although presupposing each other. One can examine a given friendship for the contradictions evident in the relationship and those occurring between the dyad and external social formations contextualizing it (Bopp & Weeks, 1984; Rawlins, 1989a). Two friends experience the former type, for example, when attempting to manage the contradictory requirements of expressive versus protective communication in their relationship (Rawlins, 1983b). By comparison, external contradictions develop when the constraints of one's marriage or job undermine freedoms negotiated between friends. Animated by such contradictions, social life is characterized by *motion*, activity, and change. The present state of any relationship or social formation is an incessant achievement.

Finally, the concept of *praxis* emphasizes the reflexive constitution of human beings and their social worlds. Human communicators are conceived as both ongoing producers and products of their own choices in encompassing and historically conditioned cultural contexts. Persons act with others to produce contexts, which, in turn, function to produce the subject as an object. The notion of praxis focuses attention on the decisions friends make in the face of objective constraints existing in their temporally and spatially specific social circumstances. Yet, a praxic view also notes that many of these constraints derive from prior choices the individual made that now manifest themselves as objective and concrete limitations on action. Accordingly, individuals are considered conscious, active selectors of possible choices from a field that is partially conceived by them, partially negotiated with others, and partially determined by social and natural factors outside of their control. The choices a person makes throughout life in concrete circumstances simultaneously generate and constrain options.

These tenets of dialectical thinking are reflected throughout the book in its persistent attempts to depict friendships as relational processes actively and continuously negotiated in enveloping matrices of social relationships and conditions. Moreover, particular relationships and changing circumstances of friendship are investigated and situated in their concrete social settings over time. Given a dialectical perspective, it was difficult for me to think of friendships apart from how, when, and where they actually occurred in the life course.

Accordingly, in considering their ongoing communicative management of dialectical exigencies, I describe how friendships participate in the challenges, satisfactions, and dramas of characteristic social configurations during each life-course stage. It becomes clear that the contradictions and activities of friendships are generated within and reciprocally shape multiple social contexts.

There are significant resemblances between dialectical and dialogical outlooks in their emphases on dynamic specificity, relational conceptions of social being, the significance of context and temporality, the avoidance of two-valued logics, and the tensions connecting fixity and flux. Even so, some distinctive contributions of dialogical thinking, especially by Bakhtin, prompted and informed this essay's reflections on the composition of *Friendship Matters*. This being so, I highlight selected ideas from Bakhtin that are crucial to this writing/rereading, followed by a brief discussion of its dialogical aspirations.

As a communication scholar, I was struck by Bakhtin's celebration of the speaking subject. Throughout his works, one hears discussions of intonation, accent, and the unique qualities of utterances and speaking situations (Bakhtin, 1981, 1984; Holquist, 1990; Todorov, 1984). Largely due to Bakhtin's ideas, the notion of *voice* is becoming a watchword for many social inquirers. As I read him, I found myself meditating on the problems and possibilities of being addressed, listening, and responding in studying friendship and the continuing challenges of representing others' speech (Bakhtin, 1981).

Bakhtin also alerts us to the manifold array of discursive genres shaping, reflecting, and stratifying social life and language. He remarks that, "Every particular utterance is assuredly individual, but each sphere of language use develops its own *relatively stable types* of utterances, and this is what we call *discursive genres*" (cited in Todorov, 1984, p. 82). In everyday and professional life, as well as in literary discourse, certain horizons of expectations develop concerning what and how language is to be used (Bakhtin, 1981). These genres of discourse are value-laden and constitute "forms for making conceptualization and evaluation concrete" (p. 289). As such, genres provide the means for collective orientations toward reality even while permitting individual variations.

Despite the patterning potential of genres, a key theme for Bakhtin (1981) is that all language use, including scholarly inquiry, is an open, generative, and contested project. *Heteroglossia,* the roiling diversity of languages, fundamentally conditions and contexualizes the meaning of utterances. All utterances are sites of struggle between centripetal forces seeking to restrict and unify verbal and ideological diversity and centrifugal forces working to decentralize and enliven language. In this inevitable and irreducible clash of languages, meanings, and perspectives, Bakhtin champions the cause of diversity over the deadening pretenses of authoritative discourse, with its (sometimes violent) insistence on having the correct vision and the last word. For my purposes, Bakhtin's concept of heteroglossia strikes at narrow images of disciplines defined by self-sealing terminologies and methodologies.

As might be expected, Bakhtin also rejects Hegelian, idealist, and teleological dialectics, which anticipate contradictions or oppositions being synthesized or resolved at a transformed level of activity; he considers them "monological" (cited in Todorov, 1984, p. 104). There is no ultimate fusion of disparate consciousnesses in Bakhtin's view. The other's consciousness is essential for constituting "events that are creatively productive, innovative, unique, and irreversible" (p. 100). Once again, alterity animates language and thought.

Last, I found Bakhtin's notion of the intertextuality of utterances to be especially useful in reflecting on the composition of my book. *Intertextuality* describes the multiple relations of every utterance to other utterances; it is the notion that "all discourse is in dialogue with prior discourses on the same subject, as well as discourses yet to come" (Todorov, 1984, p. x). Every writer's project is constituted in and through other projects, written at other times using other languages. Intertextuality, therefore, highlights the potential simultaneity of linguistic and social similarities and differences in space and time, the ongoing possibility of their juxtaposition (Holquist, 1990). Speaking of the multiple languages differentiating themselves through heteroglossia, Bakhtin (1981) stated:

> In actual fact, there does exist a common plane that methodologically justifies our juxtaposing them: all languages of heteroglossia, whatever the principle underlying them and making each unique, are specific points of view on the world, forms for conceptualizing the world in words, specific world views, each characterized by its own meaning and values. As such they all may be juxtaposed to one another, mutually supplement one another, contradict one another and be interrelated dialogically. (pp. 291–292)

Intertextuality rules out a single, unified principle of presentation while recognizing the simultaneous interrelations of multiple genres and speech acts composing texts.

Drawing on these ideas from Bakhtin, I seek to dialogue with the composition of my book, *Friendship Matters,* in the following pages. I view my engagement with this book as dialogical for several reasons. First, the book now exists as a text, a completed composition to be addressed, responded to, and questioned. So my commentary here creates a metatext, and in Todorov's (1984) words, "the metatext is actually an intertext; the utterance that describes another utterance enters into a dialogical relation with it" (p. 23). Second, the original process of composing the book—its composition— constitutes a context of discursive activity removed in time from the present, yet available for me to recollect through notes I made to myself, earlier drafts, conversation with others, as well as the accounts I produce in recalling it. These materials are juxtaposed in developing the present text. At various points that follow, a basic dialogue form is also used—asking questions and giving answers—in my attempt to address the work. Moreover, I have spent time responding to questions raised by early readers of this present text, suggesting that this chapter is already functioning to generate questions for readers or writers other than myself. This occurrence also illustrates that the activities of writing themselves can be dialogical, a question I now turn to.

How is writing dialogical? In various ways. First, writing in our field is a social activity seeking to comprehend social activity. Authors address self and others about self and others. They engage in the productive tensions of learning through questioning. Tension (hopefully) always exists because most questions that are worth asking do not come with ready-made answers. Sometimes we discover we are not asking the most edifying or revealing questions. That is, the answers we discover actually pose better questions than the one(s) we originally asked. Yet, isn't writing a more closed or controlled process than this? Not necessarily. Take this paragraph, for example. I knew I wanted to talk about the dialogics of writing here. The genre of the scholarly essay stipulates that some overview of the nature of this piece is in order. Knowing that I wanted to write a dialogical piece, therefore, found me asking the question, "How is writing dialogical?" The perceptive reader may notice at this point, however, that I have not really answered the question yet (or have I?). That is because I was (am) not entirely sure of how I would (will) answer that question until I answer(ed) it. That is why I asked it. As I progress in this paragraph and chapter, new and perhaps more useful or clear questions and answers come to me. My authorship is not complete until the work is finished and the text and I are dialogically changed in the process (Mecke, 1990). One risk of writing, like all dialogue, is that the author may be changed. Even when a book is finished being written, it can be read, responded to, and revised by any reader, including its primary author(s). The cycle of dialogue and learning can continue.

In fact, I am now writing a draft of this chapter later in time from when this prior paragraph was originally written. In my present term as author, I already tried to answer questions it provoked in early readers, such as, "How do you differentiate between dialectical and dialogical perspectives?" "How is this chapter dialogical?" My responses to these questions are found in the preceding section, that is, spatially before the provoking paragraph's actual appearance in this essay. Having registered this dialogical simultaneity, let us now turn to a discussion or narration of the writing of *Friendship Matters*.

COMPOSING *FRIENDSHIP MATTERS*

What were my purposes in writing this book? Who was my audience? How did I write this book? Or as Booth (1988) said, what was my "oath of office" as an author? (p. 208). As I recall my overall purposes, I wanted to learn as much as I could about friendship and try to write a comprehensive discussion of its many forms and circumstances across the life course. My metaphor for research is learning. I think that sometimes in our attempts to characterize or reconstruct our investigative efforts, we lose sight of that purpose or metaphor. I did not know in advance how things would turn out; I preserved my capacity to be surprised. I believe that if we can preserve our capacity to be surprised, we may learn something.

I wanted to write a discussion that was as faithful as possible to my own experiences of friendship and to the materials I was using. I also wanted to write a book that would be read by as wide a readership as possible, an inclusive type of effort. I was hoping to reach people who were interested in a robust and substantive discussion of communication in friendship, as opposed to a mere chirpy celebration of it, a bloodless scholarly tome, a literature review, or a self-help manual. My image of my audience was not monolithic, but in general, I was writing to, and hoping to constitute, a broad-minded, inquisitive, and serious general readership that also included undergraduate and graduate students as well as my colleagues who make their livings trying to understand and teach about communication, social life, and the human condition. Obviously, this implied audience for the book was also an idealized one. I view my audience for the present chapter as much more specialized. So far, this has proven to be the case, but you, as a reader, may be in the process of breaking that mold.

I wanted to create a life-course narrative that readers could identify with (or see persons that they care about in) either at various junctures or throughout the book. Perhaps some readers see their children in the childhood chapters, their students in the adolescent and young adulthood chapters, themselves if they were middle-aged in the middle-age chapters, or reflect on their own adolescence and anticipate later life.

How Did I Write This Book?

In discussing my book, some people have asked me face-to-face, or in print: "How did you do this? Where is the discussion of method?" I answer, for the most part, that instead of spending time and pages thematizing and reflecting on my position concerning such issues in the book (that I am now doing here), I simply enacted them: I wrote the book. Why? Because it was not there. I wanted to see what it would look and read like when it was finished.

I believe that writing practices compose a fundamental learning activity, a spoken and written dialogue with multiple others, genres, and moments of authorship. When I am writing, I learn things that I did not know before. In trying to render a point for an implied audience (after having read, talked with, and listened to others), knowledge (at least knowledge for me) is created in the acts of writing. I roughed out the book in light of my research activities and my folk sense of the life course, but I did not know how numerous issues concerning friendship would turn out. I thought I would see dramatic differences in friendships across life in types of friends, expectations, activities, and so on. They were not there. Friendships remain the same in a lot of ways even though circumstances change. I wanted to see where a middle-class life story goes, when pursued in this way and viewed with the optic of the communicative achievement of friendship.

From the beginning, in acknowledging the unorthodox and marginal qualities of this effort—that is, its series of paired chapters and its unusual and "unjustified" juxtaposition of textual genres—I felt free to invent and re-invent what I was doing. There is freedom working in the margins, but the line between creative marginality and alienation is a thin one. It is one thing to challenge and play with scholarly conventions; it is quite another to feel isolated or to be ignored because one's work is no longer recognized as serious inquiry. Risky study walks this line.

I have been asked by readers if and how I believe I kept from straying over this line. This is a difficult question to answer for several reasons. Multiple sets of criteria are potentially used in evaluating creative, investigative endeavors. So this "line" is more like a latticework whose composition and coordinates are susceptible to change as relevant disciplines' conventions continuously evolve due to internal and external provocation. Moreover, an author cannot really control how he or she is perceived; one audience's cutting-edge work may be yesterday's news to more avant-garde reviewers or an affront to disciplinary integrity to others. Some people, myself included, might argue that a key aspiration of scholarly inquiry is to question and press the envelope regarding what and how we know.

So, my hedges against alienation from any single matrix of evaluation involved reading widely about friendship across a variety of fields. In doing this, I learned about a range of alternatives for conducting inquiry concerning friendship as well as an emerging and overlapping array of questions that I and others thought needed to be addressed. I felt I was on the right track and was potentially already conversing with a variety of audiences in terms of conceptual and substantive issues. I also continually appraised what I was doing using the acid test of my own lived experiences and those of people of various ages whom I knew. Consequently, I went about composing answers to my questions, employing the intertextual approach to writing I describe later and trusting in the dynamics of a broad-based, lived, scholarly, and literary conversation about friendship. Situating my project in this way, I felt confident it would be taken seriously despite, if not because of, its unorthodox practices. I think unless you are doing the most scripted kind of inquiry imaginable, at some point, you have to believe that the ways you have decided to develop answers to your questions are warranted by your purposes and the resources at your disposal. In the final analysis, the extent to which you decide to stray from standard formulas for investigation thus becomes a matter of personal convictions, curiosity, and a willingness to risk rejection.

Like all utterances, most of the meaning made by a book derives from how it is responded to (Bakhtin, 1981; Bateson, 1972). Even so, as Burke recommends, I wanted to use all that is there in exploring friendship and making my case and to avoid narrowly authoritative genres. I believe all social texts are addressed to the world and available for reading; in a different language, everything is data and as Bateson (1972) teaches us, "No data are truly 'raw'" (p. xviii). Consequently, a variety of genres of texts constituted data and discourse for examination, interpretation, and eventual inclusion in the book. The interconnection of dialectical thinking and the intertextuality of dialogism invite this practice.

In reading these materials, I engaged in a combined suspension of disbelief and a hermeneutic of understanding. In Bakhtin's (cited in Todorov, 1984) words, "Every genre has its methods, its ways of seeing and understanding reality, and these methods are its exclusive characteristic. The artist must learn to see reality through the eyes of the genre" (p. 83). In perusing social science studies from a variety of fields, I read them as authors' disciplined attempts at describing people's lives and worlds, as studies using specific conventions for saying something pertinent about how people practice and live friendship. Thus, I tried to read past objectifying preoccupations and obsession with methodological issues, two practices foreign to my own scholarship and remind myself how and why these tendencies were important to the authors.

I also practiced a suspension of disbelief and a hermeneutic of understanding in reading the discourse from the interviews. Listening to and reading what these people said as sincere attempts to talk about their experiences of friendship, I heard their words as dramatizing issues and events that mattered to them in reflecting on their lives and relationships. I adopted an analogous stance in reading the literary depictions, plays, short stories, and novels. They were read as describing and enacting significant moments of relational life. All of these works were considered and heard for what they could teach me about friendship across the life course. Basically, I read these texts as composed according to different conventions utilized by social investigators, actors, narrators, and commentators for talking about social life, a mode of being common to them all.

Mirroring dialectical and dialogical assumptions, I read these various works in relation to each other; I studied relations and relations among relations. Rorty (1982) has argued and Bochner (1985) has emphasized that differences in outlooks and perspectives on inquiry are not issues to be resolved, but differences to be lived with. These different genres live together in this book. Bakhtin (1981) would describe this multivoiced and multilanguaged interanimation of genres and perspectives within the confines of one text as internally dialogic, while also allowing for external dialogue with other texts.

As part of my ongoing investigations of the communicative management of friendship, I have identified several dialectical principles in a grounded, theoretic way, studying open-ended interviews and cognate literature (Rawlins 1979, 1983a, 1983b, 1994; Rawlins & Holl, 1988). I have argued that both contextual and interactional dialectics interweave in shaping and reflecting patterns of friendship (Rawlins, 1989a). The contextual dialectics of the ideal and the real and the private and the public derive from the place of friendship in Western culture (Rawlins, 1989a). They describe cultural conceptions that frame and permeate interaction in specific friendships, yet are conceivably subject to revision as a result of changes in everyday practices. The dialectic of the ideal and the real formulates the interplay between the ideals and expectations that are typically associated with friendship and the troublesome realities and unexpected rewards of actual friendships. The dialectic of the private and the public addresses the tensions produced as the activities and decisions of friends weave in and out of public and private situations.

The following four interactional dialectics comprise tensions emerging in the ongoing communication between friends (Rawlins, 1989a). The dialectic of the freedom to be independent and the freedom to be dependent describes the contradictions of availability, obligation, absence, and copresence stemming from the voluntaristic ethic underlying friendship in Western culture (Rawlins, 1983a). The dialectic of affection and instrumentality articulates the tensions arising from caring for a friend as an end in itself versus caring for a friend as a means to an end (Rawlins, 1989a). The dialectic of judgment and acceptance describes the recurring dilemmas in friendship between providing objective appraisals of a friend's actions versus giving unconditional acceptance and support (Rawlins & Holl, 1988). Finally, the dialectic of expressiveness and protectiveness addresses the opposing tendencies to speak openly with a friend and relate private thoughts and feelings and the simultaneous need to restrain disclosures and commentary to preserve privacy and avoid burdening or hurting the friend (Rawlins, 1979, 1983b).

In writing the book, I used these dialectical principles as critical and interpretive tools for understanding and probing statistical patterns, as well as verbal depictions of predicaments friends face; they provided an intelligible frame for construing various tensions and interactional dynamics. Meanwhile, in creating this book, I also re-enacted the research practices I have employed throughout my career. That is, I worked inductively with diverse collections of texts in developing disciplined abstractions and conceptual orderings of the material I was reading (Glaser & Strauss, 1967; Lofland, 1976). Even so, my overall project was embedded in a more encompassing set of dialogical relations among utterances occurring across the life course and in and between the various textual genres that are described more in the following section. It was also shaped by my own folk grasp of a life-course narrative, my tacit understanding of what living a life meant from growing up and living in my own particular middle-class precinct of North American culture. So, my own placement in space and time also constrained how I read and utilized these texts (Holquist, 1990).

Embarking on the task of writing, I was committed to alternating chapters. I purposefully set up a tension—a dialogue—among social science, fiction, and lived experiences. In writing each of the illustrative chapters, I refused to formularize the writing process and they ended up being different. For example, the chapter addressing children's friendships is based entirely on a dialogue between my reading of social developmental accounts of childhood relationships and a collection of stories written for children about young persons' friendships. Adolescence is engaged using excerpts from in-depth interviews with adolescents as well as short stories and novels. The illustrative analysis of young adulthood is composed of three case studies of actual friendships—one male, one female, and one cross-sex pair—all based on a series of open-ended individual and dyadic interviews, as well as literary depictions. I experienced each of these chapters as an opportunity to re-invent how to write an illustrative examination, how to engage these texts, and what I could say about and with them. As the writing progressed, however, later compositional practices increasingly dialogued with prior choices, sometimes generating new possibilities, other times constraining them.

For the most part, I experienced less freedom with the social scientific texts. In many respects, these texts appear predigested, with tersely rendered and densely abstract discussions, lots of tables, and numerical descriptions. I might say that I was free to use such reports and data in different ways. Occasionally, I tried to read them dialectically in spite of themselves; for example, sometimes I interpreted minimally discussed relationships or patterns in the data as indicating dialectical tensions. However, I also found (and still find) that I tend to mimic the authoritative voice and monological rhythms of that kind of writing in those chapters. There are lots of cites derived from piecemeal efforts supporting and interruptively punctuating long strings of findings regarding friendships. Consequently, the chapters developed from that work resemble each other fairly closely in composition and tone. Although I derived a sense of the distribution of certain narrowly defined aspects of friendship in various research populations across the life course, I really did not get to know the people questioned in most of these efforts at all. I do not feel like I heard even a semblance of the participating individuals' voices. However, it also can be argued from a social scientific perspective that I am not supposed to hear them.

Except for much of the chapters concerning adolescence (Rawlins, 1989b) and young adulthood (Rawlins, 1989a) based on orthodox social scientific texts, I wrote the book's chapters in order. That is, I started with childhood and proceeded to track friendships across life. In this process, re-encountering the two chapters I previously wrote was analogous to re-encountering some of the moments in my own life that I had lived before. In fact, I wrote them in prior moments of my life, and each describes prior moments in my life, as well as those of other readers. Both types of re-encounters, both modes of narrative doubling, were contextualized by the activities of writing this book.

It was exciting and edifying to be surprised and learn new things during the writing process. For example, I changed some of the last chapters' titles. When the book was proposed, they were addressing friendships among the elderly, and "The Elderly" was the running head. However, as I continued talking with, listening to, and reading about "the elderly," I found out that most do not experience themselves as "the elderly." Instead, I heard them talking about themselves, their lives, and their friends as if they were living out their adult years; they did not speak as if they had crossed over into some "other" category. Meanwhile, my father just retired at 70 years old from practicing medicine; in observing and speaking with my father and my mother, I was further understanding the vitality of the period. Therefore, I changed the titles of the chapters to friendships during later adulthood and later life. I was trying to give voice to my perception that the men and women I encountered in person and in a variety of texts did not feel like they crossed some great divide. Now, clearly this phenomenon is likely to be different for the so-called "old–old." Moreover, experiences of later life are acutely contextualized by economics and by health (Rawlins, 1995). I have been chided for this terminology; one reviewer put scare quotes around the phrase, "later adulthood," seemingly implying, "What's going on here? Take this designation with a grain of salt; it breaks with common parlance." Yet, this is an example of a response to something I learned.

By and large, I constructed myself throughout the book in the third person, functioning as an authoritative assembler, interpreter, and renderer of these various texts. I am basically an implied presence throughout the book; I rarely, if at all, speak in the first person, self-disclose, or shoot the breeze with the reader, as I am doing now in this dialogue with you and the book. These are choices we make as writers. One adopts this role to various degrees in speaking with and speaking for other persons' words and stories. As Burke (1969) reminds us, in our attempts to provide a reflection of our conditions, we make a selection from our conditions, which is ultimately a deflection of our conditions. Choices made to write in specific ways or to describe in depth particular issues or circumstances, necessarily preempt other modes of writing and occasion minimal or no treatment of other concerns. So, the finitude of writing is a part of the finitude of life. Our inclusion or exclusion of self and others is a matter of degrees, pursued with varying extents of consciousness; it influences the extent to which writing can be truly dialogic (Rawlins, 1991).

Throughout the writing, I was positioned complexly in time in trying to develop rapport with the persons and circumstances constructed in these various accounts. I experienced these texts in a variety of ways: Charmed by the depictions of children, affected by the cares of parents and the worries of widows and widowers; at other points, annoyed, appreciative, empathetic, or simply grateful for what I was learning. For the most part, however, I attempted to be respectfully attentive; this is the stance of a hermeneutic of understanding (Ricoeur, 1970) or responsive understanding (Bakhtin, 1981).

I experienced dim remembrances of my own childhood, even as I was reminded of specific incidents or circumstances. I also tried to see these situations through the eyes of our own children. My son Brian was 7 years old when I began the book; my daughter Shelley was 4 years old. In writing the childhood chapter, I said, "Shelley and Pam are outside riding Big Wheels and they might have a fight." Shelley and Pam were outside riding Big Wheels and they might have had a fight. Guess what? By the time the book was finished, Shelley was going on 9 years old; she was in an entirely different period in the life course and Brian was almost 12 years old, entering preadolescence, no longer a child. Very different people are preserved at this moment in the writing of the book, but life goes on. In fact, Shelley is now 12 years old and Brian is 15 years old. Last week, I was showing Brian how to drive and shift a five-speed car; he is now 5 inches taller than his mom.

I aged figuratively and literally in writing the book, figuratively in trying to relate meaningfully to the circumstances of persons older than myself. The finitude of life really grabbed my attention—as well as the velocity of life and the sweetness of earlier activities and experiences, described and enacted by many of the people to whom I listened. I hear an 82-year-old woman talking about going out during college for a strawberry sundae with her best friend who had this white wool, pleated skirt. This clown spilled strawberries all over her skirt, and the narrator says, "We still laugh every time the word 'strawberries' comes up." You can almost hear young people laughing—as well as the speaker and her friend in the present—when she's talking about it. Voices call out to be heard.

I literally aged in the years spent at the word processor. I was an ethnographer of the life course; time and circumstances began to burn themselves on me. I remember writing the middle age chapter. I was in Heavilon Hall. I remember we had a pleasant dinner, it was summertime, and it was gorgeous out. I left home to go to Heavilon Hall to this musty little office and have this CRT in front of me. I heard outdoors, in this area outside my office, Frisbees scraping on the concrete, people having fun. I was typing into the CRT, "Middle-aged males are so preoccupied with success that they don't have time for friendship." I sat there typing this and I looked at the screen and thought, "You know I'm afraid if I highlight that and delete it, that I'm going to disappear!" Distancing ourselves from our writing does not guarantee we will not end up writing about ourselves anyway.

MODES OF INTERTEXTUALITY

To me, one of the most striking features of writing the book was and is its diverse embodiments and modes of intertextuality in and among the diverse genres composing the book, the relations of utterances about friendship and by friends to other utterances (Bakhtin, 1981; Todorov, 1984). I noticed intertextuality *in* the social scientific genre describing a given life-course period, the interconnections among how various researchers from multiple disciplines addressed diverse issues associated with friendship. Broad surveys of hundreds of people articulated with close-up observational studies in terms of operationally defined attributes of friendship or gender-linked patterns. The apparent overlap in foci and findings ranged from sparse to staggering in specific periods. In mustering these reasonably comparable numerical descriptions, I frequently composed modal profiles of the aspects of friendship that scholars using these methods considered worth measuring. Yet, it remained for me to make sense of them and to decide how to (re)present them. Did such data prescribe categorical images of friendship "types" and discrete "stages" in friendship and life course "development?" Could they be understood as dialectical theses susceptible to contradiction and undermining by the imprecision and relatedness of other voices, moments, and modes of understanding friendship? Were they dialogical utterances awaiting responses?

I also perceived intertextuality *in* the interview data from a given period, the relatedness among responses to diverse questions by a specific person, the connections among inductively derived themes across participants, and what they considered their most memorable experiences of friendship. How did synoptic episodes in the participants' opinions relate to how I was understanding friendship during that period in the life course? How did these incidents relate to dialectical principles I identified in other texts? What were the most moving or significant accounts? How did all of these "experience-near" texts cohere with or challenge what I already wrote about this particular period in the life course using primarily social scientific work?

Intertextuality transpired *in* the literary texts as well, with various stories and episodes in novels dramatizing closely related issues of communicating in friendship. My wife, Sandy, developed the collection of literary texts; she read them all and called my attention to rich narratives, particularly engrossing or well-written episodes, or key exemplars of dialectical principles. She focused on interactive accounts and depictions of conversation, not third person descriptions. In short, she was looking for dialogue between friends, which I then read and we talked about as friends ourselves. It did not surprise me (because I have found dialectical principles to be useful tools for under-standing friendship) that many of the best stories turned on dilemmas or ten-sions described by the dialectics. Some of these then entered the book.

I also engaged intertextuality among all of these genres *in* a given period of the life course. How does one describe the overlap and the oppositions among the genres without too much redundancy? Meanwhile, there were overlaps of what was *not* said across genres, for example, the role of desire, envy, violence, economics, or eroticism in friendship. Further, how was I to address differences of emphasis or interpretation? This challenge of dealing with differences is a fundamental concern of dialogue. Sometimes I depicted issues primarily in terms of their statistical portrayal; at other times, I used particular voices or narrated incidents to make a point. On many occasions, friendship matters were sufficiently significant, multifaceted, or common-place to be addressed from the standpoints of multiple genres.

The most intriguing intertextuality transpired throughout the genres *across* moments of the life course. I encountered examples of an event, such as divorce shaping parents' friendships, described by adult characters in a short story and by actual children in interviews. There were moments of chil-dren's friendships, like the problems of moving and being the new kid, en-acted by youths in fictional narratives and described by young people in sur-vey research reports, yet also remarked about by parents in both stories and interviews. There were recollections of childhood friendships by adolescents, childhood and adolescent friendships by young adults, and recollections from all moments of the life course by later adults. There were gendered nar-ratives depicting past moments that other voices related as their present con-cerns. There were personally stated anticipations about future interpersonal relationships compared with modal statistical descriptions of activities char-acterizing people who were already that age. I tried to listen as these diverse texts dialogued with each other, interanimating moments and events of friendship, composing and reflecting multiple life stories as well as shared exigencies.

SUSTAINING DIALECTICAL
AND DIALOGICAL QUESTIONING

Which texts "validated" which? Which were the figure and which the ground? Which were "self" and which were "other?" My senses of these texts' inter-action, including my interaction with and for them, are dialectical and dia-logical ones.

In my opinion, the textual genres composing *Friendship Matters* continu-ally interact in mutually excluding and mutually conditioning relationships (Marquit, 1981). That is, they negate each other as opposing ends of continua, while requiring the existence of each other's premises to constitute by contrast their own. They need each other to be different. Yet, if you see the relationships between social science and meaningful lived experience as solely mutually excluding and you are a devout social scientist, you may look at this book and ask, "How did you come up with these dialectics? Why were these examples of lived experience included and not others? What were your decision rules? Where is your *method?*" So it is either–or and you want to know about method according to the doctrine of orthodox social science. Yet, if it is either–or and you are a reverent interpretivist and if you are very concerned about the author's presence, you are apt to say, "How does this book connect specifically with your life? Why did you bother to include objectifying scientistic studies? Where are the accounts of your experiences of friendship in this text? Where are *you?*" Here, it is either–or and you want to know about the author's identity and activities according to the pronouncements of postmodern ethnography.

I view the mutually exclusive convictions reflected in both of these stances as constituting what Bakhtin (1981) called "false binaries." By comparison, I see these various texts and differing orientations toward inquiry as simultaneously mutually opposing and mutually conditioning issues. In this work, the social scientific depictions, the literary depictions, and the accounts of lived experience are all being compared and contrasted, presupposing and superimposing each other. This is how learning and knowing are enacted in this book. I tried to embrace and exhibit the dynamics of dialectical and dialogical relationships among these texts; I engaged them as mutually opposing and mutually conditioning utterances, speaking and answering to each other, as well as to their readers, including myself.

Such vibrant intertextuality is a feature and potential of inclusive discursive practices, which is what dialogism stands for: the chance for each voice to be heard on its own terms, as well as in comparison with coconstitutive others. Even so, I would emphatically contrast the motivating spirit of this dialogic practice with triangulation, for example, which I often hear recommended (and in some cases, enforced) as a *necessary* procedure for combining (force-fitting) deeply divergent stances toward inquiry. The kind of investigation I have been describing is not a verificationist project; it is not seeking demonstrable certainty about some social patterns or "objective" conditions that "really exist" apart from our conventions and languages for knowing them. It is not a method for determining the Truth. To the extent that triangulation invokes this stance, in my opinion, it often enacts positivist pieties; it also reinscribes a variety of traditional hypothetico–deductive motifs that I view as incoherent in the context of dialectical and dialogical thinking.

One of the clearest cases of these is the reliance on mutually exclusive categories for "coding" inherently interconnected and verbally enacted modes of social life and experience—to render them fit for formal hypothesis testing. Often these categories are then summarily described or reduced using numbers and then compared with statistical tables to determine the correct nature and extent of their relationship(s). Although these are viable procedures for warranting and testing claims within the umbrella of many positivist projects, they fly in the face of dialogism's rejection of any last word and dialectics' recognition of concrete interconnectedness, contradiction and flux.

I believe it is important to sustain some of the penchant for challenging entrenched practices that has often characterized dialectical inquiry. In my opinion, dialectical work concerning social and personal relationships emerged in direct and strident opposition to the assumptions and practices of orthodox social science. For example, in opening his eloquent, pioneering, and disturbing dialectical interrogation of American family life, *Pathways to Madness,* anthropologist Jules Henry (1965) put his cards on the table. He stated:

> I am repelled by the artificiality of experimental studies of human behavior because they strip the context from life. They take away from it the environment, without which it has no meaning, without which it has no envelope. I require the actuality of what is nowadays called the "existential human being" as he [sic] lives his [sic] real life. I have to see *that person* before me; and what I cannot see as *that actuality,* what I cannot hear as the sound of *that voice,* has little interest for me. Human life fills me with a wild, intoxicated curiosity. A result is that in my studies I try to combine disciplined observation with a comprehensive interpretation of life in its complex interrelations.
>
> In this book I offer no "typologies," because human phenomena do not arrange themselves obligingly in types but, rather, afford us the spectacle of endless overlapping. Hence I have no family "types" and no statistics, only intensive analyses of the variety of family experience. (pp. xv–xvi).

In the spirit of dialectical opposition, I argue that the antithesis instantiated by interpretive dialectical inquiry like Henry's should not be reinscribed as merely another option or perspective for the dominant orthodox thesis — that is, business-as-usual social science. There are currently clear risks that interpretive dialectical inquiry about social life is being coopted and encapsulated by mainstream knowledge producers' power structures and practices.

However, whether you acknowledge that the process of encapsulation I describe might be occurring or not could depend on how you answer questions like the following: Are reviewers using the criteria of traditional hypothetico–deductive theory building and hypothesis testing to evaluate dialectical projects? Are some writers about communication theories and perspectives asking for dialectical thinkers to see the *same* "dialectical tensions" in the social processes or relationships they examine? Are people calling for or being pressured to employ triangulation in dialectical research projects? Are people submitting dialectical work for publication including reliability checks to refute in advance questions about the "objectivity" of their inquiries (or perhaps in order to be published)? Are people using fixed response questionnaires to generate data about dialectical tensions that are then correlated with standard questionnaire data or induced categories and evaluated according to linear statistical models? Are authors treating relational dialectics or dialectical tensions as simply another variable to be factored into a standard variable-analytic description of relationships? Do people ask for the empirical testing of dialectical models?

Meanwhile, I also believe it is important to incorporate in our scholarly (and everyday) lives the penchant for inclusiveness and encouragement of different approaches to being and knowing, championed by dialogical inquiry. To a degree, this spirit inspires the simultaneity of *Friendship Matters,* its enactment of heteroglossia, and its representation and mediation of multiple texts and voices.

Dialectical, dialogical, and orthodox social scientific investigations are subsumed by the concrete social processes of accomplishing social inquiry, although they may conceive of them differently. As social actors and questioners, we can aspire to Bakhtin and other dialogical thinkers' recommendations to speak our minds and ask our questions with conviction, while remaining willing to hear others' responses and questions on their own terms.

ACKNOWLEDGMENTS

I would like to thank Elaine B. Jenks and Sandy Rawlins for their careful reading and commentary on this essay.

REFERENCES

Altman, I., Vinsel, A., & Brown, B. B. (1981). Dialectic conceptions in social psychology: An application to social penetration and privacy regulation. In L. Berkowitz (Ed.), *Advances in experimental social psychology* (Vol. 14, pp. 107–160). London: Academic Press.

Bakhtin, M. M. (1981). *The dialogic imagination: Four essays.* Austin: University of Texas Press.

Bakhtin, M. M. (1984). *Problems of Dostoevsky's Poetics.* Minneapolis: University of Minnesota Press.

Bateson, G. (1972). *Steps to an ecology of mind.* New York: Ballantine.

Baxter, L. A. (1988). A dialectical perspective on communication strategies in relationship development. In S. W. Duck, D. F. Hay, S. E. Hobfoll, W. Ickes, & B. Montgomery (Eds.), *Handbook of personal relationships* (pp. 257–273). London: Wiley.

Baxter, L. A. (1992). Interpersonal communication as dialogue: A response to the "Social Approaches Forum." *Communication Theory, 2,* 330–337.

Baxter, L. A. (1994). A dialogic approach to relationship maintenance. In D. J. Canary & L. Stafford (Eds.), *Communication and relational maintenance* (pp. 233–254). New York: Academic Press.

Bochner, A. P. (1984). Functions of communication in interpersonal bonding. In C. Arnold &

J. Bowers (Eds.), *Handbook of rhetorical and communication theory* (pp. 544–621). Boston: Allyn & Bacon.

Bochner, A. P. (1985). Perspectives on inquiry: Representation, conversation, and reflection. In M. L. Knapp & G. R. Miller (Eds.), *Handbook of interpersonal communication* (pp. 27–58). Beverly Hills, CA: Sage

Booth, W. C. (1988). *The company we keep: An ethics of fiction.* Berkeley: University of California Press.

Bopp, M. J., & Weeks, G. R. (1984). Dialectical metatheory in family therapy. *Family Process, 23,* 49–61.

Burke, K. (1969). *A grammar of motives.* Berkeley: University of California Press.

Glaser, B. G., & Strauss, A. L. (1967). *The discovery of grounded theory.* Chicago: Aldine de Gruyter.

Henry, J. (1965). *Pathways to madness.* New York: Vintage Books.

Holquist, M. (1990). *Dialogism: Bakhtin and his world.* London: Routledge & Kegan Paul.

Lofland, J. (1976). *Doing social life.* New York: Wiley.

Marquit, E. (1981). Contradictions in dialectics and formal logic. *Science and Society, 45,* 306–323.

Mecke, J. (1990). Dialogue in narration (the narrative principle). In T. Maranhao (Ed.), *The interpretation of dialogue* (pp. 195–215). Chicago: University of Chicago Press.

Rawlins, W. K. (1979, May). *A developmental and dialectical analysis of communication in friendship.* Paper presented to the annual meeting of the International Communication Association, Philadelphia.

Rawlins, W. K. (1983a). Negotiating close friendships: The dialectic of conjunctive freedoms. *Human Communication Research, 9,* 255–266.

Rawlins, W. K. (1983b). Openness as problematic in ongoing friendships: Two conversational dilemmas. *Communication Monographs, 50,* 1–13.

Rawlins, W. K. (1989a). A dialectical analysis of the tensions, functions and strategic challenges of communication in young adult friendships. In J. A. Anderson (Ed.), *Communication Yearbook 12* (pp. 157–189). Newbury, CA: Sage.

Rawlins, W. K. (1989b). Rehearsing the margins of adulthood: The communicative management of adolescent friendships. In J. F. Nussbaum (Ed.), *Life-span communication: Normative issues* (pp. 137–154). Hillsdale, NJ: Lawrence Erlbaum Associates.

Rawlins, W. K. (1991). On enacting friendship and interrogating discourse. In K. Tracy (Ed.), *Understanding face-to-face interaction: Issues linking goals and discourse* (pp. 101–115). New York: Lawrence Erlbaum Associates.

Rawlins, W. K. (1992). *Friendship matters: Communication, dialectics, and the life course.* Hawthorne, NY: de Gruyter.

Rawlins, W. K. (1994). Being there and growing apart: Sustaining friendships during adulthood. In D. J. Canary & L. Stafford (Eds.), *Communication and relational maintenance* (pp. 275–294). New York: Academic Press.

Rawlins, W. K. (1995). Friendships in later life. In J. F. Nussbaum & J. Coupland (Eds.), *Handbook of communication and aging research* (pp. 227–257). Mahwah, NJ: Lawrence Erlbaum Associates.

Rawlins, W. K., & Holl, M. (1988). Adolescents' interactions with parents and friends: Dialectics of temporal perspective and evaluation. *Journal of Social and Personal Relationships, 5,* 27–46.

Ricoeur, P. (1970). *Freud and philosophy: An essay on interpretation* (D. Savage, Trans.). New Haven, CT: Yale University Press.

Rorty, R. (1982). *Consequences of pragmatism.* Minneapolis: University of Minnesota Press.

Rorty, R. (1991). *Essays on Heidegger and others.* Cambridge, England: Cambridge University Press.

Todorov, T. (1984). *Mikhail Bakhtin: The dialogical principle.* Minneapolis: University of Minnesota Press.

5

"Going Into and Coming Out of the Closet": The Dialectics of Stigma Disclosure

KATHRYN DINDIA
University of Wisconsin, Milwaukee

The term *stigma* refers to a stable characteristic or attribute of an individual that is perceived as damaging to the individual's reputation (Goffman, 1963). Stigmas include, but are not limited to, physical disability, membership in some stigmatized group, character defects that are manifested by some discrediting event in the person's past or present, and disease. The literature on stigma disclosure includes research on disclosure of homosexuality, HIV-positive status, AIDS, sexual abuse, drug addiction, alcoholism, mental illness, epilepsy, and other stigmatized conditions, as well as occupational stigmatization (e.g., low-status occupations such as prostitutes and, more recently, animal experimenters). Individuals are stigmatized because they presently possess or display these characteristics (e.g., being HIV-positive or having AIDS), because they formerly manifested these characteristics (e.g., former drug addiction or former mental illness), or because they are associated with someone who is stigmatized (e.g., the lover, relative, or caregiver of a person with AIDS or the parent of a gay son or lesbian daughter).

Goffman (1963) classified those who are stigmatized into the "discredited" and the "discreditable." The *discredited* is one whose stigma is already known or is immediately apparent to others, such as an obvious physical disability. According to Goffman, because the stigma is difficult or impossible to conceal, whether to reveal or conceal is not an issue for the discredited. Instead, the problem for the discredited is managing the tension generated during mixed social contacts or contacts with normals (however, this may be oversimplifying the situation for the discredited, cf., Braithwaite, 1991). The *discreditable* is one whose stigma is not known about nor immediately apparent to others, such as being homosexual. Because the stigma is easier to conceal, whether to reveal or conceal is an issue for the discreditable. The major problem for the discreditable is information control, or the management of undisclosed discrediting information about self.

The purpose of this chapter is to examine stigma self-disclosure as a dialectical process. Fundamental dialectical assumptions are used to frame research findings in the literature on stigma disclosure and major theoretical and methodological implications are identified. Finally, this dialectical view of stigma disclosure is generalized to all self-disclosure.

DIALECTICAL ASSUMPTIONS

According to Baxter and Montgomery (1996), there are four shared assumptions of a dialectical perspective: contradiction, change, praxis, and totality. I illustrate how disclosure of stigmatized identities is a dialectical phenomenon by invoking these assumptions.

Contradiction

Contradiction is the fundamental, central, and unique assumption of a dialectical perspective. According to a dialectical perspective, social systems involve contradictory and opposing forces (Baxter, 1988; Baxter & Montgomery, 1996; Montgomery, 1993). Several dialectical theorists have posited openness–closedness (revealing–concealing, expressiveness–protectiveness) as a dialectical tension in relationships (cf., Altman, Vinsel, & Brown, 1981; Baxter, 1988; Bochner, 1984; Rawlins, 1983). According to a dialectical perspective, individuals continually face the contradictory impulses to be open and disclosive versus closed and protective of self or of other.

Although the term *dialectics* is not used in the literature on stigma disclosure, many of these researchers implicitly assume a dialectical perspective and posit contradiction as intrinsic to the disclosure of stigmatized identities. For example, Goffman (1963) viewed the fundamental issue for the discreditable as whether:

> to display or not to display; to tell or not to tell; to let on or not to let on; to lie or not to lie; and in each case, to whom, how, when, and where. (p. 42)

A number of researchers have described the dialectical contradiction of whether to reveal or conceal stigma. Limandri (1989) studied the disclosure of abuse, AIDS, HIV, and herpes and stated that participants in her study "were confronted with the need to tell or to conceal" (p. 76). According to Limandri, the contradictory nature of stigma disclosure is due to the fact that stigmatizing conditions contribute to feelings of shame and the wish to conceal or hide; however, those who experience such conditions also often need to confide in others and seek help from professionals.

Cain (1991), in discussing disclosure of gay sexual identity, referred to "the contradictory demands" that gay men face regarding disclosure and secrecy:

> Gay individuals, then confront a dilemma regarding how to present themselves to others. By choosing to be open, they risk being seen as different and being harassed or ridiculed; they may also risk losing friends, family ties, or their jobs. . . . Yet, by choosing not to be open, they also encounter problems. Secrecy may create a sense of distance in relationships or may lead them to feel they are dishonest with trusted others. . . . Covertness also requires them to invest considerable energy to maintain a facade of heterosexuality. (p. 72).

Wells and Kline (1987) described the double-bind of disclosure of homosexuality: Individuals want to self-disclose their homosexuality to develop relationships, but are unwilling to risk disclosure because they are afraid of being rejected. Gershman (1983) described the "Catch 22" of disclosure of homosexuality: One experiences anxiety in disclosing one's true feelings, yet failure to disclose engenders the anxiety of not being oneself. Gard (1990) argued that disclosure of HIV infection to parents involves a similar Catch 22.

Marks, Bundek, Richardson, Ruiz, Maldonado, and Mason (1992) discussed the psychological conflict involved in the decision to disclose HIV infection:

> One may feel the need to inform a significant other for purposes of support but may fear rejection from that person. Similarly, one may feel an ethical obligation to inform medical providers (e.g., dentists) but may simultaneously fear that disclosure will result in refusal of services. (p. 300)

Dindia and Tieu (1996) explicitly argued that disclosure of homosexuality is a dialectical phenomenon. Dindia and Tieu studied participants' coming out stories. Participants reported struggling with the dialectical tension of whether to reveal or conceal homosexuality. As stated by one of the study participants: "I'm really struggling with this [who to tell] for about the past year. . . . I want to tell—hard to lie—hate to lie. Something pulls the other way [not telling], I don't know what" (p. 17).

Multivocality

Baxter and Montgomery (1996) argued that dialectical contradiction is multivocal; any given contradiction has many or different meanings. Multivocal contradiction expands the conceptualization of contradiction from an oversimplified binary contradiction, like openness and closedness, to more complex contradictions, like the contradictions between expressiveness, verbal disclosure, directness, honesty, on the one hand, and concealing, indirectness, deception, ambiguity, equivocation, discreetness, and tact, on the other hand (Baxter & Montgomery, 1996).

Although the multivocality of the openness–closedness contradiction has not been elaborated in the literature on stigma disclosure (nor for that matter in the general literature on self-disclosure), there is some evidence that the contradiction between revealing and concealing stigma is multivocal. Powell-Cope and Brown (1992) discussed going public, or how persons-with-AIDS (PWA) caregivers let others know they were caring for a PWA. Powell-Cope and Brown found that AIDS family caregivers experienced both a personal and a social tension in going public. Virtually all caregivers felt the personal dilemma of going public. The major personal risk of going public was the need to protect oneself and the PWA from negative judgment and harm. The major personal benefit of going public reported by study participants was gaining support and assistance from others. In addition, a few caregivers spoke of the social and public dilemma of going public. Here, the personal need to protect self and PWA is balanced against the need to create social change. The major social risks of remaining secretive identified by caregivers were the perpetuation of homophobia and AIDS stigma, the continued escalation of the incidence of AIDS, and inadequate health and social services. The major social benefits of going public included altering the politics surrounding AIDS by increasing public awareness and the creation of a sense of community.

The studies just discussed provide evidence that contradiction is inherent in the disclosure of stigmatized identities. Stigma disclosure involves a dialectical tension between the need to reveal and the need to conceal. Individuals are simultaneously pulled in opposite directions and struggle with the contradiction of whether to reveal or conceal stigma. The dialectical contradiction between revealing and concealing stigma may be multivocal in nature, involving different meanings for different people or multiple meanings for specific individuals.

Change

The dialectical assumption of contradiction is virtually inseparable from the dialectical assumption of change; change is inherent in contradiction (Baxter & Montgomery, 1996). Although *change* is an assumption of other perspectives on self-disclosure, in particular, transactional perspectives (Dindia, 1997; Pearce & Sharp, 1973), other perspectives do not assume that contradiction is the cause of change, whereas a dialectical perspective argues that contradiction is the driving force of change (Baxter & Montgomery, 1996). The ongoing and ever-changing process of self-disclosure is the result of the inherent dialectical contradiction of the need to reveal and conceal.

Process Versus Event

A dialectical perspective on self-disclosure implies that self-disclosure is not a single, dichotomous event in which the person has disclosed or has not disclosed (e.g., is out of the closest or is not out of the closet). As stated by one participant in Dindia and Tieu's (1996) study of the dialectics of disclosure of homosexuality:

> I'm not certain whether anybody really can [come out]. . . . You can "come out" to all your friends and family and such but then you can do things like move to a more conservative area and that creates a whole new issue. You can acquire new friends and depending upon how they are it creates new issues. . . . When I moved to the Canyon . . . I ended up . . . back in the closet. The minute you step there . . . you're essentially back in. You can think of yourself, as far as I'm concerned, back in the closet every time you enter a new room. Okay? . . . There's a whole new process of coming out again as you count the ranks. (p. 18)

Although some stigma researchers have suggested that individuals either reveal or conceal their stigma, others have argued that the disclosure of stigmatized identities "is far more complex than either choosing to disclose or not disclose one's 'failing' " (Herman, 1993, p. 305). For example, Cain (1991) argued that the management of stigmatizing information is "neither simple nor dichotomous":

> It would be very difficult, if not impossible, for gay individuals to be either overt or covert all of the time . . . gay individuals may be either overt or covert in particular types of interactions or with particular people, but even then it may be difficult to categorize some interactions as either one or the other. (p. 67)

Instead, self-disclosure occurs on a continuum. Limandri (1989) studied disclosure of abuse, AIDS, HIV antibodies, and herpes and reported that disclosure ranged from nondisclosure to open and complete disclosure and that individuals disclosed at many levels in between (e.g., minimal disclosure). Similarly, Cain (1991) argued that gay individuals vary in the degree to which they are open or secretive.

Additionally, self-disclosure is an ongoing and ever-changing process. As stated by a participant in the Dindia and Tieu (1996) study: "I . . . am in the process of coming out. . . . When you say, 'heh, I'm gay.' That's the beginning. Yeah, coming out to yourself and then slowly coming out to other people as well" (p. 18). Another participant said, "I think it [disclosure of homosexuality] occurs in increments" (p. 19). He reported disclosing to a male friend, a female friend, his sister, another female friend, and his mother, in an incremental process over a 20-year period. Another respondent spoke of going through stages of disclosure: (a) if asked, would lie, (b) if asked, would say nothing, (c) "if someone asked I wouldn't deny it but I don't wear a sign" (p. 19). Other researchers have found that stigma disclosure is an ongoing process that occurs throughout a person's entire life (or at least as long as the person has the stigma; e.g., Cain, 1991; Limandri, 1989; Wells & Kline, 1987). For example, Murphy and Irwin (1992) found that methadone patients dealt with the decision concerning disclosure on an almost daily basis.

Thus, stigma disclosure is not a dichotomous and mutually exclusive phenomenon (disclosure–concealment). Self-disclosure is an ongoing, ever-changing process that is extended in time and is open-ended, not only across the course of an interaction or series of interactions, but also across the lives of individuals. Self-disclosure, like relationships, is unfinished business (Duck, 1990).

Teleological Versus Indeterminate Change

Baxter and Montgomery (1996) indicated that although all dialectical perspectives assume change, they differ in whether the change process is presumed to be teleological or indeterminate. Teleological change moves to an ideal end state. Indeterminate change is not directed toward some necessary or ideal end state. When applied to self-disclosure, indeterminate change means that self-disclosure changes, but not in a fixed pattern or sequence resulting in some specified end state (e.g., nondisclosure–minimal disclosure–full disclosure).

Some self-disclosure theorists argue that the ideal end state of self-disclosure is full disclosure. Jourard (1971) argued that to be healthy, one must disclose oneself. The "ideology of intimacy" (Parks, 1982), in which disclosure is viewed as good and beneficial to individuals–relationships and concealment is viewed as bad and harmful to individuals–relationships, is pervasive in the communication and personal relationships literatures (cf., Prager, 1995, which is based on the premise that intimacy is good for individuals and relationships).

Similarly, it is often argued in gay literature that one should come out of the closet. The cultural expectation is that gay men ought to disclose their homosexuality and that disclosing homosexuality is good: "Disclosure of homosexuality is now generally viewed in the professional literature as more desirable than secrecy; disclosure is often seen as evidence of a healthy gay identity, whereas secrecy has come to be viewed as socially and psychologically problematic" (Cain, 1991, p. 67). Indeed, movement through the stages of gay identity development, in which disclosure to others is an important step, is assumed to be positive growth. Individuals who are open are portrayed as being at advanced stages of sexual identity development; those who are closed are portrayed as being at earlier stages of sexual identity development (Cain, 1991).

However, neither full disclosure nor total concealment is possible or desirable from a dialectic perspective. Full disclosure is impossible given the dialectic interplay of opposing forces. Because self-disclosure is dialectical, one can never fully reveal oneself. The contradiction between openness and closedness can never be resolved.

Research on stigma disclosure indicates that individuals do not engage in full disclosure or total concealment. Powell-Cope and Brown (1992) studied PWA caregivers' disclosure of involvement with AIDS and found that the majority of their study participants balanced secrecy and assertiveness. Individuals lived with neither complete secrecy nor complete openness, but used varying amounts of secrecy and openness in telling others about their involvement with AIDS. Participants in Dindia and Tieu's (1996) study of disclosure of homosexuality reported the need to establish a balance between the two extremes of total concealment and total disclosure. As stated by one study participant: "I know that I've had to find a sense of equilibrium. I don't feel comfortable wearing a sign that says, 'I'm gay.' . . . But I am becoming less tolerant, as time goes on, with the 'game playing' that I did in my own head for a lot of years" (pp. 18–19).

Similarly, full disclosure (or total concealment) is not ideal from a dialectical perspective. According to a dialectical perspective, individuals need to enact some composite of openness and closedness (Rawlins, 1983). There are rewards and risks involved in disclosure as well as nondisclosure. Although disclosure of stigmatized identity can lead to acceptance, support, physiological health (Pennebacker, 1989), and so on; disclosure of stigmatized identity can also lead to the end of a relationship or loss of a job. As stated by Cain (1991), "The clinical literature, however, does not adequately account for the observation that even when gay individuals accept their sexual identity, there often remain good reasons for them to conceal it" (p. 72). Cain interviewed gay men and found that decisions regarding disclosure and secrecy were related to a variety of situational and relational factors that are independent of gay identity development. These findings suggest that clinicians and others should not automatically assume that gay individuals need to be open to be self-accepting or that gay individuals who are open have a positive self-concept and that gay individuals who are not open have a negative self-concept (Cain, 1991).

Linear Versus Circular or Spiraling Change

Some self-disclosure theorists assume self-disclosure is linear, moving in a unidirectional and cumulative fashion from nondisclosure to full disclosure (e.g., Altman & Taylor, 1973). "Peeling an onion" is the metaphor used to represent the linear process of self-disclosure. Some of the research on disclosure of stigmatized identities similarly takes a linear approach to self-disclosure. For example, MacFarlane and Krebs (1986) described the process of children's disclosure of sexual abuse as the "no-maybe-sometimes-yes" syndrome (p. 82).

Individuals do not, however, necessarily engage in a linear process of revealing more and more information about themselves. Similarly, self-disclosure in relationships does not always increase in a linear fashion. Developing or continuing relationships frequently exhibits cycles of openness and closedness and some relationships do not progress toward increased openness at all (Altman, Vinsel, & Brown, 1981). Disclosure often is cyclical because it is governed by the opposing needs to reveal and conceal.

Like Baxter and Montgomery (1996) and Conville (chap. 2, this volume), I prefer to use the analogy of spiraling rather than circular change to describe stigma disclosure. Circular change implies that self-disclosure moves back and forth (i.e., revealing and concealing and revealing) and that the process repeats in identical form (Baxter & Montgomery, 1996). Because communication is unrepeatable, the term *spiraling* better describes dialectical movement because it depicts self-disclosure as moving back and forth, but never repeating in identical form (a spiral never repeats itself as does a circle). As one moves on in time or in one's life or relationship, the spiral continues, revealing then concealing then revealing, but revealing at time $n + 1$ is not the same as revealing at time n.

Research on disclosure of stigmatized identities supports the notion of spiraling disclosure. Limandri (1989) found that some of her study participants would conceal for awhile, disclose, then retract back into concealment:

> This [deciding whether to tell or to conceal] is not a simple decision or a decision that is made only once, but rather the process simulated a swinging gate or valve that could be completely open, completely closed, or partially open . . . disclosure occurs many more times than once, . . . people can retract their disclosure at times, and . . . the process can expand and contract over time. (p. 76)

Although Dindia and Tieu (1996) found that most study participants described disclosure of homosexuality as a linear process (but see interpretation of this finding under methodological considerations at the end of this chapter), a few participants described it as spiraling. For example, one study participant described the process this way: "Coming out for me has basically moved from wanting to tell everybody to not wanting to tell anybody to kind of going in between those two" (p. 20).

Similarly, Summit (1983), in discussing children's disclosure of sexual abuse, stated that whatever a child said about sexual abuse, she or he was likely to reverse it. Summit referred to disclosure–retraction as being the normal course of children's disclosure of sexual abuse.

Sorenson and Snow (1991) developed a model of the spiraling process of children's disclosure of sexual abuse based on 630 cases of alleged child sexual abuse in which the authors were involved as therapists or evaluators. Qualitative analysis of clinical notes, conversations, audiotapes, videotapes, and reports of children's disclosure to a therapist or evaluator revealed four progressive phases to the process of children's disclosure of sexual abuse: denial, disclosure (which contains two subphases—tentative disclosure and active disclosure), recant, and reaffirm. *Denial* is defined as the child's initial statement to any individual that he or she had not been sexually abused. *Tentative disclosure* refers to the child's partial, vague, or vacillating acknowledgment of sexual abuse. *Active disclosure* refers to a personal admission by the child of having been sexually abused. *Recant* refers to the child's retraction of a previous allegation of abuse. *Reaffirm* is defined as the child's reassertion of the validity of a previous assertion of sexual abuse that had been recanted. According to this model, children typically begin by denying that they have been sexually abused and this is followed by tentative then active disclosure. Some children recant and later reaffirm sexual abuse.

Sorensen and Snow (1991) tested their model of the disclosure process in a qualitative analysis of a subset of 116 case studies from the original 630 cases involving sexually abused children from 3 to 17 years old, who were confirmed as credible victims. Seventy-two percent of the children initially denied having been sexually abused. Denial was most common when children were initially questioned by a concerned parent or adult authority figure and when children were identified as potential victims and initially questioned in a formal investigative interview. Tentative disclosure was the common middle stage for the majority of these children (78%), with only 7% of the children who denied moving directly to active disclosure. Active disclosure, a detailed, coherent, first-person account of the abuse, was eventually made by 96% of the children (including children who originally did not deny having been sexually abused). In approximately 22% of these cases, children recanted their allegations; of those who recanted, 92% reaffirmed their allegations of abuse over time.

The results of these studies provide evidence that self-disclosure does not necessarily move from nondisclosure to disclosure in a linear fashion and instead indicates that individuals may reveal, then conceal, then reveal in a spiraling manner. This is why I do not like the analogy of "coming out of the closet," and chose to use the phrase "Going Into and Coming Out of the Closet" in the title of this chapter.

Praxis

A dialectical perspective views people as both actors and objects of their own actions (Baxter & Montgomery, 1996). People are proactive actors who make communicative choices in how to deal with the contradictions and the contradictions, in turn, affect their subsequent communication actions. Praxis focuses attention on the communication actions–reactions to contradiction.

One way to view self-disclosure as praxis is to view it as a privacy regulation mechanism (Altman, 1975; Derlega & Chaikin, 1977; Petronio, 1988, 1991). Altman (1975) defined privacy as:

> an interpersonal boundary process by which a person or group regulates interaction with others. By altering the degree of openness of the self to others, a hypothetical personal boundary is more or less receptive to social interaction with others. Privacy is, therefore, a dynamic process involving selective control over a self-boundary either by an individual or by a group. (p. 6)

According to Altman, an individual desires an ideal level of privacy with others at any given point in time. A person sets a series of mechanisms in motion to adjust self-boundaries so as to realize the desired level of privacy. Self-disclosure is one such mechanism.

Communication Boundary Management Theory (CBMT; Petronio, 1988, 1991) extends privacy regulation theory and directly addresses the dialectics of disclosure. In CBMT, Petronio argued that individuals manage their communication boundaries to balance the need for disclosure with the need for privacy. The basic thesis of CBMT is that revealing private information is risky because one is potentially vulnerable when revealing aspects of the self. Receiving private information from another may also result in the need to protect oneself. To manage both disclosing and receiving private information, individuals erect a metaphoric boundary as a means of protection and as a means of reducing the possibility of being rejected or getting hurt (Petronio, 1991).

Three assumptions underlie CBMT. First, individuals erect boundaries to control autonomy and vulnerability when disclosing and receiving private information. Second, because disclosing and receiving private information is risky and may cause potential vulnerability, partners strategically regulate their communication boundaries to minimize risks. Third, decision-making rules are used to determine when, with whom, and how much private information is disclosed as well as how to respond to disclosure (Petronio, 1991).

Research on stigma disclosure provides evidence of communication boundary management in the disclosure of stigma. Terms such as *stigma management, information management,* and *information control* are used to refer to the management of undisclosed, discrediting information about self. Research demonstrates that individuals use strategies to manage their stigma and that decision-making rules guide these strategies.

Strategies of Stigma Disclosure

Goffman (1963) and Ponse (1976) suggested that stigmatized individuals utilize specific verbal strategies when revealing their stigma to others. Similarly, Marks et al. (1992) argued that disclosure of HIV infection is a reasoned action that follows from the perceived social, psychological, and material consequences of informing others. Studies show that people with a stigma evaluate the consequences of informing a particular target person before a disclosure is made and plan their disclosure accordingly (Edgar, 1994). For example, Dindia and Tieu (1996) found that individuals consciously and intentionally manage the disclosure of homosexuality. Similarly, Herman (1993) studied stigma management strategies of ex-psychiatric patients and found that almost 80% of the study participants engaged in some form of information control about their illnesses and past hospitalizations, deciding who to tell or not tell, when to tell and not to tell, and how to tell. In the following section, several commonly used strategies to regulate disclosure of stigmatized identity are discussed. The following strategies are neither mutually exclusive or exhaustive.

Selective Disclosure and Concealment. Individuals select who, what, when, where, and why to self-disclose stigma. As stated by Herman (1993), "Individuals *selectively* conceal such information about themselves at certain times, in certain situations, with certain individuals, and freely disclose the same information at other times, in other situations, with other individuals" (p. 305).

Research indicates that selective disclosure and concealment is a common strategy used to manage stigma disclosure. Herman (1993) found that ex-psychiatric patients selectively conceal their mental illness. Selective concealment took the following forms: Avoidance of selected normals, redirection of conversations, withdrawal, the use of disidentifiers (misleading physical or verbal symbols that prevent others from discovering their stigma), and the avoidance of stigma symbols (e.g., symbols of gay pride).

Primarily, people select their targets for disclosing stigma. As pointed out by Goffman (1963), one "strategy of the discredited person is to handle the risks by dividing the world into a large group to whom he tells nothing and a small group to whom he tells all and upon whose help he then relies" (p. 95). Research on stigma disclosure indicates that individuals are highly selective in choosing their targets for stigma disclosure (e.g., Dindia & Tieu, 1996; Herman, 1993; Marks et al., 1992; Murphy & Irwin, 1992; Siegel & Krauss, 1991; Wells & Kline, 1987). Target characteristics and anticipated reaction of target are the primary factors determining to whom stigma is disclosed and is discussed in the following section on decision-making rules.

People also select what to reveal–conceal. This is similar to Baxter's (1988) dialectical segmentation strategy, which differentiates topic domains into those for which self-disclosure is regarded as appropriate and those for which self-disclosure is regarded as inappropriate.

Individuals also select when and where to disclose stigma. Petronio, Reeder, Hecht, and Mon't Ross-Mendoza (1996) showed how children and adolescents select the circumstances (when and where) for disclosure of abuse.

Staging Information.   A second strategy for regulating stigma disclosure is staging information, also referred to as "testing the waters." When information is staged, the boundaries of communication are progressively relaxed (or tightened), depending on the listener's reactions to disclosure (Petronio, 1991). Specifically, the discloser reveals a minimal amount of information and tests the reaction of the target before self-disclosing in more depth or detail.

A number of researchers found that staging information is a key strategy used to manage stigma disclosure. Limandri (1989) found that disclosure of abuse, AIDS or HIV infection, and herpes usually begins with a small revelation to test the environment. MacFarlane and Krebs (1986) indicated that children frequently reveal sexual abuse in small pieces, saving the worst part until they see how the recipient reacts to the things they first disclose. Petronio et al. (1996) found that children gradually revealed abuse in a sequential fashion where each disclosure fed into the next more revealing statement. However, if at any time the children felt the recipient was not able or willing to hear, the sequence was terminated.

Dindia and Tieu (1996) also found a testing process in the disclosure of gay identity. Participants reported cautiously listening to conversations about certain topics discussed by coworkers or friends that might suggest a liberal attitude toward homosexuality. This testing was done with the explicit purpose of determining whether potential targets for self-disclosure would react positively or negatively to disclosure. Interviewees discovered how "gay friendly" their coworkers or family may be before revealing their sexual orientation.

Murphy and Irwin (1992) found that methadone patients "feel the person out about drug use" to predict possible responses of a potential target for disclosure (p. 262). Methadone patients introduced the topic of drugs and addiction and evaluated the target person's response in order to predict how a disclosure of addiction might be received. If the potential target expressed disgust and repugnance toward addicts, then the patient was unlikely to disclose addiction. If the person expressed sympathy or even ambivalence, disclosure was much more likely to occur.

Powell-Cope and Brown (1992) found that staging information was a key strategy used by PWA caregivers to manage AIDS-related stigma. Caregivers slowly painted a more complete picture of their situation by carefully selecting certain amounts and types of information to disclose. In particular, Powell-Cope and Brown found that staging information initially involved: (a) talking about a sick friend or family member, (b) elaborating that the person was very ill and had cancer or was dying, and (c) finally, disclosing that the friend or family member had AIDS, their relationship to the PWA, and the extent of their caregiving role. Staging information was advantageous for caregivers because it reduced their anxiety about being found out, allowed them to obtain support from others they did not completely trust, and protected them from others' negative reactions.

Sometimes staging information is used to determine whether to disclose to additional targets based on an initial target's reaction. For example, Herman (1993) found that disclosures to particular targets were made to test reactions by ex-psychiatric patients in which the continued disclosure of ex-patients' mental illness to other targets was contingent on responses they received to previous disclosures.

Indirect Disclosure. Another strategy for revealing stigma is to reveal it indirectly. Edgar (1994) found three dimensions of stigma disclosure, one was the degree to which it is direct–indirect. Similarly, Ponse (1976) found that inference is a frequent disclosure tactic for lesbians. Women in her study described how they make comments to others that imply their homosexuality without directly stating it. One woman said that she would make statements such as, "she and I have done this" or "she and I have done that," indirectly revealing her homosexuality (p. 332). Similarly, Wells and Kline (1987) found that approximately one third of disclosures of homosexuality were categorized as indirect rather than direct.

Almost all the participants in Dindia and Tieu's (1996) study of disclosure of homosexuality mentioned multiple instances in which they did not directly disclose they were gay; rather, they indirectly let other people know they were gay. Participants talked about dropping hints about themselves, wearing freedom rings (a symbol of gay pride), and t-shirts and caps that symbolize gay identity in a more or less explicit manner. There was evidence that individuals were consciously aware that they were indirectly communicating that they were gay. For example, one participant said:

> I don't disclose directly. I may not come out to a lot of people at work and say that I'm gay but I'll say "I'm going to Washington D.C. to see the AIDS quilt" or "I volunteer at the Milwaukee AIDS Project"—so guilt by association—I don't hide those things. (p. 31)

There was also evidence that individuals intentionally used indirect disclosure as a strategy to manage disclosure of homosexuality. For example, one male participant said:

> We celebrated our family Christmas here in Milwaukee at my apartment and I
> decided that I'm going to leave my little gay flag in my bedroom. I left that out
> and I have a poster of a guy on the wall that's not wearing much of anything.
> It's only a waist shot on up. But you can tell, a straight guy would not have that
> picture on his wall. But I left it up. And I decided ahead of time that I would
> leave that up so that anybody that would go by would see that. (p. 32)

Concealment or Nondisclosure.   Limandri (1989) found that some study participants engaged in the strategy of concealment or nondisclosure of HIV antibodies, AIDS, and abuse and would do anything possible to deny their stigma to others, including lying. Arluke (1991) found that some animal researchers concealed the fact that they did animal research. Powell-Cope and Brown (1992) found that many of the PWA caregivers in their study lived with secrecy. Specific strategies used by caregivers to pass included making excuses, lying, witholding information, changing jobs or places of residence, and avoiding certain social situations and family gatherings.

Several researchers reported that concealment was an initial strategy used to manage stigma disclosure that was often followed by some type of disclosure (e.g., Powell-Cope & Brown, 1992). For example, Dindia and Tieu's (1996) study participants reported using concealment initially and maintaining it for various lengths of time before engaging in other strategies of self-disclosure (e.g., selective disclosure). However, there are probably numerous individuals who possess discreditable stigmas and employ concealment as a life-long strategy. These people do not get included in studies of stigma disclosure.

Open and Complete Disclosure.   Alternatively, some of Limandri's (1989) study participants engaged in open and complete disclosure. Powell-Cope & Brown (1992) found that a small proportion of study participants chose to ignore AIDS stigma and to openly live with their AIDS caregiving role. Dindia and Tieu (1996), in studying disclosure of homosexuality, found open and complete disclosure to be used by 1 of 15 study participants. Most of their participants commented that they do not "wear a sign" indicating they are gay and made statements like, "You can never fully come out of the closet," but one study participant thought he was "out of the closet." This individual disclosed that he was gay in a class of 300 students, and he was on a local news program about gays in which he disclosed he was gay. As he said, "When I came out of the closet, I nuked the closet" (p. 36).

Other Strategies. Limandri (1989) found that *invitational disclosure,* in which a discloser provides sufficient cues that "something is wrong" in order to invite the respondent to request self-disclosure, is a type of stigma disclosure. Limandri, as well as Dindia and Tieu (1996), also reported reciprocal self-disclosure—stigma is disclosed in response to another person's stigma disclosure—and *responses to inquiry*—stigma is disclosed in response to a request for stigma disclosure—as common types of stigma disclosure.

Decision-Making Rules

Individuals make decisions regarding disclosure and concealment of stigma, and decision-making rules are used to determine who, what, when, where, and why to disclose stigma. Petronio et al. (1996) studied the decision rules used to grant or deny access to children's and adolescents' disclosures of sexual abuse. They found that participants in their study used three rules to grant access: (a) *tacit permission* (i.e., disclose in response to an inquiry or in response to another person's self-disclosure); (b) *selecting the circumstances* (i.e., choose a situation that makes you feel comfortable and reduces fears of disclosure); and (c) *incremental disclosure* (i.e., disclose in an incremental fashion testing the reaction to each self-disclosure before deciding whether to increase self-disclosure). Individuals denied access to disclosure of sexual abuse based on *target characteristics* (i.e., do not disclose if recipient is untrustworthy, unresponsive, or lacks understanding) and *anticipated negative reactions* (i.e., do not disclose if you anticipate negative reactions from the target including gossip and loss of control of the information).

Decision-making rules falling under the categories of target characteristics and anticipated negative reactions have been found by several other researchers. For example, Herman (1993) found that individuals select who to tell based on their perceptions of others, whether they are safe others or risky others. Dindia and Tieu (1996) found that individuals disclose homosexuality to target persons perceived as positive (warm and friendly, trustworthy, etc.) and when they anticipated a positive reaction from the target. Murphy and Irwin (1992) found methadone patients shared their stigma with those people they predicted would be understanding and accepting of their situation. Siegel and Krauss (1991) interviewed HIV-positive, gay men and found that most of them had been quite selective in deciding to whom they disclosed their infected status. Four considerations influenced whom they told: (a) fears of rejection, (b) the wish to avoid the pity of others, (c) the wish to spare loved ones emotional pain, and (d) concerns about discrimination.

Dindia and Tieu (1996), Spencer (1991), and Spencer and Derlega (1995) also found that relationship characteristics was a category of decision-making rules used to select targets. Targets were selected based on their relationship with the discloser. As stated by one participant in Dindia and Tieu's

(1996) study, "I don't come out to people that I don't know well or know at all. . . . I've gotta have some connection with them . . . have some sort of relationship with them" (p. 23). Closeness of the relationship was the most frequently mentioned relationship characteristic leading to a decision to reveal or conceal homosexuality: "It has to do with how close they are to me . . . if I get to be close to them [I tell them], I don't tell them right away" (p. 23). Study participants told friends, family, and coworkers to whom they were close; they did not tell family, friends, and coworkers to whom they were not close. Similarly, Mark et al. (1992) found that HIV-positive participants tended to inform significant others rather than less significant others. Spencer (1991) and Spencer and Derlega (1995) found that stigma self-disclosure is used to increase intimacy with a family member or significant other. In contrast, some respondents avoided coming out because they did not feel the necessary intimacy was present.

Dindia and Tieu (1996) found that the recent U.S. military policy, "Don't ask, don't tell," is a common rule used for revealing or concealing homosexuality both inside and outside the military. One woman who had been in the military reported that this was the strategy used in the military when she was in it, long before the present day policy. More interesting, a number of participants indicated that this was a common strategy used outside the military. One participant stated that she lived in an apartment directly above her parents with her lesbian lover, "They had to know but they didn't ask. So I didn't tell" (p. 35). She also talked about her brother and sister-in-law saying, "They know but they don't ask" (p. 35).

Typically, individuals do not ask or tell because the discloser or recipient does not want to talk about it or hear about it. Several participants in Dindia and Tieu's (1996) study reported friends and relatives that they believed did not want to hear they were gay, and consequently, they did not disclose homosexuality. One participant broke up with her lover and her father literally told her, "I don't want to hear about it [being gay], but go talk to someone" (p. 36). The study participant said, "He was trying to be supportive but he doesn't want to talk about it. So that's why I don't tell him" (p. 36). One participant did not tell his father because, "He made it clear a long time ago that he doesn't want to hear certain things. So I'll respect that" (p. 36).

The "Don't ask, don't tell" rule exists because stigma disclosure is a taboo topic (Baxter & Wilmot, 1985), a topic that is off limits in a relationship, a family, or an organization such as the military. For example, one woman in Dindia and Tieu's (1996) study referred to her relationship with her parents, saying, "Sex is something we don't talk about in the first place. You're not going to talk about being in love with another woman [when you don't talk about sex]" (p. 23). She went on to say that she did not disclose this information to anyone in her family, saying, "That's not how my family is" (pp. 23–24).

Similarly, several participants in Dindia and Tieu's (1996) study indicated that in some cases of explicit disclosure of homosexuality, a rule was made never to talk about it again. For example, one study participant told his father, and his father's reaction was, "Okay. As long as you don't bring it into my house or as long as you don't ever talk about it" (p. 36).

There is considerable overlap in the literature between decision-making rules and strategies for disclosing or concealing stigma. However, decision rules are the cognitive component of disclosure strategies. "Don't disclose to people who are . . ." and "don't disclose to people who will react . . ." are decision rules guiding the strategy of selective disclosure and concealment. That is individuals selectively reveal–conceal information about themselves based on target characteristics and anticipated negative reactions of the target. Similarly, "Choose a situation that makes you feel comfortable and reduces fears of disclosure" is a decision rule guiding the strategy of selective disclosure and concealment (i.e., selecting where and when to disclose stigma). "Disclose in an incremental fashion, and if at any time you feel the recipient is not able or willing to hear, terminate the disclosure" is a decision rule guiding the strategy of staging information. "One should disclose as a response to an inquiry or in response to another person's self-disclosure" is the decision-making rule that leads to reciprocity of self-disclosure and self-disclosure in response to a request for self-disclosure. Finally, the decision-making rule, "Don't ask, don't tell," can lead to strategies of total or selective concealment or to indirect disclosure.

In brief summary of this section, self-disclosure is both an action and reaction to the dialectical contradiction between the need to reveal and conceal. Self-disclosure viewed as a boundary-control mechanism provides a view of self-disclosure as praxis. Self-disclosure strategies are employed to manage communication boundaries and to balance the need to reveal with the need to conceal. Decision-making rules guide these strategies.

Totality

The fourth and final core assumption of a dialectical perspective is *totality*, the assumption that phenomena can be understood only in relation to other phenomena. According to Baxter and Montgomery (1996), the assumption of totality implicates three issues: where contradictions are located, interdependencies among contradictions, and contextualization of contradictions.

The Location of Contradiction

The dialectical view of stigma disclosure described in this chapter locates the contradiction of revealing–concealing stigma at all social levels—individuals, relationships, and society. However, the primary location of the contradiction of whether to reveal or conceal is located in the individual. Powell-

Cope and Brown (1992) provided an excellent example of how the tension of going public exists at a societal level:

> Going public is embedded in a society that distinguishes between a private and public self. The American value of individualism and the constitutional right to privacy encourage people to keep the personal private and to solve personal problems with self-reliance. Because of the cultural emphasis on privacy, deception and secrecy are considered acceptable strategies to protect oneself from other's judgments. At the same time, Americans value participation in public spheres of life. . . . The American legacy of democracy validates public assertion of one's beliefs as a social right, a responsibility, and for some, a moral imperative. Therefore, the conflicting values of privacy and public participation were particularly problematic for AIDS family caregivers. (p. 572)

Baxter and Montgomery (1996) argued that dialectical contradictions are located in the interpersonal relationship rather than the individual. I agree that the contradiction of whether to reveal or conceal exists at the level of the relationship. However, the tension of whether to reveal or conceal stigma transcends any particular relationship and ultimately rests in the individual. Individuals must decide whether to reveal their stigma to anyone and if so, to whom. In interviewing individuals about their coming out stories (Dindia & Tieu, 1996), I heard participants describe an internal struggle occurring in themselves rather than an external struggle occurring between people. Similarly, they reported a struggle that transcended and was not specific to any relationship, signifying that the contradiction of whether to reveal or conceal is primarily an intrapersonal rather than an interpersonal contradiction.

Dialectical contradiction is also located in dyads and groups (e.g., couples and families) when the stigma is seen as belonging to the dyad or group rather than an individual. In this case, the dyad or group must decide whether to reveal or conceal beyond the boundaries of the dyad or group (see Petronio, 1988). An example is when a family must decide whether to reveal or conceal that a family member's death was due to AIDS.

In sum, the primary location of the tension of whether to reveal or conceal stigma resides at the level of the social unit that owns the stigma and must decide whether to reveal or conceal it to others. Typically, this is an individual, but it may be a dyad or a group. Following from this, I also argue that the primary location of the tension of whether to reveal or conceal any information resides at the level of the social unit (i.e., individual, dyad, or group) that owns the information.

Interdependencies of Contradiction

Dialectical tensions are interrelated. In particular, the contradiction between revealing–concealing is interrelated with the contradiction of autonomy–connection. Typically, disclosure fosters connection and concealing fosters autonomy. Recursively, connection fosters disclosure and autonomy fosters concealment. Both Dindia and Tieu (1996) and Spencer (1991) found that coming out disclosures were made based on the level of closeness in a relationship or a desire to be closer to the other person (connection) and that some refusals to come out were related to a lack of intimacy felt in the relationship with the other person (autonomy) and no desire to become closer. Cain (1991) found that one of the reasons given by gay men for why they disclose their sexual preference to others was to build the relationship (connection) with the person to whom they were disclosing. Alternatively, Spencer (1991) illustrated how revealing stigma can create autonomy and concealing stigma can create connection. Spencer, in discussing gay and lesbian adolescents and young adults who want to come out to their parents, stated that gay sons and lesbian daughters must choose between maintaining intimacy with their parents and sacrificing their personal identities in the family (i.e., connection and concealment) versus sacrificing intimacy in favor of the need to maintain their identity as sexual persons (i.e., autonomy and disclosure). The link between various dialectical contradictions needs to be examined more in the personal relationships literature in general and in the literature on stigma disclosure in particular.

Contextualization of Contradiction

A third issue implicated in the assumption of dialectical totality is the contextualization of dialectical contradiction. A dialectical perspective assumes that contradiction varies from one context to another, obligating dialectical scholars to study contradictions *in situ*. Self-disclosure is contextualized and the context affects self-disclosure. From a dialectical perspective, it makes little sense to study self-disclosure between strangers (e.g., the stranger-on-the-train phenomenon) unless this is the context to which one is generalizing.

Implicitly, the literature on stigma disclosure takes into account the societal context. Goffman (1963) emphasized that the negative social meaning placed on an attribute by society is more important than the attribute itself. Thus, what constitutes a stigma is socially defined. Similarly, who is stigmatized versus who is normal is socially defined. An obvious implication of this is that individuals are likely to disclose to others who are also stigmatized and who are in the "back places where persons of the individual's kind stand exposed and find they need not try to conceal their stigma" (Goffman, 1963, p. 81). For example, it has been shown that methadone patients are quite open with fellow patients, fellow drug users, narcotics sellers, and clinic counselors (Murphy & Irwin, 1992).

Explicitly, there is limited research on the role of context in the literature on stigma disclosure. As stated earlier, the effect of target characteristics on stigma disclosure was studied (e.g., Dindia & Tieu, 1996; Limandri, 1989; Petronio et al., 1996). Similarly, Petronio et al. (1996) studied the circumstances (when and where) surrounding children's and adolescents' disclosure of sexual abuse.

Self-disclosure is also contextualized by the relationship between the discloser and the recipient. Research indicates that the level of intimacy of the relationship affects stigma disclosure (Cain, 1991; Dindia & Tieu, 1996; Limandri, 1989; Spencer, 1991; Spencer & Derleag, 1995). Self-disclosure is also contextualized by the life stage of the discloser and recipient. According to Nussbaum (1989), one cannot understand communication without first discovering the individual and relationship developmental processes of which it is part. Spencer (1994), in discussing adolescent–parent self-disclosure, illustrated this point: "The long relationship past and future not only invoke issues of developmental change in the children's own cognitive and emotional growth, but the child's individual development implies relationship changes with parents as the child grows to adolescent and eventually to adult" (pp. 61–62). When applied to self-disclosure, this means that one must study self-disclosure not only within the context of the relationship, but also within the life spans that contextualize the relationship.

Although there is little to no research examining self-disclosure in the context of individual and relationship development, there is a great deal of research examining self-disclosure in the context of identity development. Goffman (1963) was the first to discuss the role of self-disclosure in stigmatized identity development. Goffman referred to the similar "moral career" of persons who have a particular stigma, arguing that these people tend to have similar learning experiences regarding their stigma and go through a similar sequence of personal adjustments. The stigmatized person learns and incorporates the society's point of view regarding the particular stigma in the first phase of this process. In the second phase, the person learns that he or she possesses a particular stigma and the consequences of possessing it. Learning to pass or conceal the stigma constitutes the third phase. In the fourth phase, the stigmatized individual "can come to feel that he should be above passing, that if he accepts himself and respects himself he will feel no need to conceal his failing" (p. 101). According to Goffman, self-disclosure fits into the process here.

Similarly, self-disclosure is conceived as one of the phases in the coming out process. *Coming out,* in popular American culture, refers to public disclosure of a gay or bisexual identity. However, in scholarly literature, *coming out* refers to the larger developmental process of acquiring a gay identity of which disclosure is only a part (Paradis, 1991). Several models of gay identity development have been presented in the clinical literature (cf., Berger, 1983; Berzon, 1992; Cass, 1979; Coleman, 1982; Mazanec, 1995; Plummer, 1975). These models organize major milestone events in a sequential process and include disclosure of one's sexuality to others as a major milestone (Cain, 1991). For example, Coleman (1982) described a 5-stage model; coming out is the second stage, in which individuals begin the process of self-disclosure to others. Berzon (1992) described a turning point process in which disclosure to a nongay person is the third turning point and disclosure to family, friends, and coworkers is the seventh and final turning point.

Disclosure in these models is typically viewed as a developmental task (Coleman, 1982). For instance, Wells and Kline (1987) stated that "prerequisite to the emergence of a positive homosexual identity is the communication of one's sexual orientation to significant others" (p. 191). According to McDonald (1982), "achieving a positive gay identity appears to be contingent upon disclosing one's sexual orientation to significant nongay others" (p. 54).

The emphasis on disclosure and identity development dominates the literature on stigma disclosure to the degree that other situational and relational factors have been virtually ignored. Cain (1991) argued that models of identity formation fail to adequately recognize the social factors that shape the disclosure of stigmatized identities. He went on to argue that decisions regarding disclosure and concealment are related to a variety of situational and relational factors that are independent of gay identity development. The link between identity development and disclosure assumed in models of identity development had several ramifications according to Cain. In particular, decisions related to disclosure and secrecy were viewed primarily in terms of individual psychological factors rather than social influences. The literature portrays gay men's decisions to disclose or conceal their sexual preferences as a consequence of a developmental stage rather than other contextual factors. Findings from his study suggest that identity development is an important consideration in self-disclosures of gay identity, however, it is only one of several factors that affect and are affected by stigma disclosure. Other aspects of context should not be ignored.

METHODOLOGICAL IMPLICATIONS

In general, research on self-disclosure is incompatible with the dialectical assumption of change. Self-disclosure in the communication and psychology literature is primarily studied as an act or an event. Research from this perspective focuses on individual messages or behaviors. The unit of analysis is typically the utterance or the thought unit and typical research variables include intimacy, amount, valence, accuracy, clarity, and flexibility of self-disclosure (Cline, 1982). Research from this perspective attempts to identify the causes and effects of self-disclosure and studies self-disclosure as the independent or dependent variable.

There is some research on self-disclosure in the communication literature that begins to examine the process of self-disclosure. Time-series analysis of conversational sequences (Dindia, 1982, 1984; Spencer, 1993b) and ethnog-

raphy of natural conversation (Spencer, 1993a, 1994) have been used to examine short conversational sequences centering around self-disclosure. In
particular, these studies focus on the comments occurring directly before and
after a self-disclosure. However, these studies implicitly or explicitly assume
that self-disclosure is a one-time event, occurring within the confines of a single conversation, typically within a single utterance. VanLear (1987) examined the process of self-disclosure across six conversations between zero-
history dyads. VanLear's study identifies patterns of self-disclosure across
conversations, including changes in levels of self-disclosure and reciprocity of
self-disclosure. However, even VanLear's study treats the act of self-disclosure
(i.e., the utterance) as the unit of analysis.

Although some of the research on stigma disclosure invokes the "self-disclosure as action or event" perspective (e.g., Edgar, 1994; Wells & Kline,
1987), much of the research is compatible with the dialectical assumption of
change. Interview and observational methods are regularly used to elicit conversational sequences of self-disclosure that extend across a particular conversation to multiple conversations and sometimes to the life-long process
of self-disclosure (cf., Dindia & Tieu, 1996; Limandri, 1989; Sorenson &
Snow, 1991).

However, it should be noted that the stigma disclosure research that uses
narrative to examine self-disclosure may be biased in portraying self-disclosure as a linear process. For example, Dindia and Tieu (1996) found that participants in their study described disclosure of homosexuality as a linear rather
than a spiraling process. It is possible that this result is an artifact of the interview protocol. Dindia and Tieu asked participants to tell their coming-out
story in a chronological manner. This may have suggested how the inter-
viewee should format the narrative. The idea of a story or chronology typically suggests a linear format in Western culture, which may have made it difficult to get at the circular nature of disclosure.

GENERALIZABILITY OF THE DIALECTICS
OF STIGMA DISCLOSURE

The dialectical contradiction between the need to reveal and the need to conceal is not limited to stigma disclosure, but is generalizable to self-disclosure
of all private and risky information about self. As Goffman (1963) pointed
out, the problem of stigma control is not a case of a few who are stigmatized
and the majority who are not:

> Stigma management is a general feature of society, a process occurring wher-
> ever there are identity norms. The same features are involved whether a major
> differentness is at question, of the kind traditionally defined as stigmatic, or a

picayune differentness, of which the ashamed person is ashamed to be ashamed. (p. 130)

All people suffer some discrepancy between their ideal identity and their actual identity and thus are faced with the problem of identity management and must make decisions regarding self-disclosure.

Disclosing private and risky information about self is a dialectical phenomenon in which all the assumptions of a dialectical perspective apply: contradiction, change, praxis, and totality. Self-disclosure of private and risky information involves a contradiction of whether to reveal or conceal and the process of disclosing such information is indeterminate rather than teleological and spiraling rather than linear. Dialectical strategies of self-disclosure, such as selective disclosure, concealment, and staging information, are employed to manage personal boundaries and to deal with the contradiction of whether to reveal or conceal. Finally, self-disclosure is contextualized in the individual, the relationship, and society. The metaphor, "coming out of the closet," should be changed to, "going into and coming out of the closet," to reflect the dialectical nature of stigma disclosure. In addition, this metaphor should be extended beyond the social realm for which it has been traditionally applied (e.g., disclosure of homosexuality, AIDS, HIV-positive status) to the disclosure of all private and risky information about self.

ACKNOWLEDGMENTS

The author would like to thank Barbara Montgomery and Leslie Baxter for their helpful feedback on an earlier version of this manuscript.

REFERENCES

Altman, I. (1975). *The environment and social behavior: Privacy, personal space, territory, and crowding.* Belmont, CA: Wadsworth.

Altman, I., & Taylor, D. A. (1973). *Social penetration: The development of interpersonal relationships.* New York: Holt, Rinehart, & Winston.

Altman, I., Vinsel, A., & Brown, B. H. (1981). Dialectic conceptions in social psychology: An application to social penetration and privacy regulation. In L. Berkowitz (Ed.), *Advances in experimental social psychology: Vol. 14* (pp. 107–160). New York: Academic Press.

Arluke, A. (1991). Going into the closet with science: Information control among animal experimenters. *Journal of Contemporary Ethnography, 20,* 306–330.

Baxter, L. A. (1988). A dialectical perspective on communication strategies in relationship development. In S. W. Duck (Ed.), *A handbook of personal relationships* (pp. 257–273). Chichester, UK: Wiley.

Baxter, L. A., & Montgomery, B. M. (1996). *Relating: Dialogues and dialectics.* New York: Guilford.

Baxter, L. A., & Wilmot, W. W. (1985). Taboo topics in close relationships. *Journal of Social and Personal Relationships, 2,* 253–269.

Berger, R. (1983). What is a homosexual: A definitional model. *Social Work, 28,* 132–141.

Berzon, B. (1992). Developing a positive gay identity. In B. Berzon & R. Leighton (Eds.), *Positively gay* (pp. 3–15). Milrose, CA: Celestial Arts.

Bochner, A. (1984). The functions of human communication in interpersonal bonding. In C. Arnold & J. Bowers (Eds.), *Handbook of rhetorical and communication theory* (pp. 544–621). Boston: Allyn & Bacon.

Braithwaite, D. O. (1991). "Just how much did that wheelchair cost?" Management of privacy boundaries and demands for self-disclosure by persons with disabilities. *Western Journal of Speech Communication, 55,* 254–274.

Cain, R. (1991). Stigma management and gay identity development. *Social Work, 36,* 67–73.

Cass, V. C. (1979). Homosexual identity formation: A theoretical model. *Journal of Homosexuality, 4,* 219–235.

Cline, R. J. (1982, May). *Revealing and relating: A review of self-disclosure theory and research.* Paper presented at the International Communication Association Convention, Boston.

Coleman, E. (1982). Developmental stages of the coming out process. *Journal of Homosexuality, 7,* 31–43.

Derlega, V. J., & Chaikin, A. (1977). Privacy and self-disclosure in social relationships. *Journal of Social Issues, 33,* 102–115.

Dindia, K. (1982). Reciprocity of self-disclosure: A sequential analysis. In M. Burgoon (Ed.), *Communication Yearbook 6* (pp. 506–530). Beverly Hills, CA: Sage.

Dindia, K. (1984, May). *Antecedents and consequents of self-disclosure.* Paper presented at the meeting of the International Communication Association, San Francisco.

Dindia, K. (1997). Self-disclosure, self-identity, and relationship development: A transactional/dialectical perspective. In S. Duck (Ed.), *Handbook of personal relationships* (2nd ed., pp. 411–426). Chichester, UK: Wiley.

Dindia, K., & Tieu, T. (1996, November). *Self-disclosure of homosexuality: The dialectics of "coming out."* Paper presented at the Speech Communication Association Convention, San Diego.

Duck, S. W. (1990). Relationships as unfinished business: Out of the frying pan and into the 1990s. *Journal of Social and Personal Relationships, 7,* 5–29.

Edgar, T. (1994). Self-disclosure behaviors of the stigmatized: Strategies and outcomes for the revelation of sexual orientation. In R. J. Ringer (Ed.), *Queer words, queer images* (pp. 221–237). New York: New York University Press.

Gard, L. (1990). Patient disclosure of human immunodeficiency virus (HIV) status to parents: Clinical considerations. *Professional Psychology: Research and Practice, 21,* 252–256.

Gershman, H. (1983). The stress of coming out. *The American Journal of Psychoanalysis, 43,* 129–138.

Goffman, E. (1963). *Stigma: Notes on the management of spoiled identity.* Englewood Cliffs, NJ: Prentice-Hall.

Herman, N. J. (1993). Return to sender: Reintegrative stigma-management strategies of ex-psychiatric patients. *Journal of Contemporary Ethnography, 22,* 295–330.

Jourard, S. M. (1971). *The transparent self* (Rev. ed.). New York: Van Nostrand.

Limandri, B. (1989). Disclosure of stigmatizing conditions: The discloser's perspective. *Archives of Psychiatric Nursing, III,* 69–78.

McDonald, G. (1982). Individual differences in the coming-out process for gay men: Implications for theoretical models. *Journal of Homosexuality, 8,* 47–60.

MacFarlane, I., & Krebs, S. (1986). Techniques for interviewing and evidence gathering. In K. MacFarlane & J. Waterman (Eds.), *Sexual abuse of young children* (pp. 67–100). New York: Guilford.

Marks, G., Bundek, N., Richardson, J., Ruiz, M., Maldonado, N., & Mason, J. (1992). Self-disclosure of HIV infection: Preliminary results from a sample of Hispanic men. *Health Psychology, 11,* 300–306.

Mazanec, M. J. (1995, November). *Border work by gays, lesbians, and bisexuals: Coming out on the borders of experience.* Paper presented at the Speech Communication Association Convention, San Antonio.

Montgomery, B. M. (1993). Relationship maintenance versus relationship change: A dialectical dilemma. *Journal of Social and Personal Relationships, 10,* 205–224.

Murphy, S., & Irwin, J. (1992). "Living with the dirty secret": Problems of disclosure for methadone maintenance clients. *Journal of Psychoactive Drugs, 24,* 257–264.

Nussbaum, J. F. (1989). Life-span communication: An introduction. In J. F. Nussbaum (Ed.), *Life-span communication: Normative processes* (pp. 1–4). Hillsdale, NJ: Lawrence Erlbaum Associates.

Paradis, B. A. (1991). Seeking intimacy and integration: Gay men in the era of AIDS. *Smith College Studies in Social Work, 61,* 260–274.

Parks, M. (1982). Ideology in interpersonal communication: Off the couch and into the world. In M. Burgoon (Ed.), *Communication yearbook 5* (pp. 79–108). New Brunswick, NJ: Transaction Books.

Pearce, W. B., & Sharp, S. M. (1973). Self-disclosing Communication. *Journal of Communication, 23,* 409–425.

Pennebacker, J. W. (1989). Confession, inhibition, and disease. In L. Berkowitz (Ed.), *Advances in experimental social psychology: Vol. 22* (pp. 211–244). New York: Academic Press.

Petronio, S. (1988, November). *The dissemination of private information: The use of a boundary control system as an alternative perspective to the study of disclosures.* Paper presented at the Speech Communication Association Convention, New Orleans, LA.

Petronio, S. (1991). Communication boundary management: A theoretical model of managing disclosure of private information between marital couples. *Communication Theory, 1,* 311–335.

Petronio, S., Reeder, H. M., Hecht, M. L., & Mon't Ross-Mendoza, T. (1996). Disclosure of sexual abuse by children and adolescents. *Journal of Applied Communication Research, 24,* 181–189.

Plummer, K. (1975). *Sexual stigma: An interactionist account.* London: Routledge & Kegan Paul.

Ponse, B. (1976). Secrecy in the lesbian world. *Urban Life, 5,* 313–338.

Powell-Cope, G. M., & Brown, M. A. (1992). Going public as an AIDS family caregiver. *Social Science Medicine, 34,* 571–580.

Prager, K. J. (1995). *The psychology of intimacy.* New York: Guilford.

Rawlins, W. (1983). Openness as problematic in ongoing friendships: Two conversational dilemmas. *Communication Monographs, 50,* 1–13.

Siegel, K., & Krauss, B. J. (1991). Living with HIV infection: Adaptive tasks of seropositive gay men. *Journal of Health and Social Behavior, 32,* 17–32.

Sorensen, T., & Snow, B. (1991). How children tell: The process of disclosure of child sexual abuse. *Journal of the Child Welfare League of America Inc.. LXX,* 3–15.

Spencer, T. (1991, June). *To come out or not to come out: A test of self-disclosure theories applied to adolescent-parent relationships.* Paper presented at the Third International Network on Personal Relationships Conference, Normal, IL.

Spencer, T. (1993a, June). *The use of a turning point conversation task to stimulate nearly natural conversation.* Paper presented at the Fourth International Network on Personal Relationships Conference, Milwaukee, WI.

Spencer, T. (1993b, November). *Testing the self-disclosure reciprocity hypothesis within the context of conversational sequences in family interaction.* Paper presented at the annual meeting of the Speech Communication Association, Miami, FL.

Spencer, T. (1994). Transforming relationships through ordinary talk. In S. Duck (Ed.), *Under-*

standing relationship processes IV: Dynamics of relationships (pp. 58–85). Thousand Oaks, CA: Sage.

Spencer, T., & Derlega, V. J. (1995, February). *Important self-disclosure decisions: Coming out to family and HIV-positive disclosures.* Paper presented at the Western States Communication Association convention, Portland, OR.

Summit, R. C. (1983). The child sexual abuse accommodation syndrome. *Child Abuse and Neglect, 7,* 177–193.

VanLear, C. A. (1987). The formation of social relationships: A longitudinal study of social penetration. *Human Communication Research, 13,* 299–322.

Wells, J. W. & Kline, W. B. (1987). Self-disclosure and homosexual orientation, *Journal of Social Psychology, 127,* 191–197.

6

Dialectic Empiricism:
Science and Relationship Metaphors

C. Arthur VanLear
University of Connecticut

> *A theory is just a model of the universe, or a restricted part of it,*
> *and a set of rules that relate quantities in the model to observations*
> *that we make. It exists only in our minds and does not have*
> *any other reality (whatever that might mean). . . . [It] is*
> *always provisional. . . . You can never prove it.*
> —Hawking, 1988, pp. 9–10

I have been asked to present my approach to dialectics in relationships as the representative of traditional social and behavioral sciences. Rather than logical positivism, the philosophy of science I subscribe to is *dialectic empiricism*. This approach privileges the empirical: Not because of a belief in a single parsimonious truth that is knowable and demonstrable, but because of the assumption that an explanation or interpretation of events will be most useful if it is consistent with observations that are intersubjectively reliable in a frame of reference. I view research as a process of persuasive argumentation in which data and results constitute the evidence, and the method and theory are the warrants (Anderson, 1987).

I am also considered more traditional than most other authors in this book because my research methods are quantitative and I use statistical tests of evidence. Such methods are shunned by many dialectical scholars in the postmodernist tradition. This chapter adopts a philosophy of science based on a dialectic tension between discovery of empirical reality and symbolic construction of experience. I show how my approach allows for a variety of research methods—both qualitative and quantitative. In addition, I present my own understanding of the dialectic tensions evidenced in the dynamics of interpersonal relationship emergence. This chapter pictures science, mathematics, evolution, and dialectics as metaphorical systems that can be used together to provide useful insights into personal relationships.

RETHINKING TRADITIONAL SCIENCE

In 1776, Laplace argued that given Newton's equations, if one could only determine the position and velocity of every object in the universe, one could predict the future forever with complete certainty. This optimism led some social scientists to search for equally deterministic laws of human behavior that could be known with the same degree of certainty. Modern philosophy of science has put an end to that idyllic view of the universe (Campbell, 1994; Feyerabend; 1963, 1965; Suppe, 1974).

One of the biggest blows to this assumption was the discovery of Heisenberg's (1930) *uncertainty principle*.[1] This principle has two implications that go far beyond Quantum theory:

1. Any measurement contains error.
2. All observation implies an inherent interaction between the observer and the observed (Kaplan, 1964).

To observe, one must observe in some way and using some method. The choices a scientist makes about what to observe and how to observe it affect and constrain what constitutes the data, so that the data are as much a function of the creative choices of the observer as a reflection of reality. The positivist ideal of the objective observer dispassionately recording a directly apprehended raw reality is an inherently unattainable myth.

Logical positivism holds that a valid theory is one in which the properties of the theory have an isomorphic correspondence to the reality that they represent (Suppe, 1974). Operationalizations and their corresponding observations must completely exhaust the meaning of the theoretical terms. Not only is this impossible given the uncertainty principle, but also because of the nature of observation and meaning (the representation of observation). First, meanings can only be identified in a context or frame of reference (Bateson,

---

[1]Heisenberg (1930) demonstrated that the more precise the measurement of the position of a subatomic particle, the less precise the measure of velocity, and the more precise the measure of velocity, the less precise the measure of position. The act of observing changes the behavior of what is observed. There are many arguments against logical positivism. Those presented here are illustrative and relevant to the position advocated by this chapter. Heisenberg's arguments were most persuasive to traditional scientists because they were presented by a scientist, in the language of science, using accepted tests of evidence.

1972): They are always relative. Second, we must apprehend reality through the mediation of our senses (which science tells us are patterns of electro-chemical activity in our central nervous system). In order to be understood, by ourselves and others, that experience must be encoded into a symbolic–cognitive representation. The representations of experience, whether in a scientific theory or otherwise, are always only abstractions and are only meaningful given a frame of reference. Our knowledge seems absolutely true only to the extent that we are incapable of stepping outside the frame of reference in which the knowledge claim is based.

As an alternative to objectivity, some scholars postulate that reality is socially and symbolically constructed (Berger & Luckmann, 1967). Because all knowledge is perceptual, perception is inherently personal, and perception depends on one's physical and social position in the world (Deetz, 1985); knowledge exists only in a frame of reference. Because frame of reference includes one's position in society, which is not objective but created by the culture and learned from it, our understanding is inherently social and symbolic. These symbolic constructions are then reified by treating them as if they are real (just as we can learn them by watching others treat them as real) and interpreting the reactions of others from within that interpretive frame. When others refuse to accept our frame of reference, we assume they are mad or bad (i.e., deluded or deceitful). Even if we could step outside our usual interpretive frame of reference, we must still operate in some frame of reference, and we have no objective basis for evaluating its adequacy. This view of understanding pictures explanation (knowledge) as inherently circular. The knower cannot be separated from what is known.

THE CONSTRUCTION (INTERPRETATION)/ DISCOVERY (REALITY) DIALECTIC

On the other hand, the argument that reality is only a social and symbolic construction is too extreme for many people. After all, traditional science has offered knowledge claims that are useful and persuasive to consumers of knowledge. Likewise, it is intuitively and empirically apparent to most people that there is a real reality, even if we cannot know that reality directly and with certainty. If I wake in the night disoriented and stub my toe on something unseen and unexpected, the sensation is precipitated by a physical event and probably precedes my socially contextualized, symbolic construction. At some level, it is independent of my symbolic construction.

If these arguments are circular and if there can be no positive answer to them, then in order to proceed with research or scholarship, we must make assumptions. Such assumptions form the foundation on which less abstract issues about personal relationships can be addressed.

- Assumption I: There is an objective reality that exists independent of our apprehension of it, but that reality is not directly knowable with certainty.
- Assumption II: Our understanding of reality is always indirect, mediated, and meaningful only in a frame of reference: Understanding is always a relative interpretation.

These assumptions form the basis of a dynamic tension between the discovery of objective reality and the symbolic construction of reality—a dialectic of inquiry. Discovery implies something existed *a priori,* independent of the person who found it. Construction implies the person participated in its creation. The unity of these opposites is apparent. We must have symbols and interpretations to understand and grasp a concept like *reality,* let alone represent it. Yet, interpretations must be of something. The fact that we have interpretations at least implies the existence of an interpreter. So the notion of reality and interpretation imply each other. The dynamic tension between discovery and construction is the driving force behind the process of empirical research.

- Assumption III: Interpretation, if it is scientific and useful, is also to some degree constrained by empirical reality.

It is possible for two interpretations of the same event to be equally valid given that they are made from two different positions or perspectives. However, it is also possible for two interpretations or representations to differ because one is less constrained by, or sensitive to, empirical reality, although what that means can only be assessed in the frame of reference of a theory and metatheory.

Science attempts to explicitly structure empirical constraints or infer the constraints from reliable (i.e., intersubjectively agreed on) observations. If we can explicitly set out our expectations before the observation, provide explicit, detailed information about what counts as evidence, and if others operating from within our frame of reference agree that the evidence provides compelling support (not proof) of our claim, then we have a traditional scientific empirical approach. Through this process of structured observation with a priori tests of evidence, traditional science places its knowledge claims at risk at the point of analysis as well as in the peer review process. This is not to say that the process of doing science usually corresponds to the idealized description of the scientific method.[2] The fact that hypotheses and opera-

---

[2]In the process of doing science, a study rarely proceeds exactly as described in the textbooks. Ideas are included after data analysis has begun. When the original hypothesis is not supported by the preplanned tests, new tests are conducted, additional control variables included, instruments are modified, refined, and so on. Unexpected results are interpreted or rationalized and interesting possibilities fuel speculation. The ego and values of the scientists, the conservative traditions of the scholarly community, and the sources of funding all influence what gets researched, what constitutes acceptable evidence or arguments, what is important, and therefore, what gets published.

tionalizations are presented a priori means that the observer's expectations must influence what is observed, how it is observed, and how it is interpreted. As scientists, we attempt to be explicit about how the observer's expectations constrain the results.

Typically, logical positivism is pictured as a hypothetical deductive approach, and grounded theory and ethnography are pictured as inductive approaches. One implication of the construction–discovery dialectic is recognizing research that features an interplay between inductive and deductive processes. Research questions and nondirectional hypotheses are as acceptable as directional hypotheses. Theories and expectations form the interpretive context for assessing results. Unexpected patterns in the data, failure to support a hypothesis, and so on should lead to revision of theory and provide a heuristic basis for new ideas.

Dialectic empiricism is data based regarding its research methods. Yet, it recognizes that the meanings of empirical observations (explanations) are not absolute, but relative and fallible. A community of scholars, operating in a common frame of reference, who accept certain tests of evidence, make predictions or ask questions to test the practicality and usefulness of a theory and then modify the theory to account for new information. Logical positivism demands consistency and abhors contradiction. Dialectics expects inconsistency and contradiction as a natural outgrowth of the dynamic tensions between functional oppositions.[3] Most scholars approach the discovery–construction dialectic by selecting one pole of the duality and rejecting the other. I suggest acceptance of the dynamic tension as a natural part of a dialectic research process.

METHODS, MODELS, AND METAPHORS
OF DIALECTIC EMPIRICISM

We learn in high school that a metaphor compares the unknown with the known. Explanation or theory, whether scientific or not, is often, to some extent, metaphorical. A dialectic is essentially a metaphor that is general enough to apply to a wide variety of human experiences that can be symbolically cast as dynamic oppositions. We see how mathematics offers a particularly useful metaphorical system for the modeling of human relationships, even their dialectical dynamics.

Given we cannot directly apprehend a raw reality, we automatically translate our observations into a symbolic system and organize those symbols into a description or explanation. Because much of this process is automatic and

---

[3]This does not mean that dialectics is irrational or illogical. When empirical evidence and strong arguments point to two apparently contradictory conclusions, positivism would ask "Which is right?" but dialectics would ask "Is there a dialectic tension that is responsible for this contradiction?"

preconscious, we may not realize that a translation has occurred and may even confuse the symbolic representation for the reality.

In the process of empirical research, we attempt to be deliberate about how we structure our observations and how we translate and retranslate them into an analytically useful symbolic system. For the conversation analyst, this translation usually takes the form of a highly structured transcript written in a conventionalized symbol system. For the ethnographer, it often takes the form of field notes and later illustrative vignettes in the published paper. For the quantitative researcher, this translation takes the form of a number system that is treated as nominal, ordinal, or interval. We choose what symbolic system to translate our observations into based on its utility for analysis, our preconceived notions of the nature of the theoretical construct, and our research tradition. Whatever symbolic, metaphorical system we choose to translate and organize our observations into, it constrains and focuses our ultimate interpretation of the data.

The conventionalized structure of the conversation analyst's transcript is a useful reconstruction for highlighting or reifying certain features of the conversation that are considered important in that frame of reference. Other features, like many nonverbal cues and cognitions, usually do not get represented and consequently, are not the focus of the final explanation.

The ethnographers' field notes represent their observations as descriptions of selected events translated into their native language. This has the advantage of representing the observations in a symbol system similar to the one the social actors and readers use to enact and make sense of their own social episodes. In the research report another translation and reorganization occurs in which selected vignettes are presented and interpreted in terms of some theoretical constructs (*social rules, roles, cultural myths, dialectic contradictions*, etc.), which are basically metaphors with general features. Specialized jargon (*text, narrative, dialectics*, etc.) provide general metaphorical systems that permit the analyses and explanations to be integrated with other similar analyses and explanations. The goal is to present "disciplined abstractions" (Lofland, 1976), "thick description" (Geertz, 1973) or expose the "taken for granted" assumptions of everyday life (Garfinkel, 1967). The power of such an analysis is not based on its generalizability, but on its insight into subtleties and novel ways of understanding what casual observation would picture as mundane and unremarkable or what another frame of reference would interpret quite differently. Of course, interpretive researchers want readers to make applications of their conclusions beyond the specific cases studied.

Quantitative methods are neither inherently more empirical nor less interpretive than these other methods. Quantitative methodology also involves the translation of observation into a symbolic metaphorical system (i.e., mathematics). Such a translation assumes that we can symbolically identify multiple cases of a similar category of observations (nominal frequencies), identify a symbolic ordering of observations or constructs (ordinal ranks), or that we can treat the coding of experiences or observations as if they were a specific distance from certain other observations or experiences (interval scales).

Typical quantitative methods attempt to place the expectations and knowledge claims at risk at the point of analysis. Given an a priori test of evidence (e.g., an alpha level, effect size, or confidence interval), researchers may conclude that the evidence does not warrant the conclusion expected: Many quantitative studies fail to reject the null hypothesis. Quantitative methods are no less interpretive than qualitative methods. Rather, the nature of the tests of evidence differ somewhat, and the way in which the interpretation is first placed at risk may differ.

Translation of observation or experience into a mathematical system is useful for several reasons. First, numbers representing nominal frequencies, ordinal ranks, or interval scales are useful metaphors that imply a certain way of organizing and thinking about our observations or experiences. Second, such a symbolic system permits us to aggregate or summarize a large number of observations or experiences and submit those representations to very precise methods of analysis. This is a powerful advantage because it provides an argument for the generality of the metaphor (or model) or for prediction of future values (if the evidence is persuasive given the reader's assumptions). However, unlike symbolic systems like language, quantification sacrifices thick description, subtlety of meaning, and the sense of having been there for analytic precision, generality, and prediction.

Haley (1963) argued that one of the main barriers to a theory of human relationships is that our language tends to reduce relationships down to the characteristics of individuals: Our language does not have an adequate vocabulary or syntax for describing relationships. Watzlawick, Beavin, and Jackson (1967) argued that because the syntax of mathematics is designed to describe and analyze relationships between quantities or values, it can also be extremely useful for describing relationships between people. They called for a calculus of human relationships.

A relationship involves at least two individuals who are aware of each other and are influenced by each other (Berger, 1993). The opposite of a relationship is independence. Operationally, a human relationship can be said to exist when peoples' feelings, thoughts, or behaviors are not statistically independent of each other (Cappella, 1996; Rogers, 1993).

A minimal definition of a relationship does not restrict the form of the mathematical relationship between partners' scores: It can be a positive or negative correlation or regression (Cappella, 1996), a nonlinear association (VanLear, 1990, 1992), a contingent interaction effect (VanLear, 1992), the matching and timing of cyclical patterns (VanLear, 1991), a probabilistic stochastic association between behavioral choices (VanLear, 1987; VanLear & Zietlow, 1990), or an association that is nonstationary, such that it changes over time (VanLear, 1987; VanLear & Trujillo, 1986). Likewise, the association may be mutual adaptation in which both partners exercise influence over each other or it can be asymmetric, such that one person's behavior dominates or entrains the behavior, thoughts, or feelings of the other (Cappella, 1996; Gottman, 1979, 1982), in which case, the form of mathematical association can be an analogue for relational control (VanLear, 1996).

Watzlawick, Beavin, and Jackson (1967) also argued that human relationships are "systems" (another metaphor), and therefore, "nonsummative." The explanation of the whole cannot be reduced to the sum of the parts. This implies that a mathematical metaphor of human relationships should not be a simple summative equation. Likewise, dialectic explanations do not lend themselves to static, additive, linear models that are the stock and trade of most traditional quantitative researchers. Of course, these traditional techniques are typically used as tools to test hypotheses or answer questions, not as relational analogues. As tools, these techniques may have limited uses if they do not impose a linear view of dialectics. Yet, they must be used with caution. Furthermore, if a dialectic is a dynamic tension between oppositions, the analogue should usually be dynamic, implying a time-series model.

Science traditionally seeks to identify patterns (i.e., redundancies across space and time). "If we recognize a pattern across a large enough number of cases, it permits us to 'generalize' to other unobserved cases. If we recognize a pattern over a long enough period of time, it permits us to 'predict' it will continue into the future" (VanLear, 1996, p. 36). However, relational dialectics also recognizes a dialectic tension between predictability and novelty (Baxter, 1988) that grows out of the dialectics of similarity versus difference and stability versus change (Altman, Vinsel, & Brown, 1981).[4] Research from this perspective not only looks for patterns across relationships and across time, but it may also be interested in deviations from those patterns, not just as error, but as meaningful choices (Baxter & Montgomery, 1996).

Scientific interpretations must be based on observations. Interpretations can only be made using a symbolic system. The symbolic system used to represent observations (to self and others) constrains and effects their interpretation. A key methodological implication of the discovery–construction

---

[4]Predictability and novelty has a direct mathematical analogue in information theory. If knowledge of X_1 reduces uncertainty about X_2 by virtue of a redundant pattern in the data, then information is a function of the predictability or novelty of an event. Information, uncertainty, and pattern are linked by the same mathematical definition. However, the discovery or creation of the mathematics of chaos (Baker & Gollub, 1990) has shown that certain, relatively simple, deterministic systems, in which the dimensions are related by nonlinear equations, can produce a course of evolution that is essentially unpredictable.

dialectic is that all empirically based research involves the translation of pre-consciously coded observations to a symbolic system for further reorganization (analysis) and interpretation. Whatever the paradigm used to structure observations and whatever the symbolic system used to organize and interpret these data, the process of data analysis involves the construal of patterns in the translated data. These patterns are then metaphorically associated with previously known or observed patterns as part of the interpretive process. In general, this process is quite similar whether the research is qualitative or quantitative. Whereas qualitative analyses can offer subtle, contextually embedded thick descriptions, quantitative analyses offer a group of metaphors with precisely known qualities that can be used to analogue relationships and tests of evidence that provide arguments for the range of applicability of a model.

DIALECTICS IN INTERPERSONAL RELATIONSHIPS

Both relationships and the communication that creates them are multileveled phenomena. My understanding of the dialectics of interpersonal relationships posits that dynamic, unified oppositions exist at the *individual* level (i.e., a person's cognitive, interpretive construction in a relationship context and resulting individual behavior), the interpersonal or *relational* level as a characteristic of the relationship itself, and at the group or *societal* level as a characteristic of a larger social system. Due to space constraints, this chapter only discusses the individual and relational level (see Baxter & Montgomery, 1996; Montgomery, 1992).

Sources of Dynamic Tension

This chapter uses evolution as a metaphor for relationship emergence. Social evolution selects those patterns of relating that are adaptive and functional. However, people and groups experience dialectic tensions because both sides of an opposition may be functional, adaptive, and desirable. Therefore, social evolution is a result of ongoing adaptations to dialectic tensions. Because multiple choices or adaptations are functional, no one choice permanently resolves the dialectic tension.

The most basic source of motivation is survival of the individual, group, and species. Survival of individual members of a group is necessary for survival of the group. However, at times, individuals are sacrificed for the good of the group. To survive, individuals and groups have evolved both special purpose systems that consist of specific functions (e.g., hunger, thirst, sex) and general purpose systems, which are abilities that can meet a variety of needs and functions (e.g., the capacity for abstract symbolic thought and symbolic communication systems; Buck, 1984).

To survive and prosper in a complex competitive world, human beings form relationships and band together into groups that provide both special and general functions. At least a temporary mate is necessary for procreation (a special function). However, a permanent mate can enhance survival by either sharing functions or providing complementary functions (providing added protection, food, shelter, or emotional support, etc.). Mothers are necessary for birth and nurturing, but they also may provide socialization, emotional support, and so on. Relationships may have a primary, special purpose but evolve to provide multiple functions.

Emotions are motivational systems that evolved to promote survival (Buck, 1984). For example, fear can save our lives in dangerous situations and emotional bonds of attachment form the basis of maternal nurturing, as well as other functional affiliations. Some motivational emotional states (e.g., happiness vs. sadness, affection vs. repulsion, and fear vs. confidence) can be thought of as oppositional pairs. Although these reactions are based on chemical activities in the central nervous system, they can be activated or constrained by situational, symbolic, and social factors (Buck, 1984). Some motivational emotional states are primarily for individual preservation (e.g., fear), and others are primarily social and inherently involve a relationship context (e.g. affection). Emotional states can produce spontaneous behavioral responses (e.g., facial affect displays and fight or flight) and can also be expressed symbolically as disclosures, compliments, threats, and so on. People experience a variety of conflicting emotions in complex situations over the course of a relationship (Shaver, Morgan, & Wu, 1996). We may be attracted to, and then repulsed by, the same person; we may be fearful at times and curious or confident at other times. We attach meaning to these experiences such that conflicting emotions can produce dynamic tensions between symbolically construed oppositions.

Instrumental efficacy is a source of motivation both for individuals and for larger social relational systems. Individuals have certain desires and engage in certain behaviors to fulfill those desires. Likewise, relationships and larger social systems have functions and goals and engage in coordinated joint action to fulfill them. Yet, there may be tension between functions or joint actions of the system. For example, a decision-making group may need to maintain a degree of unity or cohesion to accomplish its function, yet too much cohesion may stifle dissent and the critical testing of ideas (i.e., group think) and produce a poor decision (Fisher, 1980). This could be viewed as a dialectic tension between cooperation and competition. Various instrumental joint actions and episodes can be defined as oppositions and relational partners must jointly negotiate the dynamic tension arising from these oppositions.

Finally, morals and values can form the basis for both individual behavior and the joint actions of larger social systems. Morals and values are evaluations or judgments about what is good and what is bad. They can arise because they are functional for a group and its survival. "Do unto others as you would have them do unto you" can create a very functional group norm. What is morally right or wrong is a socially based symbolic construction. People like to think that their behaviors and values are consistent. However, values often come into conflict and the moral implications of behaviors depend on interpretation. People may say they respect others' right to privacy, but they may also want to know certain things about their partner's personal life. People might hold individual freedom to be a primary value, but still believe that people should obey the norms and rules of their group. Such conflicting values and morals create dynamic tensions.

These sources of motivation interact to create dynamic tensions that can be viewed as dialectic processes. For example, fear is functional and can lead to flight that saves the person, yet a society may view courage as a valued trait and that too may be functional at the level of the group (e.g., an individual overcomes his or her fear to save other members of the group). We only understand courage if we have experienced or know what fear is. Yet, our fear and subsequent flight only become cowardice when juxtaposed symbolically against our understanding of courage. The dynamic tension of a dialectic process arises out of the fact that both sides of an opposition can be functional and desirable.

Manifestations of Relationship Dialectics

Relationships are constituted by the process of interpersonal communication and, therefore, relationship dialectic contradictions are negotiated through communication. When people communicate, they not only communicate semantic content about a topic, but they also communicate a definition of the relationship. People emotionally react to others and these reactions often generate spontaneous behaviors that are received and responded to by the other (Buck, 1984). People present self (Goffman, 1959) and react to the self-presentation of others (McCall & Simmons, 1978), whether explicitly or implicitly. People use symbolic behavior to accomplish pragmatic functions and because such functions are accomplished vis-à-vis another person, these pragmatic functions impact the nature of the relationship between communicators (Fisher, 1978; Watzlawick et al., 1967). We cannot avoid negotiating the nature of our relationships that emerge through the patterned interstructuring of relational functions between communicators. Therefore, communication involves both a content and a relational level (Watzlawick, et al., 1967).[5]

---

[5] A pragmatic paradox, or double bind, occurs when there is a contradiction between messages at different levels of communication (Bateson, 1972). This version of relational dialectics views these mixed messages as one kind of manifestation of dialectical contradictions and the tension between opposites.

Baxter and Montgomery (1996) pointed out the multivocal nature of relationship dialectics. There are many dialectic tensions in interpersonal relationships and they are related in complex ways. The dialectics of constructive interpretation versus discovery of reality, stability versus change, similarity versus difference, and novelty versus predictability are general enough to apply to any area of human activity and so might be termed *generic*. The family of *relationship dialectics* are unique to and inherent in the conduct of interpersonal relationships. Relationship dialectics include, but are not limited to, independence versus connection, dominance versus deference, and expression versus restraint. These dialectic tensions have manifestations at the individual and relational levels.[6]

Manifestations at the Individual Level

The independence versus connection dialectic is basic to personal relationships because a relationship by definition must minimally involve some kind of connection between people's thoughts, feelings, or behaviors (Rogers, 1993). However, the very formation of a connection between people sets up a dialectic tension between autonomy versus attachment or independence versus relationship. We are social animals; we need connections with others to live in a complex world. Yet, engaging in any relationship means surrendering a degree of autonomy. To some extent, being in a relationship requires that the other is taken into account in one's personal actions. Whereas a strong bond or commitment is often desirable, people in our culture value their autonomy. Contradictions arise because people desire both autonomy and connection to another. Once we decide to engage in a relationship with another person, the connection dialectic is not resolved but must be continually handled and negotiated.

At the individual level, this dialectic is related to the dynamic tensions between desires for autonomy versus commitment, attraction versus repulsion, self-concern versus concern for other, and identification versus differentiation. These cognitive dilemmas also manifest as a tension between behavioral choices: approach versus avoidance, association versus privacy, and sharing versus possessiveness.

Individuals display a healthy self-interest necessary to keep from being exploited. However, people also show concern for others (altruism), which is likewise functional in helping to preserve beneficial relationships so that they (and the larger group) are mutually benefited. Likewise, individuals experience a sense of identification with others like themselves, but they also wish

---

[6]I use the term *relationship dialectics* to refer to dialectic processes at a variety of levels that are unique to human relationships. I use the term *relational* to refer to a concept that cannot exist at the individual level, but implies a dyadic or higher system level.

to differentiate themselves from the group. My foster son identifies with his ethnic culture (Puerto Rican). Yet, he does not want to be just another Puerto Rican. He wants to be the "coolest Puerto Rican sax player" in the "hood." His identification is based on highlighting the commonalities and similarities with the group; his differentiation is based on distinguishing himself from the group(s). Identification versus differentiation is an intrapersonal manifestation of the similarity versus difference dialectic.

Many scholars argue that interpersonal relationships inherently involve the negotiation of relational control (Fisher, 1978; Rogers & Bagarozzi, 1983; Watzlawick et al., 1967). The need for efficacy usually underlies the exercise of influence and control. Autonomy implies freedom from others, but any relationship implies constraints on freedom. Yet, a relationship may allow more control over the world than the individual can achieve alone. Connection to another cannot be accomplished without the negotiation of control, which can be viewed as a dialectic process.

There are times when a person must be assertive, exercise leadership, or even be demanding. There are also times when one should defer to others or subordinate one's desires to the needs of others for the sake of the relationship or larger goals. Individuals engage in domineering or assertive behavior and submissive, deferring, or subordinating behavior (Rogers & Bagarozzi, 1983).

There is also a dialectic tension between expression of self versus privacy or restraint. By engaging in open disclosure of private and personal information, speakers share something of their inner selves and may thereby analogically communicate trust as well as provide information necessary for a closer relationship. Even the nonverbal expression of emotion makes the internal world of one person accessible to the other. Silence, restraint, evasion, or suppression of emotional expression may at times be appropriate or functional, but can also communicate closedness or relational distance. Rawlins (1983) discussed the dialectic tension between candor and restraint, and Altman et al. (1981) pointed out the need for people in relationships to be both open to the other and to maintain physical, psychological, and communicative privacy. However, expression is only part of the communication process. Communication implies interaction in which the expressive behavior of one person is received and responded to by another.

Manifestations at the Relational Level

Whereas individuals in a relationship context experience dialectic tensions and these result in individual behaviors, a dynamic tension between oppositions may exist as a property of the relationship itself. Such relational dialectics are not simply reducible to the summation of behaviors and perceptions of individuals.

When the thoughts or feelings of two individuals are compared, we can characterize the result as similar or different (agreement vs. disagreement, understanding vs. misunderstanding, etc.), which are properties of the relationship. There is a dynamic tension between similarity versus difference. Relationships often benefit from the similarities or commonalities between the dispositions, thoughts, and feelings of communicators. However, there is strength in diversity. Some differences complement each other. At the lowest levels of abstraction, no two people are, or should be, exactly alike. At the highest levels of abstraction, all people share some things in common at some point in time.

Behaviorally, a relational level dialectic can be manifest as a dynamic tension between symmetrical versus complementary or reciprocal versus compensatory patterns of interaction. There are times when it is functional in a relationship to reciprocate similar behaviors. For example, reciprocation of self-disclosure can promote growth in the closeness of a relationship that is not one-sided. However, there are times when it is appropriate for two people to exchange different or opposite behavioral functions. There are times when one person's disclosure should not be met with a counterdisclosure, but with a supportive listening ear or even a tactful evasion. This is not just another case of expression versus restraint, but is a dynamic tension between the reciprocation of expression and a compensation for the other's expression. Bateson (1972) argued that either symmetrical (reciprocal) or complementary (compensatory) patterns can be *schismogenetic:* They can spiral out of control. For example, when Person A is domineering, Person B may respond with domineering behavior to maintain equality, but Person A then feels compelled to engage in further domineeringness, and the partners get locked in an escalating struggle for relational control. However, partners can also get caught in a rigid complementary relationship in which one person must always be domineering and the other submissive, and this is just as dysfunctional. The solution is a more flexible parallel relationship pattern (Rogers & Bagarozzi, 1983; VanLear & Zietlow, 1990; Watzlawick et al., 1967) in which (a) partners engage in both symmetrical and complementary patterns of interaction or (b) the roles in complementary interaction are not rigidly defined so that both partners engage in both kinds of functions (e.g., leader and follower, discloser and confidant). Neither party alone can ensure a parallel relationship. It emerges from the negotiation of the patterns produced by the joint actions of both relational partners. Later, we see how a parallel relationship can be enacted by either the application of a contingency principle or by cyclical alternation.

Reciprocal patterns can be identified for attraction versus repulsion (e.g., approach–approach; avoidance–avoidance), expression versus restraint (e.g., disclosure–disclosure), and control (e.g., domineering–domineering), and so on. Compensatory patterns can also be identified for attraction versus repulsion (e.g., approach–avoidance), expression versus restraint (e.g., deep disclosure–restraint, evasion, or small talk), and control (e.g., domineering–deference), and so on.

RELATIONSHIP EMERGENCE

Traditionally relationship formation has been treated as a developmental process (Altman & Taylor, 1973; Knapp, 1978; VanLear & Trujillo, 1986). Relationships are seen as developing through a series of sequentially ordered stages or phases (e.g., orientation, exploration, growth, and commitment). The communication in each phase fulfills a function that is prerequisite for movement to the next phase.

Baxter and Montgomery (1996) critiqued the "monologue of progress" characteristic of traditional developmental models. I agree with much of their critique. Picturing relationship emergence as progressive development is one of many valid ways to organize and punctuate the process of relating. My approach allows for certain progressive directional processes to co-exist with cyclical and multifinal processes.

The Dialectic Praxis of Relating

Whitehead's (1929) famous dictum that an entity's " 'being' is constituted by its 'becoming,' " is a key to the dialectic principle of praxis and also to this view of relationship emergence (p. 35). The definition of a relationship is found in its interactive history. I do not view relationships as merely the cognitive symbolic images individuals hold about their associations with others (although these are important products of the process). Rather, relationships exist between people in the process of relating (Rogers, 1993). As a communication scholar, I view the process of relating and the process of interpersonal communication as virtually the same thing. Of course, at times it is convenient to conceptually freeze this dynamic process and talk about relationships, as if they were semistatic structures. The course of relationship evolution is a function of how people handle their individual dialectic tensions and how partners negotiate their relational dialectics.

Handling the Dialectic Tensions of Relating

As people act in response to the dialectic tensions they experience in their relationships, their behaviors affect their partner, and are responded to by their partner. The patterns of these interactions in turn set up relational-level dialectics that must be negotiated by the joint actions of both parties to the relationship. This process defines the course of relationship evolution.

People are continually confronted with dialectic contradictions between approach versus avoidance, independence versus connection, expression versus restraint, assertiveness versus deference, and so on. They deal with these dialectic tensions in a variety of ways (Baxter, 1988, 1990; Baxter & Montgomery, 1996). I focus on four dynamic responses to dialectic contradictions and tensions: (a) redefinition, (b) balancing, (c) contingent selection, and (d) cyclical alternation.

People can semantically handle dialectic contradictions by redefining one side of the opposition so that it does not appear to contradict the other side. For example, if cooperation is the expected or valued response, individuals may redefine their argumentative responses as "discussion." Lack of honest, candid disclosure is seen as "discretion" or "tact," rather than "evasion." Redefinition may be used because of the value judgments associated with one side of a dialectic or to maintain an appearance of consistency when engaging in contradictory behaviors. If relationship evolution is a function of how we handle dialectic contradictions, redefinition of a dialectical contradiction may impact the subjective definition of the relationship.

Another way individuals can respond to a dialectic tension is by responding in a moderate or neutral way and avoiding the extremes of either pole of the opposition, thus balancing the two poles (Baxter, 1988). For example, when experiencing a dialectic tension between the desire to be domineering and the need to defer to another, one could attempt to communicate neutrality or equality. Likewise, when experiencing the contradictory tendencies toward both openness and closedness, one might attempt to be moderately open.

At the relational level, patterns of interaction can emerge that are neither symmetrical nor complementary. For example, the so-called "transitory" patterns of relational control (e.g., one-up to one-across; one-down to one-across) are frequent patterns that were interpreted as "safe interaction" that might avoid symmetrical and complementary schismogenesis.

The effectiveness or consequences of balancing may be examined empirically. VanLear and Zietlow (1990) found that frequent use of the one-across (or neutral) control category was associated with marital satisfaction in a variety of different types of marriage. VanLear (1990) found nonlinear (quadratic) relationships between husbands' sharing and their wives' satisfaction, such that husbands who engaged in moderately high amounts of sharing in their marriage had wives who were more satisfied than those who engaged in either too much or too little sharing. These are only a few examples from my own research that indicate balancing may be useful. Choosing moderation may be one way of effectively coping with tensions between two opposite extremes. However, it is probably not always possible or desirable to simply sit on the fence by selecting a neutral or moderate response.

People can achieve balance by alternating between poles of a dialectic process. When responses are averaged over time (either mentally by the participants or operationally by a researcher) the mean usually tends toward moderation, even though a specific behavior in a given situation at a given point in time may not be moderate. For example, VanLear and Zietlow (1990) found that certain complementary patterns of interaction were dissatisfying if they were employed either too often or too seldom because indices of the amount of interaction structure for these patterns, aggregated across the conversation, had a nonlinear (quadratic) association with marital satisfaction. A dialectic interpretation is that a parallel relationship keeps either pole of the opposition from dominating. There are two principles that people can use to alternate between poles of the dialectic: contingency and cycling.

Contradictory dialectic tendencies can be handled by applying a contingency principle. Contingency involves selecting one pole of the dialectic in some situations or under certain conditions and selecting the other pole of the opposition (or the neutral point) in other situations. The response selected is contingent on the situation. For example, the situation may indicate whether it is appropriate to exercise leadership (e.g., when one is the most knowledgable or experienced) or to defer to the lead of another (e.g., when one has less knowledge or status). Likewise, Rawlins (1983) showed how under certain conditions friends are open and candid with each other and under other conditions, they may be tactful or restrained. Contingent responding produces alternating responses over time, but the alternation is not periodically patterned unless the situational contingencies are periodically spaced in time (which may happen). A useful contingency model involves more than the recognition that the selection of responses depends on the situation. Rather, one should ideally show what responses are used or are appropriate under what situations. Despite the logic of the contingency principle, the alternatives are still opposites and the attraction to both poles can still create contradictions and tension.

There are numberless possible situational contingencies, but the nature of the relationship, its relational history, the episode being enacted, and the behavior of one's relational partner seem to be important. For example, the extent of openness and disclosure in a relationship is contingent on the point in its relational history (Altman & Taylor, 1973; VanLear, 1987) with less openness early in the relationship than later in time. Likewise, relational control behavior choices are contingent on the point in the relationship's life cycle (Zietlow & VanLear, 1991), the type of relationship, and episode being enacted (Williamson & Fitzpatrick, 1985).

In addition, whether or not one chooses to disclose or refrain from disclosure is contingent on the behavior of one's relational partner (VanLear, 1987), such that partners often (but not always) follow a reciprocity norm. Relational control behaviors are also highly contingent on the control choices of the other. It is this contingency that sets up the relational dialectic between symmetry and complementarity. These relational patterns themselves can be negotiated based on a contingency principle, such that certain patterns are more frequently selected in certain types of relationships or in certain types of episodes (Williamson & Fitzpatrick, 1985).

Contingent responding can result in a balanced pattern of responding over time if the contingencies that call for selection of one pole are canceled out by the contingencies that suggest use of the other pole of the opposition. Yet, this need not always happen. If contingencies are not patterned over time or normative across relationships, they tend to produce a multifinal (multiple sequence) course of relationship evolution.

People may also respond to dialectic tensions by alternating between oppositions (e.g., openness vs. closedness, dominance vs. deference, and symmetry vs. complementarity) in a cyclical pattern over time (Altman et al., 1981; Fisher & Drecksel, 1983; VanLear, 1991). With cycling, the alternating is patterned by time rather than by the situation such that there is a regular pace or rhythm.

Fisher and Drecksel (1983) found cyclical alternation between symmetrical and complementary patterns of relational control in socially isolated peer relationships. They interpreted this as one way in which couples enact parallel relationships. VanLear (1991) found evidence of cycles of openness and closedness in relationships for both behavior and perception. The cycles were regular but complex: for example, smaller cycles of openness occurred in conversations nested in longer cycles across conversations.

There are several reasons to expect regularity in dialectic alternation (VanLear, 1991, 1996). First, regularity of cycling provides people with a degree of predictability and stability in their lives. Second, there are natural physiological rhythms that can produce regular behavioral patterns (Warner, 1996). Third, people's social lives are entrained to regularly scheduled periodic events and activities (work, school, church, dinner, etc.). Finally, by regularly pacing periodic behavior, we can coordinate our behaviors and activities with others (VanLear, 1996; Warner, 1996). Regular cycles can have the effect of creating a sense of balance because neither pole of the dialectic dominates indefinitely and the alternation is symmetrical over time. However, this dialectic perspective does not assume that maximum predictability and regularity is always desirable or that relationships always seek a balanced state.

Predictability Versus Novelty

People and relationships must deal with the generic dialectics like predictability versus novelty as they negotiate the relationship dialectics of independence versus connection, dominance versus dependence, and expression versus restraint. In fact, predictability or novelty can only be assessed in terms of some other aspect of the relationship.

Relationship evolution is, in part, a function of the dialectic of stability versus change (Altman et al., 1981). It is said, "The more things change the more they remain the same," but it is also said that "the only constant is change." People and relationships need both stability and change. People require stability for predictability so they know what to expect and how to behave. However, people require variation as well. Relationships must have a degree of stability for people to coordinate their behavior and accomplish joint goals. However, relationships can become too stagnant (Knapp, 1978) or too rigid (Gottman, 1979; Rogers & Bagarozzi, 1983). Both structure and flexibility are desirable (VanLear & Zietlow, 1990). There is a dynamic tension between stability and change and flexibility and structure regarding how we handle and negotiate all of the dialectic processes in interpersonal relationships.

Stability can refer to a constant state over time (no change) or to a regular dynamic periodic pattern over time (a cycle). Change can be planned or unplanned, smooth or erratic. Yet, how can relationships be both changing and stable?

Communicators may handle the stability–change dialectic by how they choose to punctuate the process of relating. What looks like progressive change over a short span of time may look like a part of a periodic cycle if extended over a longer period, or what looks like a stable cycle, for a period may undergo recalibration or change when viewed from a longer temporal horizon. Likewise, frequent fluctuations that may indicate very rapid cycling may evidence a directional trajectory when smoothed or averaged across the ups and downs over a long period of time.

Given these multiple possibilities, stability and change can be viewed as simultaneously present in a multidimensional, multilevel process. While certain aspects of the relationship may be undergoing change (e.g., intimacy), others may be stable (e.g., control). Likewise, a relationship may be undergoing change in the level of variable values (e.g., the communication may become more intimate), but the variable relationships and processes that generated that change may be stationary (e.g., the norm of reciprocity).[7] In this way, despite change at one level in the relationship, a degree of stability and predictability is maintained. Elsewhere (VanLear, 1996) I suggested:

> The degree of stability or change evidenced by a communication process depends upon the variables observed, the level of analysis, the temporal scope or horizon of the study or model, and the punctuation of the continuous temporal

---

[7]Time-series analysis distinguishes between stationarity of variable levels and stationarity of process (i.e., variations in variable relationships over time). Elsewhere (VanLear, 1996), I likened this to the distinction between first-order and second-order change. Relationships may gradually grow or change through changes in variable levels (*first-order change*). However, a more fundamental qualitative change in the relationship may occur when the processes that generate the variable levels change (*second-order change*).

stream. . . . Communication processes . . . are likely to exhibit stability and change contemporaneously. . . . The degree of stability or change in a communication process is a matter of perspective as well as detectable redundancy (pp. 58–60).

There is also a dialectic tension between similarity versus difference across relationships. At the lowest levels of abstraction, no two relationships are exactly alike. However, by definition, all relationships share some things in common at the highest levels of abstraction. There may be similarities across relationships because what works may be replicated across relationships and social norms arise that promote such commonality. If all relationships were unique, people would have no guide for how to behave in them. However, diversity across relationships can also be functional to a society. Some differences can be complementary. Likewise, the more diversity in abilities and functions provided by different relationships in a group or society, the more likely it is that the group has the resources to meet the demands of any situation.

Dynamically, relationships may take similar developmental trajectories or different courses of evolution. The degree of homogeneity in the process depends on the variables and functions considered, their level of abstraction, and the level of analysis. In short, it is a matter of perspective as much as empirically detectable uniformity (VanLear, 1996). In some ways, relationships are characterized by homogeneous developmental processes. In other ways, relationship evolution is multifinal.

Social evolution selects those patterns of relating that are adaptive and functional. If dialectic tensions exist because both sides of an opposition can be functional or adaptive, the responses to these dialectic tensions may potentially produce multiple courses of relationship evolution. Yet, if a given sequence is functional, it may be repeated across relationships.

The dialectic tension between predictability and novelty (Baxter, 1988) grows out of the twin dialectics of similarity versus difference and stability versus change. A stable pattern over time promotes predictability, even if that pattern is unique to the person or relationship. However, change is unpredictable to the extent that its progression is different from other cases and is not regular over time. Yet, predictability versus novelty is also a matter of perspective for both relational partners and for relationship researchers. However, given a specific set of operationalizations and applications, it becomes an empirical issue.

Toward a Model of Relationship Emergence

The general model of relationship emergence has three components. The first is a set of relationship dialectic oppositions or relationship dimensions (e.g., openness vs. closedness and dominance vs. deference). The second is a temporal function or trajectory describing the course of the variable(s). The third is a dynamic principle of coordination or relating. The resulting model has a temporal horizon and a range of generality that can be tested for stationarity and homogeneity, given appropriate operational applications of the metaphor/model.

The temporal function of relationship emergence can be a scheduled trajectory, in which values at any point in time predict values at a distant point in time. Scheduled trajectories can be directional (linear, curvilinear, or phasic), a periodic cycle, or some combination (a progressive cycle).[8] They can result from planning, rule-governed behavior, or some natural process. If a scheduled trajectory is adaptive and functional, it may be supported by social norms and, therefore, become replicated across relationships. Scheduled trajectories favor the predictability side of the predictability–uncertainty dialectic and can act as a template to assess deviations against.

Even when there is a scheduled trajectory, there is usually an unscheduled or stochastic component. There are usually on-the-spot changes and adaptations based on unforeseen contingencies and disruptions that affect the course of relationship evolution (VanLear, 1996).[9] At some level of abstraction, evolution is multifinal.

One important contingency is the behavior of the other party to the relationship. The minimal definition of a relationship requires that the thoughts, feelings, or behaviors of the communicators affect each other, such that there is some adaptation or coordination of one to the other (Cappella, 1996). Coordination can also be scheduled or unscheduled. Relational partners can coordinate by matching and timing their scheduled behaviors and trajectories or they can adapt to the immediate behaviors of the other. The influence can be mutual (A affects B and B affects A) or one party to the relationship can dominate the other (A affects B, but B does not affect A). Mutual adaptation can usually be identified as reciprocal (A matches B and B matches A), or

---

[8]Scheduled trajectories that are directional can be modeled by linear or curvilinear trend analyses. Scheduled trajectories that are cyclical can be modeled by Fourier or Spectral analytic techniques (VanLear, 1991; VanLear & Watt, 1996). In fact, any time series (cyclical or not) can be represented by a series of sinusoidal functions. The simpler and more regular the process, the simpler the mathematical model needed to adequately represent it. Most scheduled trajectories have finite temporal horizons based on their range of stationarity.

[9]In a stochastic model, the best predictor of a variable value is a value immediately proceeding it, and values further away provide successively poorer predictions. Stochastic variation over time can be based on a systematic process (auto correlation or moving average), or it can take the form of a *random walk,* where each successive value is close to the immediately preceding value, but the direction of its movement from that value is random. A stationary time series can be modeled as the sum of scheduled trajectories (both directional and cyclical) plus a stochastic component (VanLear, 1996). Nonstationary processes require a second-order explanation. A nonstationary model is more complex, but is represented as a relationship X time interaction.

compensatory (A and B respond in opposite ways). These coordination patterns can be stationary (the same pattern of adaptation persists over time) or nonstationary (the pattern of adaptation varies over time). Nonstationary patterns of interaction can be based on contingency or cyclical alternation.

An Example: Openness in Relationship Emergence

Considerable research supports a view of gradual reciprocal increase in openness of self to other over time as relationships develop (Altman & Taylor, 1973; VanLear, 1987). This process promotes reduction of uncertainty, mutual understanding, trust, and relational growth. This suggests a scheduled directional trajectory of breadth and depth of self-presentation and accessibility of self to other.

Altman et al. (1981) argued that early linear models of interpersonal openness were over simplified because they ignored cyclical variations in openness based on a dialectic tension between openness and closedness. There are times when people are open and accessible and times when they are private and closed to the other. There are times when relational partners are candid and honest with each other, and times when they are restrained, circumspect, tactful, or even evasive or communicatively distant. Both types of responses can be functional, appropriate, and adaptive (at least at times). Given the dialectic tension between stability and change, Altman et al. (1981) proposed that regular cycles of openness versus closedness allow for stability in the relationship, whereas progressive changes in the frequency, duration, and amplitude of these cycles over the course of its history provide a sense of growth. Early in the relationship the frequency of cycling is high, but the amplitude (height) of the cycles is small. As relationships progress, there should be a systematic increase in the height of the cycles. Finally, they suggest that for successful relationships, partners should match and time their cycling behavior.

Based on the Altman et al. (1981) model, VanLear (1991) conducted two studies of communicative openness and found: (a) Relationships were characterized by cycles of communication openness versus closedness; (b) cycles were complex such that shorter cycles were nested in longer cycles; (c) the amplitude of the cycles were higher for long-term relationships; (d) communicators generally matched and timed their cyclical behaviors; and (e) stable relationships had flatter amplitudes than deteriorating relationships.

Figure 6.1a represents the first four findings and is a model of the scheduled trajectories and scheduled coordination. This figure shows smaller cycles nested in longer cycles that increase in amplitude over time. The increasing amplitude results in a gradual increase in the overall baseline level of openness over time. Relational partners match and time their cyclical behavior. The smooth regular curves make it clear this is a scheduled trajectory and

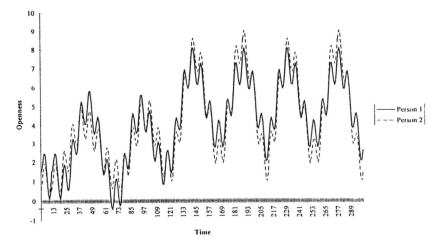

FIG. 6.1a. Dialectics of openness in relationship evolution: Scheduled coordination of two scheduled trajectories.

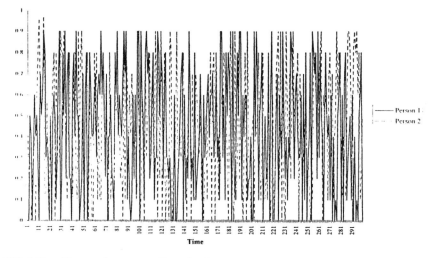

FIG. 6.1b. Two random uncoordinated series.

the coordination is based on matching and timing the two scheduled trajectories. Figure 6.1b depicts two random unrelated series. Figure 6.1c takes these same two scheduled trajectories and adds a random stochastic component from Fig. 6.1b to each person's time series and then adjusts each person's score for the random variation in their partner's immediately preceding score, thereby building unscheduled coordination (i.e., reciprocity) into the model. Figure 6.1d presents exemplary data from an actual relationship dur-

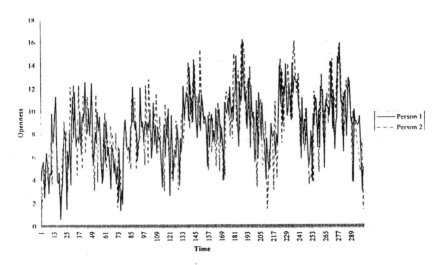

FIG. 6.1c.   Scheduled and unscheduled coordination.

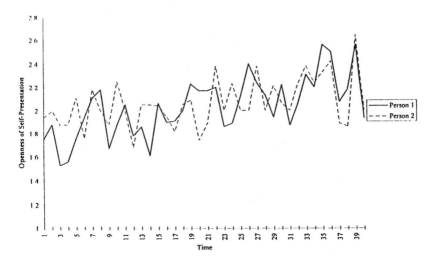

FIG. 6.1d.   Openness in relationship formation: Actual data from two relational partners.

ing the formation process. It shows an overall increase in openness and matched and timed cycles of openness behavior by both partners.

Figure 6.1a was generated from a mathematical model based on Fourier Analysis plus a linear trend (see VanLear, 1991; VanLear & Watt, 1996). The techniques used to model scheduled trajectories produce relatively smooth patterns. If partners follow a scheduled trajectory, this model should account for a substantial portion of the variance. However, relationships typically experience unscheduled disruptions that lead to on-the-spot adaptations in behaviors that, in turn, lead to responses by the relational partner. Stochastic techniques model values as a function of other proximal values (of self and other) and can, therefore, model the types of adjustments and adaptations participants make in response to these unscheduled events. The combination of both scheduled and unscheduled processes allow relational partners to experience relationship evolution as both predictable and novel.

This model is basically stationary. We could also include variation in mutual adaptation over time to represent second-order change. For example, it has been suggested that reciprocal adaptation is more likely early in the relationship than latter. Such a contingency principle requires alterations in this example.

CONCLUSIONS

For over a decade I have been using the metaphor of relational dialectics to help me organize and clarify some of my thinking about interpersonal communication and relationship processes. Some scholars begin with the assumption that the world is a series of dialectical contradictions and proceed to an explanation of their subject from there. I start with a set of assumptions about the world, science, communication, and relationships. I find that many of these are usefully organized by the metaphor of dialectics. Once the dialectic metaphor is accepted, it then provides a wealth of heuristic ideas and directions for research and theory.

A metaphor never evokes exactly the same image in everyone. My use of the dialectic metaphor differs somewhat from other authors in this volume and even those scholars whose work I have referenced. In translating their concepts and insights into my theoretical structure, I unavoidably altered their meaning.

My English teachers warned me against mixing my metaphors. My mentor, B. Aubrey Fisher, warned me of the dangers of blindly combining concepts from theoretical perspectives with differing fundamental assumptions. Although I shamelessly mixed my metaphors, I tried to be clear about my basic assumptions and how they shape my understanding of concepts derived from various sources.

I had several goals for this chapter. First, was to explicate a set of metatheoretical assumptions that allow a postpositivist, scientific view of dialectics. Next, I attempted to show that such an approach allows a variety of research methods, both qualitative and quantitative. Third, I presented my view of some of the sources and manifestations of dialectic tensions in personal relationships. I then presented a view of relationship evolution based on how people handle their dialectic contradictions. The general model of relationship emergence pictures relationships as evolving along both regular scheduled trajectories and irregular unscheduled trajectories. Finally, an example was provided based on Altman, Vinsel, and Brown's (1981) model and my own empirical work.

Neither the empirical research cited here, nor any future research will "prove" the "validity" of this framework. However, if my assumptions can be accepted by others, the resulting research may be persuasive as to the applicability and usefulness of this metaphorical system. Our emergent understanding of interpersonal relationship processes is a nonsummative product of a multivocal conversation. I hope this chapter is a useful contribution to that ongoing dialogue.

ACKNOWLEDGMENTS

The author gratefully acknowledges the helpful direction and comments provided by Lesley Baxter and Barbara Montgomery, but takes total responsibility for the content of this chapter.

REFERENCES

Altman, I., & Taylor, D. A. (1973). *Social penetration: The development of interpersonal relationships*. New York: Holt, Rinehart & Winston.

Altman, I., Vinsel, A., & Brown, B. (1981). Dialectic conceptions in social psychology: An application to social penetration and privacy regulation. In L. Berkowitz (Ed.), *Advances in experimental social psychology: Vol. 14* (pp. 76–100). New York: Academic Press.

Anderson, J. A. (1987). *Communication research: Issues and methods*. New York: McGraw-Hill.

Baker, G. L., & Gollub, J. P. (1990). *Chaotic dynamics: An introduction*. Cambridge, England: Cambridge University Press.

Bateson, G. (1972). *Steps to an ecology of mind*. New York: Ballantine.

Baxter, L. A. (1988). A dialectical perspective on communication strategies in relationships development. In S. Duck, D. F. Hay, S. E. Hobfoll, W. Iches, & B. Montgomery (Eds.), *Handbook of personal relationships* (pp. 257–273). London: Wiley.

Baxter, L. A. (1990). Dialectical contradictions in relationship development. *Journal of Social and Personal Relationships, 7*, 69–88.

Baxter, L. A., & Montgomery, B. M. (1996). *Relating: Dialogues and dialectics*. New York: Guilford.

Berger, C. R. (1993). Revisiting the relationship construct. *Personal Relationship Issues, 1*, 25–27.

Berger, P. L., & Luckmann, T. (1967). *The social construction of reality: A treatise in the sociology of knowledge*. Garden City, NJ: Anchor.

Buck, R. (1984). *The communication of emotion*. New York: Guilford.

Campbell, D. T. (1994). The social psychology of scientific validity: An epistemological perspective and a personalized history. In R. Shadish & S. Fuller (Eds.), *The social psychology of science*. New York: Guilford.

Cappella, J. N. (1996). Dynamic coordination of vocal and kinesic behavior in dyadic interaction: Methods, problems, and interpersonal outcomes. In J. H. Watt & C. A. VanLear (Eds.), *Dynamic patterns in communication processes* (pp. 353–386). Thousand Oaks, CA: Sage.

Deetz, S. (1985). *Interpretive research methods in communication.* Paper presented at a special Conference on Qualitative Methods in Communication Research, University of Wisconsin-Milwaukee.

Feyerabend, P. K. (1963). How to be a good empiricist: A plea for tolerance in matters epistemological. In B. Baumrin (Ed.), *Philosophy of science: The Delaware seminar* (Vol. 1, pp. 3–40). New York: Wiley.

Feyerabend, P. K. (1965). Problems of empiricism. In R. Colodny (Ed.), *Beyond the edge of certainty* (pp. 145–260). Englewood Cliffs, NJ: Prentice-Hall

Fisher, B. A. (1978). *Perspectives on human communication.* New York: Macmillan.

Fisher, B. A. (1980). *Small group decision making.* New York: McGraw-Hill.

Fisher, B. A., & Drecksel, G. L. (1983). A cyclical model of developing relationships: A study of relational control interaction. *Communication Monographs, 50,* 66–78.

Garfinkel, H. (1967). *Studies in ethnomethodology.* New York: Prentice-Hall.

Geertz, C. (1973). *The interpretation of cultures.* New York: Basic Books.

Goffman, I. (1959). *The presentation of self in everyday life.* Garden City, NY: Doubleday.

Gottman, J. M. (1979). *Marital interaction: Experimental investigations.* New York: Academic Press.

Gottman, J. M. (1982). Temporal form: Toward a new language for describing relationship. *Journal of Marriage and the Family, 44,* 943–962.

Haley, J. (1963). *Strategies of psychotherapy.* New York: Gune & Stratton.

Hawking, S. (1988). *A brief history of time.* New York: Bantam.

Heisenberg, W. (1930). *The physical principles of the quantum theory* (C. Eckart & F. C. Hoyt, Trans.). New York: Dover.

Kaplan, A. (1964). *The conduct of inquiry: Methodology for behavioral science.* New York: Harper & Row.

Knapp, M. L. (1978). *Social intercourse: From greeting to good-bye.* Boston: Allyn & Bacon.

Lofland, J. (1976). *Doing social life.* New York: Wiley.

McCall, G. J., & Simmons, J. L. (1978). *Identities and interactions: An examination of human associations in everyday life.* New York: The Free Press.

Montgomery, B. M. (1992). Communication as the interface between couples and culture. *Communication Yearbook, 15,* 475–507.

Rawlins, W. K. (1983). Openness as problematic in ongoing friendships: Two conversational dilemmas. *Communication Monographs, 50,* 1–13.

Rogers, L. E. (1993). The concept of social relationship from an interactional pragmatic view. *Personal Relationship Issues, 1,* 20–21.

Rogers, L. E., & Bagarozzi, D. A. (1983). An overview of relational communication and implications for therapy. In D. A. Bagarozzi, A. P. Jurich & R. W. Jackson (Eds.), *Marital and family therapy: New perspectives in theory, research and practice* (pp.48–78). New York: Human Sciences Press.

Shaver, P. R., Morgan, H. J., & Wu, S. (1996). Is love a "basic" emotion? *Personal Relationships, 3,* 81–96.

Suppe, F. (Ed.). (1974). *The structure of scientific theories.* Urbana: University of Illinois Press.

VanLear, C. A. (1987). The formation of social relationships: A longitudinal study of social penetration. *Human Communication Research, 13,* 299–322.

VanLear, C. A. (1990). Communication and marital satisfaction: Social desirability and nonlinearity. *Communication Research Reports, 7,* 38–44.

VanLear, C. A. (1991). Testing a cyclical model of communicative openness in relationship development: Two longitudinal studies. *Communication Monographs, 58,* 337–361.

VanLear, C. A. (1992). Marital communication across the generations: Learning and rebellion, continuity and change. *Journal of Social and Personal Relationships, 9,* 103–124.

VanLear, C. A. (1996). Communication process approaches and models: Patterns, cycles, and dynamic coordination. In J. Watt & C. A. VanLear (Eds.), *Dynamic patterns in communication processes* (pp. 35–70). Thousand Oaks, CA: Sage.

VanLear, C. A., & Trujillo, N. (1986). On becoming acquainted: A longitudinal study of social judgment processes. *Journal of Social and Personal Relationships, 3,* 375–392.

VanLear, C. A., & Watt, J. (1996). A partial map to a wide territory. In J. Watt & C. A. VanLear (Eds.), *Dynamic patterns in communication processes* (pp. 3–33). Thousand Oaks, CA: Sage.

VanLear, C. A., & Zietlow, P. H. (1990). Toward a contingency approach to marital interaction: An empirical integration of three approaches. *Communication Monographs, 57,* 202–218.

Warner, R. M. (1996). Coordinated cycles in behavior and physiology during face-to-face social interaction. In J. Watt & C. A. VanLear (Eds.), *Dynamic patterns in communication processes* (pp. 327–352). Thousand Oaks, CA: Sage.

Watzlawick, P., Beavin, J. H., & Jackson, D. D. (1967). *Pragmatics of human communication: A study of interaction patterns, pathologies, and paradoxes.* New York: Norton.

Whitehead, A. N. (1929). *Process and reality.* New York: Macmillan.

Williamson, R. N., & Fitzpatrick, M. A. (1985). Two approaches to marital interaction: Relational control patterns in marital types. *Communication Monographs, 52,* 236–252.

Zietlow, P. H., & VanLear, C. A. (1991). Marriage duration and relational control. *Journal of Marriage and the Family, 53,* 773–785.

7

Choice Points for Dialecticians: A Dialectical–Transactional Perspective on Close Relationships

Barbara B. Brown
Carol M. Werner
Irwin Altman
University of Utah

We believe dialectic research has reached a point where scholars' decisions can yield chaos or community. We can either be soloists playing from different scores or an ensemble developing variations on a common set of themes. Both are equally valid forms of music or scholarship. Nevertheless, at this time, we argue for an integrative and unified approach—the ensemble form of dialectic thinking. A review of our own and others' dialectic work shows that greater commonality in dialectic approaches will require attention to choice points concerning substance of dialectic oppositions, temporal aspects of dialectic functioning, participants in dialectic processes, and the holistic nature of dialectics.

BACKGROUND ON OUR APPROACH TO DIALECTICS

The three defining features of our initial dialectic approach continue to prove useful: opposition, unity, and change (Altman, Vinsel, & Brown, 1981). Whereas much of the literature in the 1960s and 1970s focused exclusively on openness and self-disclosure, we viewed openness and closedness as mutually defining and inseparable features of viable interpersonal relationships. Our dialectic approach, like those of others, presumed that people change with respect to oppositional processes as circumstances, goals, and relationships evolve.

We also have found useful some dialectic features that are not widely shared. First, we believe oppositional qualities are interdependent, lending meaning to each other, but also having unique features that allow either pole of the opposition to be studied in its own right. This view presumes that we examine two positively defined and related concepts such as openness and closedness (i.e., "functional opposition," Baxter & Montgomery, 1996, pp. 8–9), rather than openness and not openness (that is, a positive quality and its negation).

We also assume that oppositional forces arise from pervasive aspects of human behavior and society, so that both openness and closedness, for example, are omnipresent. Chronic and total openness, a complete fusion of self and other, destroys the self and its ability to contribute distinctively to the relationship. Similarly, chronic and total closedness destroys the strands of connection essential to any relationship. Although either openness or closedness may predominate at one time or another, both remain vital to the relationship, and their unity is ongoing.

Finally, we do not assume a nirvana or ultimate state toward which all social relationships strive, unlike scholars who posit balance, homeostasis, equilibrium, or predictability as ultimate relationship goals. Instead, we assume that many temporal patterns of stability and change in relationship processes are possible and viable. Thus, relational partners are not presumed to be seeking any singular, permanent, or overriding relational goal.

OUR APPLICATIONS OF DIALECTICS

We have worked with a variety of dialectic oppositions over the years. The dialectic of openness and closedness provided the model for Altman's (1975) analysis of privacy regulation, which helped to unify and synthesize a range of literature on self-disclosure, personal space, territoriality, and crowding. Later, a more formal conceptual analysis described how the dialectics of openness–closedness and stability–change characterized dyadic relationships (Altman, Vinsel, & Brown, 1981). A variety of other studies also examined how decorations, rituals, and celebrations reveal the dialectic of individual and communal identity for persons, families, and neighbors (Altman & Gauvain, 1981; Brown & Werner, 1985; Gauvain, Altman, & Fahim, 1983; Werner, Altman, Brown, & Ginat, 1993). An analysis of cultural practices involving courtship, weddings, and placemaking revealed historical and cultural changes in the interplay of an autonomy–connection dialectic in husband–wife relationships and the relationship between the couple and their families (Altman, Brown, Staples, & Werner, 1992). In polygynous marriages, dialectic tensions operate within each husband–wife dyadic tie and in relationship to the communal family in which it is embedded (Altman & Ginat, 1996). In sum, our dialectic approach has been a flexible but sturdy tool in the study of a wide range of relationships across cultures, times, places, and social units.

TRANSACTIONALISM AND DIALECTICS

In the last decade, we began to ground our dialectic approach in a transactional world view (TWV; Altman & Rogoff, 1987). The TWV treats interactions and relationships as "a spatial and temporal confluence of people, settings, and activities that constitutes a complex organized unity" (Altman & Rogoff, 1987, p. 24). In this view, any attempt to understand persons abstracted from their contexts is incomplete.

Similarities of TWV and Dialectics

The TWV and our dialectical approach agree in certain respects. Both presume that humans are active and goal-seeking, with behaviors and goals changing as a result of internal and external circumstances. Neither of the two approaches endorses an ultimate teleological direction to human activity.

Enhancements Offered by a TWV

First, the TWV provides a more compelling and comprehensive approach to holism than did our early work on dialectics. For us, holism in dialectics focused on the unity of oppositional processes, such as openness and closedness. Transactional holism is completely compatible with the unity of opposites, but also incorporates physical settings, social contexts, and the actions of participants as integral aspects of events. For example, in Christmas celebrations there is a holistic unity to the cultural traditions, environmental artifacts (the home decorations, trees, lights, gifts, and other aspects of Christmas), the participants and their actions, and the rhythm and pace of the celebrations (Werner, Haggard, Altman, & Oxley, 1988). Thus, the TWV more explicitly states that holism involves understanding how varied levels and types of behaviors work together and how varied life domains, such as courtship, weddings, and placemaking create a whole fabric of experience. In sum, the TWV explicitly states that people, psychological processes, temporal processes, and places are intrinsic aspects of any behavior one studies.

Second, the TWV more clearly states philosophical assumptions regarding causality and generality than do most dialectical approaches. Because of its focus on holism, the TWV does not focus primarily on antecedent–consequent, cause–effect relationships, known as *Aristotelian efficient* causes. Instead, a transactional approach emphasizes *formal causes,* that is, the patterns that characterize changing aspects of an event. For example, throwing a rock is an efficient cause that explains breaking a window. The formal cause of the broken window involves characterizing the "laws of trajectories, force, and tension . . . that constrain (or permit or dictate) a broken-window outcome" (Bates, 1979, p. 138). The TWV does not neglect efficient causes, but recognizes that an exclusive focus on efficient causes results in an incomplete understanding of events. The meaning of the rock goes beyond understanding that it caused the window to shatter; the rock is more fully understood as an object with possible actions that are formed, in part, by the context in which the rock is located. A search for formal causes seeks to describe and understand the complex and variegated contextual patterns that constitute an event.

Differences Between TWV and Dialectics

Dialectic and transactional approaches differ somewhat in their assumptions about the generalizability of concepts. Dialectic approaches vary among themselves with respect to whether they presume the existence of universal dialectic oppositions and generalizable processes. Our particular approach to dialectics has emphasized universal oppositions, which we believe are inherent in the very definition and nature of relationships, such as openness and closedness (Altman & Chemers, 1980). At the same time, we recognize that dialectic processes play out in very different and particular ways, depending on the cultural, temporal, social, and physical aspects of any situation (Altman & Chemers, 1980). For example, our research on neighborhood relationships illustrates how people differentially express and create interdependence over time or across different neighborhoods (Altman & Chemers, 1980; Brown & Werner, 1985; Oxley, Haggard, Werner, & Altman, 1986). Some people may become involved in group celebrations and others may decorate or maintain their homes in ways that reflect and promote neighborly engagement. The decorative devices themselves may be specific to the season and the neighborhood. Therefore, the underlying process of becoming engaged with neighbors appears to be universal, but the occasions, techniques, and temporal patterning of engagements differ across situations.

Although not necessarily a difference in the two perspectives, the TWV explicitly acknowledges that there are multiple observers to an event—including participants *and* researchers—and that different perceptions, interpretations, and meanings are assigned to events. The implication is that a dialectic researcher should appreciate and seek out the multiple psychological positions held by varied participants in an event.

Our efforts to integrate the TWV with dialectics and our review of more recent dialectic work suggests a set of choice points to help our own research program and to reach out to other researchers in hopes of a common vocabulary and set of understandings.

CHOICE POINTS IN DIALECTIC THEORY
AND RESEARCH

Will the Study of Social Relationships Presently Benefit More From a Centrifugal Multiplication or a Centripetal Convergence of Dialectic Oppositions?

Dialectic research has undergone a stimulating and open growth phase, wherein every new publication appears to suggest yet another set of dialectic oppositions. Researchers often follow their own set of assumptions, definitions, and methods without regard to those of others. We have observed that some researchers use identical terms to refer to different processes or disparate terms for the same processes. We suggest that dialectic research is in danger of fracturing to the point where researchers lack a common understanding of dialectics, especially with respect to the nature of oppositions. We believe it is time to reflect and seek some common ties across the diversity of dialectics. In order for a new paradigm to flourish in the long run, it must be rendered comprehensible to others and especially to other contributing researchers (Kuhn, 1970).

As an illustration of both richness and a threat to comprehensibility, Werner and Baxter (1994) noted that researchers use 18 different but related sets of oppositional terms to refer to aspects of interpersonal integration and separation. These include stability–self-identity, connection–autonomy, integration–differentiation, intimacy–identity, intimacy–detachment, and intimacy–freedom. Such terminological proliferation raises the possibility that the same terms mean different things or that different terms may have the same meaning. To seek synthesis of knowledge and to avoid definitional confusion, we believe that it is useful to identify a limited number of underlying or general dialectics and we offer a proposal in the following section.

In addition, commonality can be achieved by asking scholars to describe their conceptions of how their terms oppose and are unified. Although oppositions can be defined in a variety of ways (Baxter & Montgomery, 1996), most scholars agree that dialectic approaches involve interdependent, unified oppositional processes. Open implies closed or intimacy can imply superficiality. By asking researchers to be specific about what properties are in opposition, it will be clearer how concepts like stability–self-identity (Askham, 1976), intimacy–autonomy (Conville, 1991) and intimacy–detachment (Masheter & Harris, 1986) might all be related to a common underlying dialectic.

As previously stated, a primary way to create clarification of meaning is to seek out common substantive themes underlying dialectic oppositions. Baxter (1993) and Werner and Baxter (1994) proposed that integration–separation, expression–nonexpression, and stability–change are three common dialectic themes that synthesize a vast number of alternative conceptualizations. In keeping with these efforts, we propose that all relationships involve three fundamental and interdependent oppositional aspects of social relationships: engagement, affect, and regulation.

Engagement refers to the degree and level of integration, involvement, connection, openness, interdependence, or association that relationship partners have with one another, in opposition to their degree and level of being individuated, uninvolved, disconnected, closed, independent, or separate from one another.

Some amount of engagement is a prerequisite for a relationship; indeed, engagement concepts have been central to social theorists for a long time. Classical sociological perspectives often acknowledge or imply an engagement type of dialectic (Cooley, 1902; Mead, 1934; Schutz, 1966). Self and society are twinborn in their view, with one's identity and well-being dependent on the existence and operation of the other.

Similarly, Baxter and colleagues (1988; Werner & Baxter, 1994), in a more explicitly dialectical approach, posited that connection–autonomy or integration–separation dialectics address a fundamental issue of people relating to one another. This opposition varies across relationships in terms of the relative dominance of each oppositional force. In some relationships, one partner may prefer more autonomy, whereas the other prefers more connection; other couples may agree that a particular level or changing interplay of autonomy and connection across the history of the relationship is desired. These oppositions do not reflect a hydraulic model, wherein greater autonomy implies lesser connection. In some relationships, partners' connections to one another allow them to exercise greater autonomy. Thus, autonomy and connection operate as a true dialectic, with each quality present in the relationship in a holistic way, but in complicated blends that shift over time.

The engagement dialectic, like all dialectics, operates among a variety of social units—individuals, couples, and groups. Montgomery (1992) has stated that dialectic relations between couples and society, for example, define and facilitate social existence. Autonomy provides couples a sense of worth and special character, but also provides society with innovative or deviant relationships that facilitate societal change. Couples' actions may create unique norms thereby expressing greater autonomy in their relationship with society, whereas actions that endorse societywide norms express greater connection to society. Couples who choose to create their own unique norms do not do so in a vacuum—they do so with an understanding of what an act of uniqueness means in their relationship with society. Thus, highly autonomous actions are not necessarily independent of society.

The dialectical and transactional perspectives provide a useful counterpoint to research that presumes individuals or couples operate relatively autonomously, without recognizing any individual's or couple's embeddedness in society (see review by Markus & Kitayama, 1994). Markus and Kitayama (1994) traced this bias to Western cultural values of individuality in social and physical settings: "Americans are likely to create and live within settings that elicit and promote the sense that one is a positively unique individual who is separate and independent from others" (p. 573). Recent reviews of developmental psychology (Fogel, 1994), social psychology (Miller & Prentice, 1994), and our own work on cross cultural aspects of courtship, weddings, and placemaking (Altman, Brown, Staples, & Werner, 1992) advocate a renewed emphasis on individual–group interdependencies. We believe that processes of engagement highlight an appreciation for the interdependencies between social actors and social units.

Affect involves a range of positive and negative emotions and actions associated with a relationship. Positive affective qualities include acceptance, approval, agreement, enjoyment, satisfaction, friendliness, liking, and love. Negative affective counterparts include rejection, disapproval, disagreement, aversion, dissatisfaction, hate, dislike, and hostility. Positive and negative aspects of emotional experience often go hand in hand, as in experiences of ambivalence, mixed emotions, and complex blends of varied emotions. These emotional qualities occur within individuals, between members of a relationship, and between groups.

Affective evaluations are useful in steering individuals and groups away from dangerous relationships or helping motivate individuals and groups toward desired personal or relational goals. Positive affective aspects of relationships often constitute a goal in and of themselves, and relationship viability is often linked to affective qualities of the social bond.

Affective evaluations are also central to person perception (Zebrowitz, 1990), communication (Rawlins & Holl, 1988), and small group dynamics (Bales, 1950). Clinical psychologists also proposed that relationships are characterized by dimensions of positive and negative affect, such as love and hate (Leary, 1957; Sullivan, 1953) or attack and active love (Benjamin, 1993). Although emphasizing affect, many clinical approaches do not provide dialectical models. Instead, they treat positive and negative affect as alternatives along a continuum, not as unified oppositional processes. An exception is found in some of the ideas of Leary (1957), who suggested that positive and negative affective qualities are blended in healthy relationships. He stated that being frank and forthright was a way of expressing negative affect in the context of a positive relationship. For Leary, as for dialecticians, dysfunctionality involves any quality carried to an extreme or inflexible level. For example, the extreme form of forthrightness might involve a destructive attack.

By acknowledging the oppositional affective qualities of social bonds we support Duck and Perlman's (1985) critique of a "positivity bias" in personal relationship research, in which such research proceeds as if relationships are "pure hotbeds of emotional positivity" (p. 11). According to Duck and Perlman, and consistent with a dialectical perspective, researchers should emphasize the waxing and waning of positive and negative experiences in relationships and not overplay the positive side of social bonds. For example, although most individuals strive for positive relationships instead of negative ones, the natural course of relationships involves both positivity and negativity. Intimate friendships give rise not only to self-acceptance, trust, and rapport, but also to insecurity, jealousy, and resentment (cited in Rawlins, 1992, p. 55); positively valued partners often perceive one another to have negative qualities that call forth negative affective aspects of the relationship; relationship behaviors that were once positively valued later become irritants (i.e., "fatal attractions," Felmlee, 1995). At one point in time, individuals often make independent evaluations of positive and negative aspects of their social relationships (Henderson-King & Veroff, 1994), confirming the existence of ongoing positive and negative forces.

Regulation involves oppositional processes of making decisions or creating rules and norms to guide the relationship. Oppositional qualities involved in regulation can include dominating, controlling, and offering direction versus submitting, resisting, and accepting direction. They can also involve differing ideas of how the parties to a relationship coordinate or coregulate the relationship. There may be tensions between cooperative and competitive processes, between relying on past procedures or forging new ones or between offers and counteroffers with respect to the activities, meanings, and directions of the relationship.

Regulatory processes are essential to relationships because relationships require coordination and some technique for making decisions that carry the relationship forward (Wiemann, 1985). Altman (1975) posited that regulation is essential for individuals and groups. Both need to regulate their interactions in order to have a sense of identity—where one's boundary ends and another's begins—as well as effectiveness. Groups preserve their identity and lines of action through their regulation of both members and outsiders. Without regulation, it would be impossible to coordinate all parties to a social unit.

The processes of coordination and regulation are fundamental and ongoing, in part, because of the absence of fixed or immutable relationship goals. Recall that in a transactional approach, there is no teleological end state, such as balance or homeostasis, to simplify and provide a predictable or ultimate direction to relationships. Instead, parties create ongoing working agreements, intentionally or unintentionally, that resolve some of the fundamental contradictions inherent in multiple goals, conflicting commitments, and varied preferred futures. Parties are unlikely to be in complete accord with respect to setting or accomplishing goals in relationships or to understand fully each other's perspective. These differences feed into temporary and shifting but necessary rules for sustaining the relationship.

Regulation processes may be easiest to understand as dialectic oppositions involving dominance and submission, in which one party submits, obeys, and defers and the other demands, takes the lead, or dictates. This theme of a vertical dimension to relationships is common in the communication literature (Burgoon & Hale, 1984; Millar & Rogers, 1987). From a dialectical perspective, superordinate and subordinate roles are not fixed and static. A relationship may involve one person taking the lead on one relationship goal (e.g., spending less money) whereas the other takes the lead on another (i.e., selecting entertainment). Yet, fulfilling goals in both domains can often be incompatible, fueling some of the waxing and waning of regulatory processes. Alternatively, individual needs and aspects of the social and historical context may change, resulting in a reconfiguration of dominating and subordinating processes.

Simmel (1908/1950) believed that superordination and subordination were fundamental aspects of social life and emphasized how those in subordinate roles may actively define and lend meaning to the role of the superordinate person. Thus, the relationship involves two actively constructing parties, not one actor and one passive recipient. As a dialectician, Simmel believed that good relationships involve regulation, but that extreme and rigid dominance relationships are not viable.

Other social and clinical psychologists confirm the centrality of regulatory processes, such as control, treating them as basic human needs (Sullivan, 1953), intrinsic to group dynamics (Bales, 1950), or salient in certain phases of group decision making (Schutz, 1966). Similarly, research on abusive relationships, communal and exchange relationships, or family relationships often deal with issues of destructive or constructive interpersonal regulation.

Traditional social psychology also details the mechanisms individuals use to regulate others, seek regulation by others, or respond to bids for regulation by others. This research often deals with individualistic and discrete instances of regulation, rather than placing regulation in a general framework of relationships. Nevertheless, concepts such as equity, obedience, conformity, persuasion, interpersonal influence, reactance, perceived control, and others attest to the pervasiveness of regulatory issues in human behavior. Finally, much of the work on scripts, roles and rules in society specifies how regulation operates in terms of division of labor, relationship responsibilities and taboos, and the like (Allan, 1993).

Regulation involves micro- and macrolevels of social conventions and constructions. At a very microlevel, regulation can involve the development of standards for turn taking in conversation (Wiemann, 1985); it can include division of responsibility in a relationship, as in the classic studies of socioemotional and task-oriented leaders in small groups (Bales, 1950). Regulation may also involve a variety of decision making, influence, and persuasion processes in relationships (Steil & Weltman, 1992). At a cultural level, it may involve scripts, prescriptions, and proscriptions for roles in relationships. A dialectic approach to regulation is complex, involving a variety of sources of both freedom and mutual constraints in the service of advancing multiple personal and relational goals.

Regulation is often construed as a relationship goal, without recognizing its existence as part of a dialectic process. Thus, Baxter and Montgomery (1996) criticized the uncertainty reduction paradigm for ignoring the fact that humans often relish uncertainty. Similarly, our earlier dialectic formulation (Altman, Vinsel, Brown, 1981) questioned traditional balance and consistency models for suggesting only one end state toward which interpersonal regulation proceeds. Thus, our dialectic–transactional perspective suggests that total regulatory structure and order is unlikely. The focus, instead, is on the analysis of changing regulatory processes as relationships unfold and evolve.

We propose that the dialectics of engagement, affect, and regulation allow researchers to focus on long-standing themes in relationships in a new way. We do not believe that these three dialectic oppositions encompass the total range of interpersonal dialectics to be studied. They also do not offer a simplistic account of human behavior; the next section shows the richness inherent in the themes as they blend together. Yet, we believe that they capture many of the concepts of interest to dialecticians and other scholars in the multiple disciplines involved in research on personal relationships.

Is It Useful to Examine Dialectic Oppositions
One at a Time, Singly, or as an Interrelated Set?

We conceive of engagement, affect, and regulation as naturally interdependent in operation and definition. For example, some degree of engagement is necessary before one can set the tone for affect and regulation. Similarly, affective orientations are usually expressed in accordance with a certain degree of engagement and acceptable methods of regulation. Different regulation strategies may be chosen depending on whether one desires love, respect, fear, or some combination of all three and in the context of certain levels of engagement. Also, different interrelationships among affect, regulation, and engagement are considered culturally appropriate for different roles (e.g., boss, friend, or spouse). Thus, although each dialectic may be profitably studied separately, we believe it is also useful to examine their interdependencies.

Many conceptualizations of social relationships recognize two or more processes from the triad of affect, regulation, and engagement. For example, although Bales' initial interaction coding scheme classified utterances as either involving affect or instrumentality (regulation), his reformulation (Bales & Cohen, 1979) required simultaneous scoring of affective and regulatory domains. Similarly, clinical theories include both affective and regulatory processes (emotional contact and power for Sullivan, 1953, and affiliation and control for Benjamin, 1993, and Leary, 1957).

Others assert the importance of a combination of affect and engagement. For Denzin (1984), a symbolic interactionist, "emotionality lies at the interaction of the person and society, for all persons are joined to their societies through the self-feelings and emotions" (p. x). Fogel, a developmental psychologist, advocated rejecting the view of emotions as solely involving individualistic biological reactions that sometimes erupt into social expression; instead he conceived of emotions as ongoing and inherently linked to aspects of social engagement (Fogel et al., 1992).

Other scholars propose three central dimensions similar to engagement, affect, and regulation. For example, Schutz (1966) hypothesized that inclusion, affection, and control were fundamental human needs, although he did not articulate dialectic oppositions. In the realm of nonverbal behavior, Patterson (1984) proposed that involvement, control, and intimacy combine in complex ways. Montgomery (1992) suggested that control, affection, and affiliation are important aspects of relationships. Simmel's (1908/1950) statement that "concord, harmony, coefficacy . . . must nevertheless be interspersed with distance, competition, repulsion" provides an early dialectic view that seems to blend aspects of engagement, affect, and regulation (p. 315).

There are some advantages to recognizing the simultaneous functioning of the three dialectic processes. First, it illuminates probable gaps in research. In retrospect, our earlier use of the individual–community identity dialectic to study the celebration of holidays included affect and engagement, but largely excluded regulation (Brown & Werner, 1985). That is, we examined how people invested neighborhood celebratory engagements with positive affective qualities (i.e., pride and liking) and negative affective qualities (i.e., resentment), but we did not inquire how neighbors regulated relationships by creating occasions for and constraints on neighborliness.

Conversely, Werner and Baxter's (1994) proposed expression–nonexpression dialectic focused on informational qualities of interactions or what partners reveal and conceal from one another. Yet, they do not seem to explicitly address the emotional power of what is revealed and concealed. Montgomery (1992) detailed how nonverbal immediacy behaviors signal engagement; however, it would also be useful to examine the affective qualities of immediacy, with both acrimonious arguments and intensely loving encounters accompanying immediacy. Thus, by explicitly recognizing the interplay of engagement, affective, and regulatory qualities as intrinsic and interdependent, we go beyond purely structural or atomistic accounts of the connections and separations in relationships to encompass important and experientially rich affective and regulatory processes in relationships.

Other gaps become apparent when one dialectic opposition appears to be more complex than its counterpart. For example, in the commonly used autonomy–connection dialectic, it appears that *autonomy* is often used to combine engagement and regulation, whereas *connection* is used to refer exclusively to engagement (without suggesting regulatory processes). Consider how, in an attachment–differentiation dialectic, *attachment* often connotes both positive affect and engagement, a blend, whereas *differentiation* connotes relatively pure disengagement or independence (using *integration* instead of *attachment* clearly focuses on a single dimension). When treating multiple dialectic processes, consistent treatment requires that if both poles of one dialectic are addressed, then both poles of other dialectics should be addressed as well.

Second, we also see the three dialectics as providing a useful bridge to much of the historical and contemporary work in interpersonal relationships. As our previous review demonstrates, nondialectical research often focuses on the substance of relationships, including concepts involved in engagement, regulatory, and affective processes. Dialectical approaches provide more flexible and comprehensive views of the opposition, unity, and change inherent in such processes. We believe acknowledging the classical contributions of nondialecticians opens a useful dialogue with the larger, more traditional field of relationship research and helps to focus efforts on areas of research that are of longstanding importance to the fundamental challenges of human relationships.

Third, recognizing the blending of the three dialectics opens new lines of inquiry into relationship viability. The three dialectics may operate to temper what otherwise might become an extreme, dysfunctional dialectic, wherein one oppositional quality engulfs the relationship. Thus, Gottman (1979) found that married couples' arguments are less destructive if the negative affect communicated by one partner is acknowledged by the other partner instead of being met by a countercomplaint, suggesting how a regulatory strategy can curb excessive negativity. Also, marriages that tend toward a dialectic extreme on one feature, such as those with substantial coercion (high dominance as regulation but without affective regard) or avoidance (disengagement), are less satisfying (Crohan, 1992). In keeping with our nonteleological view of the world, we suspect that viable relationships use many patterns of engagement, affect, and regulation. Most important, research suggests that the three dialectics may change and temper each other in ways that sustain relationships and prevent one oppositional quality from becoming too extreme.

Is Stability–Change a Separate Dialectic, or Is It an Aspect of All Dialectic Processes? How Are Time and Change Conceived, and How Do Dialectic Processes Unfold?

Our own and others' favorite dialectics have always involved an opposition between stability and change (or predictability–novelty, or similar terms). Although separating this dialectic highlights the importance of temporal issues, we always discuss stability and change in reference to substantive aspects such as openness and closedness (Altman, Vinsel, & Brown, 1981). We now propose that temporal processes of stability and change are not a substantively distinct dialectic, but are a property or feature of all dialectic oppositions. Thus, we recommend dealing with the stable and changing aspects of engagement, affect, and regulation, thereby locating temporal qualities in the essence and definition of all dialectic processes.

The transactional world view also suggests additional ways of thinking about the temporal unfolding of dialectic processes, namely, that change is internal and integral to events, and that social events should be studied in natural temporal units rather than according to an external clock. This is consistent with dialectic approaches that assume an irregular ebb and flow of events, according to changing needs and circumstances (Altman, Vinsel, & Brown, 1981). Unfortunately, current statistical models are not always amenable to the study of such temporal irregularities and more flexible statistical models are needed.

The TWV, which acknowledges multiple perspectives of an event, also encourages greater attention to complex temporal features and associated phenomenological experiences of dialectic processes (Werner, Altman, & Brown, 1992; Werner, Haggard, Altman, & Oxley, 1988). What is a daily rhythm and how do couples coordinate their separate temporal rhythms to achieve satisfactory engagement, affective, and regulatory processes? How does the temporal scale or duration of events contribute to their meaning? How does the increasing pace of wedding preparations contribute to the experience of the event and the dynamics of engagement, affective, and regulatory processes? These and other temporal qualities are part and parcel of relationships and need to be explored systematically.

Is Dialectic Holism of Opposites Compatible With a TWV of Holism of an Event? How Does Either Conception of Holism Guide Our Understanding of Dialectic Processes?

First, whereas our dialectic perspective originally focused on the unity and holism of oppositional processes, we, only recently, extended the TWV to include a dialectical perspective. The TWV accepts but does not mandate an examination of the holism of opposites. Transactional explorations of place attachment, for example, have rarely acknowledged both positive and negative affective qualities implicit in bonds with environmental settings (see review by Brown & Perkins, 1992). Just as it is useful for the transactional researcher to consider the oppositional qualities of an event, likewise the dialectician may want to consider the holistic qualities of a transactional unity.

Second, our TWV encourages dialecticians to examine how physical environments are chosen, created, and support or constrain particular blends of dialectic oppositional processes. Physical proximity, territorial mechanisms, verbal and nonverbal behaviors, cultural traditions and artifacts, and temporal qualities all contribute to the unfolding of dialectic processes in relationships. In contrast, many dialecticians have privileged verbal communication, such as conversations, accounts, and other reports of interaction, as the primary source of evidence for dialectic processes. There are exceptions, however, in the work of other dialecticians (Georgoudi, 1983; Montgomery, 1992), who have advocated what we consider to be a transactional approach to holism. For example, Rawlins (1989) situates dialectic processes "in their spatio-temporal cultural setting" (p. 159). Baxter and Montgomery (1996) root dialectics in a temporal and spatial "chronotope," using Bakhtin's approach. We believe these concepts will help encourage a different conceptualization of data to be collected in dialectic research.

What Are Suitable Social Units of Analysis?

Some authors focus on dialectic processes in dyadic relationships, others note relationships between individuals and society. A transactional view presumes that multiple social relationships co-exist, with all the complexities entailed by co-existence. Spouses cannot conveniently enact their marital relationship separately from their other relationships as parents, employees, friends, in-laws, or neighbors. Dialectic processes may involve many different, but embedded social units. Thus, Baxter's (1993) and Werner and Baxter's (1994) focus on dyads led them to describe dyadic dialectics as internal, with all other participants' influences treated as external. A transactional approach reminds us that designations like "internal" and "external" are necessary for creating a manageable research task, but that the relationships themselves do not correspond to internal or external boundaries—the relationships are simultaneous and overlapping.

Acknowledging the simultaneous operation of multiple social units also provides a new perspective on relationships. For example, our original dialectic analysis (Altman, Vinsel, & Brown, 1981) described different trajectories of a dyadic relationship. We did not exploit the possibility that the growth or deterioration of relationships might be related to opportunities and constraints arising from work, family obligations, or other of life's many realities and commitments. Our more recent work acknowledges the simultaneous interdependence of social units (Brown, 1992; Brown, Werner, & Altman, 1994). For example, in a transactional analysis of courtship, weddings, and placemaking, we focused on how couples are intricately connected to kin, friends, and the broader culture; how couple members related to one another; and how individual participants are connected to families, friends, in-laws, and others (Altman, Brown, Staples, & Werner, 1992). Thus, even if one is interested in one particular social unit, such as married couples, explicit recognition and clear delineation of other social units involved in engagement, affect, and regulation processes can enrich and add precision to an understanding of marital relationships.

OVERVIEW

The field of dialectics is thriving, so much so that its energy and diversity of ideas almost border on information overload. Given the remarkable proliferation of dialectic concepts, we proposed three pervasive and broadly conceived dialectic oppositions that might help anchor some of these concepts in a common vocabulary. Engagement, affective, and regulatory processes are evident or implicit in the work of both nondialectical and dialectical researchers, reflecting potentially universal processes in social relationships. *Engagement* refers to managing degrees of interdependence, a fundamental task for relationships. *Affect* includes blends of positive and negative processes and reflects fundamental social ways of relating. *Regulation* involves opposing decision making and operational processes in relationships. These three processes are seen as interdependent, with the blends of the three providing much of the richness of relationships. Conversely, research that overlooks one or more of the three processes reveals only a partial understanding of relationships.

We also articulated the mutualities and complementarities of our dialectical and transactional perspectives and suggested that research on personal relationships incorporate both approaches. Of particular importance, the TWV is distinctive in its call for the study of social, physical, temporal, and psychological aspects of social relationships; its emphasis on multiple observers of an event; and its recognition of the idea of formal cause or the search for coherent patterns of relationships.

We also proposed that concepts of stability and change apply to all dialectics instead of constituting their own dialectic oppositions. In addition, dialectic oppositions operate across many social units (dyads, families, neighborhoods, etc.). To the extent that research focuses on one social unit, it is useful to keep in mind that a chosen social unit does not exist in a vacuum, but functions in relationship to other social units as well.

Taken together, we have delineated a series of choice points and decisions facing dialectically oriented scholars. Too often, these choice points have only been implicitly addressed, with insufficient attention given to the consequences of these choices. If dialectically oriented work is to prosper, it is important that we make decisions and choices consciously and with forethought. This chapter articulated key decision domains and the choices we selected for our future research and theorizing. We invite dialogue with respect to whether these choice points and our decisions are also useful tools for other dialectically oriented scholars.

REFERENCES

Allan, G. (1993). Social structure and relationships. In S. Duck (Ed.), *Social context and relationships* (pp. 1–25). Newbury Park, CA: Sage.

Altman, I. (1975). *Environment and social behavior: Privacy, personal space, territory, and crowding.* Monterey, CA: Brooks/Cole.

Altman, I., Brown, B. B., Staples, B. A., & Werner, C. W. (1992). A transactional approach to close relationships: Courtship, weddings and placemaking. In B. Walsh, K. Craik, & R. Rice (Eds.), *Person–environment psychology* (pp. 193–241). Hillsdale, NJ: Lawrence Erlbaum Associates.

Altman, I., & Chemers, M. M. (1980). *Culture and environment.* Monterey, CA: Brooks/Cole.

Altman, I., & Gauvain, M. (1981). A cross-cultural and dialectic analysis of homes. In L. S. Liben, A. H. Patterson, & N. Newcombe (Eds.), *Spatial representation and behavior across the life span* (pp. 283–320). New York: Academic Press.

Altman, I., & Ginat, J. (1996). *Polygamous families in contemporary society.* New York: Cambridge University Press.

Altman, I., & Rogoff, B. (1987). World views in psychology: Trait, interactional, organismic, and transactional perspectives. In D. Stokols & I. Altman (Eds.), *Handbook of environmental psychology: Volume 1* (pp. 1–40). New York: Wiley.

Altman, I., Vinsel, A., & Brown, B. B. (1981). Dialectic conceptions in social psychology: An application to social penetration and privacy regulation. In L. Berkowitz (Ed.), *Advances in experimental social psychology: Vol. 14* (pp. 107–160). New York: Academic Press.

Askham, J. (1976). Identity and stability within the marriage relationship. *Journal of Marriage and the Family, 38,* 535–547.

Bales, R. F. (1950). *Interaction process analysis: A method for the study of small groups.* Reading, MA: Addison-Wesley.

Bales, R. F., & Cohen, S. P. (1979). *SYMLOG: A system for the multilevel observation of groups.* New York: The Free Press.

Bates, E. (1979). Response to Brainerd versus Aristotle with Piaget looking on. *Behavioral and Brain Sciences, 1,* 138–139.

Baxter, L. A. (1988). A dialectic perspective on communication strategies in relationship development. In S. W. Duck (Ed.), *A handbook of personal relationships* (pp. 257–273). New York: Wiley.

Baxter, L. A. (1993). The social side of personal relationships: A dialectic perspective. In S. Duck (Ed.), *Social contexts and relationships: Understanding relationship processes* (Vol. 3, pp. 139–169). Newbury Park, CA: Sage.

Baxter, L. A., & Montgomery, B. M. (1996). *Relating: Dialogues and dialectics.* New York: Guilford.

Benjamin, L. S. (1993). *Interpersonal diagnosis and treatment of personality disorders.* New York: Guilford.

Brown, B. B. (1992). The ecology of privacy and mood in a shared living group. *Journal of Environmental Psychology, 12,* 5–20.

Brown, B. B., Altman, I., & Werner, C. W. (1992). Close relationships in the physical and social world: Dialectic and transactional analyses. In S. Deetz (Ed.), *Communication yearbook 15* (pp. 509–522). Newbury Park, CA: Sage.

Brown, B. B., & Perkins, D. D. (1992). Disruptions in place attachment. In I. Altman & S. Low (Eds.), *Place attachment* (pp. 279–304). New York: Plenum.

Brown, B. B., & Werner, C. M. (1985). Social cohesiveness, territoriality, and holiday decorations: The influence of cul-de-sacs. *Environment and Behavior, 17,* 539–565.

Brown, B. B., Werner, C. M., & Altman, I. (1994). Close relationships in environmental context.

In A. L. Weber & J. H. Harvey (Eds.), *Perspectives on close relationships* (pp. 340–350). Boston: Allyn & Bacon.

Burgoon, J. K., & Hale, J. L. (1984). The fundamental topoi of relational communication. *Communication Monographs, 51,* 193–214.

Cooley, C. H. (1902). *Human nature and the social order.* New York: Scribner.

Conville, R. L. (1991). *Relational transitions: The evolution of personal relationships.* New York: Praeger.

Crohan, S. E. (1992). Marital happiness and spousal consensus on beliefs about marital conflict: A longitudinal investigation. *Journal of Social and Personal Relationships, 9*(1), 89–102.

Denzin, N. K. (1984). *On understanding emotion.* San Francisco: Jossey-Bass.

Duck, S., & Perlman, D. (1985). The thousand islands of personal relationships: A prescriptive analysis for future explorations. In S. Duck & D. Perlman (Eds.), *Understanding personal relationships: An interdisciplinary approach* (pp. 1–15). Beverly Hills, CA: Sage.

Felmlee, D. H. (1995). Fatal attractions: Affection and disaffection in intimate relationships. *Journal of Social and Personal Relationships, 12* (2), 295–311.

Fogel, A. (1994). Development and relationships: A dynamic model of communication. In J. B. Slater (Ed.), *Advances in the study of behavior, Vol. 24* (pp. 259–290). New York: Academic Press.

Fogel, A., Nwokah, E., Dedo, J. Y., Messinger, D., Dickson, K. L., Matusov, E., & Holt, S. A. (1992). Social process theory of emotion: A dynamic systems approach. *Social Development, 1,* 122–142.

Gauvain, M., Altman, I., & Fahim, H. (1983). Homes and social change: A cross-cultural analysis. In N. R. Feimer & E. S. Geller (Eds.), *Environmental psychology: Directions and perspectives* (pp. 80–218). New York: Praeger.

Georgoudi, M. (1983). Modern dialectics in social psychology: A reappraisal. *European Journal of Social Psychology, 13,* 77–93.

Gottman, J. M. (1979). *Marital interaction: Experimental investigations.* New York: Academic Press.

Henderson-King, D. H., & Veroff, J. (1994). *Journal of Social and Personal Relationships, 11,* 509–534.

Kuhn, T. (1970). *The structure of scientific revolutions.* Chicago: The University of Chicago Press.

Leary, T. (1957). *Interpersonal diagnosis of personality: A functional theory and methodology for personality evaluation.* New York: Ronald Press.

Markus, H. R., & Kitayama, S. A. (1994). A collective fear of the collective: Implications for selves and theories of selves. *Personality and Social Psychology Bulletin, 20,* 568–579.

Masheter, C., & Harris, L. (1986). From divorce to friendship: A study of dialectic relationship development. *Journal of Social and Personal Relationships, 3,* 177–190.

Mead, G. H. (1934). *Mind, self, and society.* Chicago: University of Chicago Press.

Millar, F. E., & Rogers, L. E. (1987). Relational dimensions of interpersonal dynamics. In M. E. Roloff & G. R. Miller (Eds.), *Interpersonal processes: New directions in communication research* (pp. 117–139). Newbury Park, CA: Sage.

Miller, D. T., & Prentice, D. A. (1994). The self and the collective. *Personality and Social Pyschology Bulletin, 20,* 451–453.

Montgomery, B. M. (1992). Communication as the interface between couples and culture. *Communication Yearbook, 15,* 475–507.

Oxley, D., Haggard, L. M., Werner, C. M., & Altman, I. (1986). Transactional qualities of neighborhood social networks: A case study of "Christmas Street." *Environment and Behavior, 18,* 640–677.

Patterson, M. L. (1984). Intimacy, social control, and nonverbal involvement: A functional approach. In V. J. Derlega (Ed.), *Communication, intimacy, and close relationships* (pp. 105–132). New York: Academic Press.

Rawlins, W. K. (1989). A dialectic anlaysis of the tensions, functions, and strategic challenges of communication in young adult friendships. *Communication Yearbook, 12,* 157–189.

Rawlins, W. K. (1992). *Friendship matters: Communication, dialectics, and the life course.* New York: de Gruyter.

Rawlins, W. K., & Holl, M. (1988). Adolescents' interactions with parents and friends: Dialectics of temporal perspective and evaluation. *Journal of Social and Personal Relationships, 5,* 27–46.

Schutz, W. C. (1966). *The interpersonal underworld.* Palo Alto, CA: Science & Behavior Books.

Simmel, G. (1950). *The sociology of Georg Simmel.* (K. Wolff, Trans.). New York: Macmillan. (Original work published 1908)

Steil, J. M., & Weltman, K. (1992). Influence strategies at home and at work: A study of sixty dual career couples. *Journal of Social and Personal Relationships, 9,* 65–88.

Sullivan, H. S. (1953). *The interpersonal theory of psychiatry.* New York: Norton.

Weimann, J. M. (1985). Interpersonal control and regulation in conversation. In R. L. Street & J. N. Capella (Eds.), *Sequence and pattern in communicative behavior* (pp. 85–102). London: Edward Arnold.

Werner, C. W., Altman, I., & Brown, B. B. (1992). A transactional approach to personal relationship: physical environments, social contexts, and temporal qualities. *Journal of Social and Personal Relationships, 9,* 297–323.

Werner, C. M., Altman, I., Brown, B. B., & Ginat, J. (1993). Celebrations in personal relationships: A transactional/dialectic perspective. In S. Duck (Ed.), *Social context and relationships* (pp. 109–138). Newbury Park, CA: Sage.

Werner, C. M., & Baxter, L. A. (1994). Temporal qualities of relationships: Organismic, transactional, and dialectical views. In M. L. Knapp & G. R. Miller (Eds.), *Handbook of interpersonal communication* (2nd ed., pp. 323–379). Newbury Park, CA: Sage.

Werner, C. M., Haggard, L. M., Altman, I., & Oxley, D. (1988). Temporal qualities of rituals and celebrations: A comparison of Christmas Street and Zuni Shalako. In J. E. McGrath (Ed.), *The social psychology of time: New perspectives* (pp. 203–232). Beverly Hills, CA: Sage.

Zebrowitz, L. A. (1990). *Social perception.* Monterey, CA: Brooks/Cole.

8

Dialogism and Relational Dialectics*

BARBARA M. MONTGOMERY
Millersville University

LESLIE A. BAXTER
University of Iowa

INTRODUCTION

Our goal in this chapter is to describe a pattern of thinking about interpersonal communication that we call "relational dialectics." Partly because of the norms of scholarship and partly because of our own styles, we emphasize here a systematic, logically asserted version of relational dialectics more than an analogic, holistic vision. Yet, the latter vision is every bit as important to grasp because it extends understanding of our dialectical perspective beyond its central assumptions and questions to how those assumptions and questions are integrated into a dialectical view of relationships. So before we sprinkle the body of this chapter with references to people like Mikhail Bakhtin, Michael Billig, Irv Altman, and other scholars who have influenced our conceptual understanding of dialogism and dialectics, we would like to turn your thoughts momentarily to people like Duke Ellington, Anita Baker, and Marcus Roberts, who have influenced our understanding of its spirit.

Jazz has much in common with our notions about dialectics. Jazz is musically identified by its inclusiveness and its improvisation. Jazz musicians have open invitations to "sit in on a gig," to lend their unique vocal and instrumental sounds to the event, and they readily encourage each other to stretch their musical contributions beyond the givens to the potentials of the moment. Collaboration is in the service of spontaneous creativity. The musi-

---

*This chapter is adapted with permission by Guilford Publications, Inc. from *Relating: Dialogues and Dialectics* (1996) by Baxter and Montgomery.

cal score and deep structures of jazz provide just enough guidance to allow for coordination in making music, but an accompanying irreverence for the music as written allows for the synergy of improvisation. Players, composer, and even audience jointly participate in a creative dialogue that characterizes good jazz (Oldfather & West, 1994).

This same spirit permeates our notion of relational dialectics. It is a way of understanding social interaction that is marked by a healthy dose of irony, a sense that things are both what they seem to be and something else as well. Irony entertains both belief and doubt, both hope and despair, both serious-ness and play, and in these kinds of complexities, it hints at the very nature of relational dialectics. Creativity is another hallmark. Relational dialectics de-mands that we reach beyond our ready-made vocabularies of generalized central tendencies to appreciate the uniqueness of each communicative mo-ment. Inclusiveness is key as well. Our notion of relational dialectics respects different meaning systems, is attuned to their distinct voices, and so, repre-sents a multivocal social reality. Last, we wish to stress the sense of fluidity and unfinalizability that characterizes our relational dialectics approach. All is becoming, but never becomes.

The metaphor of jazz conveys these qualities well. Jazz is musically identi-fied by its inclusiveness and its improvisation; coordination of unique, some-times discordant voices happens in the service of spontaneous, creatively synergistic music. So imagine a bit of Arturo Sandoval or Eddie Palmieri playing in the background as you read this chapter, and let that analogic metaphor frame the logic-based assertions that follow.

CONCEPTUALLY DIFFERENTIATING RELATIONAL DIALECTICS

On the generic conceptual foundations of contradiction, change, praxis and totality, we have constructed a version of dialectics heavily influenced by the dialogic thinking associated with Mikhail Bakhtin (1981, 1984, 1986). Bakhtin wrote the bulk of his work in the Soviet Union in the 1920s and 1930s. Critical of the rigidity that he perceived in Stalinist dialectical materi-alism, he worked at the intellectual and geographic fringes of Soviet society, largely for political reasons. Because of his marginalized status, his work was slow to be published and even slower to be translated. Nevertheless, since its rediscovery in the 1970s and 1980s, Bakhtin's perspective has gained new stature in areas such as literary criticism, social theory, rhetoric, and commu-nication.

The essence of Bakhtin's dialogic view holds that dialogue—both as an actual, real-time, interpersonal process and as a conceptual metaphor for understanding more abstract cultural, historical, and relational phenomena—is the glue that holds social existence together. Here, we can only sketch the implications of Bakhtin's dialogism for extending and reframing the basic notions of dialectics. We present a more developed treatment of these themes in a recently published book that not only traces the historical roots and contemporary developments of dialectical thinking about relationships, but also describes the implications of a dialogic dialectics for creating alternatives to established lines of communication and relationship research (Baxter & Montgomery, 1996).

A Dialogic View of Contradiction: Centrifugal-Centripetal Dynamics

Without exception, dialectical scholars explicitly proclaim that contradiction is a ubiquitous aspect of social relationships and that communication plays a most significant role in the ongoing experience of contradictions. We wish to make four additional observations about contradiction that differentiate relational dialectics from other dialectical views.

First, dialectical contradictions are not represented well with simple, binary oppositions, which has been the tendency among most scholars currently working from a dialectical perspective, including ourselves. We have come to realize that it is much too simple and mechanistic to reduce the dialectics of relationships to a series of polar oppositions like certainty versus novelty, autonomy versus connection, and openness versus closedness. Rather, contradictions are better conceived as complex, overlapping domains of *centripetal* or dominant forces juxtaposed with *centrifugal* or countervailing forces. Thus, the centripetal relational feature of certainty is countered by several centrifugal oppositions that co-exist—certainty–unpredictability, certainty–novelty, certainty–mystery, certainty–excitement, and so on. Although each of these dynamic juxtapositions is worthy of study, taken together, they form a knot of functional and interdependent contradictions that add validating depth and richness to a scholarly treatment of relational interaction. Similarly, connection as a centripetal force in personal relationships is in dynamic and opposing associations with a host of centrifugal forces like autonomy, privacy, self-assertion, and independence. Understanding connection in personal relationships depends, then, on exploring this range of associations. Openness and closedness also consist of a knot of oppositions rather than a simple binary pair. Openness–lying, openness–discretion, and openness–silence are but a few. Our dialogic view of dialectics commits us to describing such knots of socially situated contradictions.

Second, we are uncomfortable in distinguishing primary from secondary contradictions, although many do (e.g., see Brown et al., chap. 7, this volume), and we have done so in the past. Such a distinction now seems premature to us, given the current level of understanding of relationships. We are persuaded by Fitch's (1994) argument that asserting a common core of contradictions presumes a level of cultural homogeneity that is not warranted. It also assumes a progressive, cause–effect patterning, whereby primary contradictions beget secondary contradictions that we have not observed in our study of everyday interactions. We emphasize, instead, dynamic, indeterminant patternings that characterize systems of contradictions. We invoke this notion of causation in its most general sense to indicate that the ongoing interplay between opposite tendencies is what drives change.

Third, we hold that there is no finite set of contradictions in personal relationships to be discovered. As Billig (1987) notes, infinite possibilities for relational oppositions exist, depending on historically, culturally, and relationally salient topics of conversation. Another way of thinking about the limitless potential for contradictory themes is Bakhtin's (1984) notion that social moments are polyphonic, involving multiple, fully valid voices representing different perspectives, no matter the issue. Thus, as couples cocreate their relational world in the dynamic context of a society, they are bound to realize differences, oppositions, and contradictions. The issue of the moment, the agenda of the day, the expectations of the era are all breeding grounds for centripetal and centrifugal forces. The most meaningful challenge for scholars is not to catalog the definitive set of contradictions in personal relationships, but to contribute to the understanding of the processes by which couples create, realize, and deal with dialectical tensions.

Fourth, unlike other dialectical approaches in which discrete domains, such as individuals, relationships, and society, are demarcated and characterized by their respective sets of contradictions, we locate contradictions in the process of relating that occurs between and among people. As we elaborate in the following section, the individual and the social are dialogically inseparable. The individual self becomes only in relating, and relating both produces and reproduces an historical–cultural–social milieu. Contradictions, thus, are relational phenomena.

Monologic, Dualistic, and Dialogic Visions of Change

Relational dialectics is infused with dialogism and so can be distinguished from alternative monologic and dualistic views. Monologic approaches treat communication as one-sided and univoiced. As in a monologue, the focus is on sameness, on the centripetal to the neglect of the centrifugal–centripetal dynamic, which creates a fiction of consistency and completeness. We see this fiction in scholarly representations that privilege unidirectional development and maintenance of openness, interdependence, trust, certainty, and a host of other assumed-to-be-positive qualities in personal relationships (for a review, see Montgomery, 1988). We see it in a preoccupation with the individual as the unit of analysis and the relegation of the other to "merely an object of consciousness, and not another consciousness . . . [whose response] . . . could change everything in the world of my consciousness" (Bakhtin, 1984, p. 293). All of these instances elevate the tedious sameness of one voice speaking.

Dialectical views are not immune to monologism. Approaches that stress transcendence of dialectical contradictions through synthesis often equate transcendence with resolution and resolution with achieving a univoiced perspective. For instance, Conville (1992) seems to assume that "the dialectic disappears" with transcendence and second-order change, and he allows for long periods free from dialectical stress between relational transitions (p. 138). Weeks and his colleagues (e.g., Bopp & Weeks, 1984) take a similar view in their explication of the dialectics of family functioning. This monologic notion is foreign to our view of relational dialectics. Instead, we view transcendence not as resolution, but merely as a reframing of a dialectical tension that serves to perpetuate it in a new form. "Friends," grappling with the contradictions between their platonic history of behavior and their sexual attraction for each other, may reframe their relationship as "lovers," but still have to grapple with tensions between spiritual and passionate caring. Foreground tensions may recede to background, but they never are resigned to speaking their presence in one voice; they always require at least two, usually many more.

Dualism, in contrast to monologism, acknowledges and gives expression to countervailing forces in relationships. A dualistic conceptualization contends that couples are open sometimes and closed other times and are aware of the pressures to do both in the relationship. Yet, dualistic views do not emphasize the ongoing, indeterminant interplay of complex, contradictory elements. Instead, they tend to treat contradictory elements either as simple polarities or as independent forces. As simple polarities, each element is assigned to opposite anchoring points on a single dimension. Communication between relational partners is perceived to slide between each polarity, being more open or more closed, more autonomous or more connected, more honest or more dishonest, more competent or more incompetent. Thus, the complexities of interpersonal interaction are reduced to a series of binary oppositions in a zero-sum game. Alternatively, some researchers treat contradictory elements as if they were independent, relegating them to parallel but virtually unrelated relational spheres of existence. For example, extensive research exists on self-disclosure and its binary opposite, privacy regulation. However, this research is dualistic so long as each phenomenon is conceived to be definitionally, developmentally, and behaviorally independent. Indeed, much of the research on these two themes has proceeded in just this way, emphasizing the parallel oppositions of openness and privacy regulation, but ignoring their interactive unity (for exceptions, see Brown et al., chap. 7, this volume).

By contrast, a dialogic approach emphasizes how parties manage the simultaneous exigency for both disclosure and privacy in their relationships and, especially, how the "both/and"ness of disclosure and privacy is patterned through their interplay across the temporal course of their relationship. Dialogic approaches, including relational dialectics, implicate a kind of in-the-moment, interactive multivocality, in which multiple points of view retain their integrity as they play off each other. Dialogism, thus, detours communication scholars from the search for shared meanings and balanced, homeostatic solutions by celebrating the multiplicity in perspectives. The "truth" of relationships, then, is not tied to any single consciousness or idealization of merged consciousnesses, but is premised on an ever-present multiplicity of meanings and points of view. Partners may be aware of the complex centripetal and centrifugal forces in their relationship, and they certainly act in particular, patterned ways to deal with those forces, but those forces are never transcended. Partners cannot simply choose to be either open or closed, either supportive of the other or assertive of the self, or either interdependent or independent. They must act in ways that express both the prevailing centripetal themes and the implicated centrifugal themes, simultaneously. These ways are not usually found in the happy mediums of compromise and balance, but more typically, in messier and more inconsistent unfolding practices of the moment.

Additionally, those practices of the moment reflect an interactive dynamic among the various centripetal and centrifugal themes, such that they are constantly in a state of redefining themselves, recalibrating their intensities, and reorganizing their relevancies to the communicative moment. This interactive, dynamic aspect of dialogic thinking is critical.

The distinctions we make among monologic, dualistic, and dialogic visions of change have implications for understanding all aspects of relating, but perhaps the significance is best illustrated by considering the issue of relationship change, more commonly called "relationship development." Our view of relationship change has made us suspicious of the very term *development* because it implicates monologic progress, a presumption of unidirectional, linear, usually quantitative and cumulative change toward some idealized or preferred end state. In sharp contrast, we propose that a relationship begins with the interplay of contradictory voices and a relationship ends with dialogic silence. Between these points in time/space, we propose the concept of dialogic complexity as an alternative to the concept of progress to describe change. By *dialogic complexity,* we refer to a relational system that is characterized by a knot of contradictions that stimulate multidirectional, spiraling, qualitative and quantitative change that has meaning in its own right rather than in relation to some anticipated end state. Dialogic complexity is captured by simultaneous moreness and lessness on a variety of contradiction-based characteristics, for example, more and less interdependence, more and less openness, and so forth. Thus, relationships move both "upward" and "downward," both "toward" and "away from," and both "forward" and "backward." However, centrifugal movement is not framed as regressive; the various spatial metaphors of "downward," "away from," and "backward" are stripped of their negative connotations of non-progress. Thus, movement and change assume a rightful and significant meaning in the moment. Following from this, acquaintanceship, friendship, and romantic attachment cease to be seen as less developed forms of the idealized relationship of marriage, but stand conceptually on their own ground with attendant dialogic complexities. Middle periods of relationships cease to be defined as holding patterns of homeostatic equilibrium associated with achieving idealized destinations, but instead are seen as periods of dynamic and ongoing improvisational change that sustain the relationship. The result is a portrait of relationship process as dynamic flux, or as Bakhtin would have it, inexhaustible possibilities.

Communication, Relationships, and Praxis

Foremost in our thinking is the assumption that personal relationships are constituted in communication. We use the term, *communication,* judiciously and with specific meaning. For us, it captures the spirit of Bakhtin's (1984) dialogism, Billig's (1987) rhetorical argumentation, and Bateson's (1972) relational view. It encompasses, simultaneously, referential and relational information. It is an interactive, involving, and situated process that produces multiple meanings that simultaneously both differentiate and connect participants. Communication is the vehicle of social definition; participants develop their senses of self, partners develop their senses of their relationship, and societies develop their senses of identity through the process of communication.

The term *communication* implicates the full range of human actions—verbal and nonverbal, vocal and nonvocal, intended and unintended, sincere and contrived—that can be meaningfully interpreted in interpersonal settings. Thus, language and utterances are important informational elements in our relational dialectics perspective, but so too are such factors as intonation, style, pacings and rhythms, gestures, gazes, and myriad other actions that figure in interpretations of meanings.

We also recognize a unique kind of communication that is possible in personal relationships and makes personal relationships possible. Shotter (1993) begins to capture its essence with his notion of *joint action,* a special form of communication not understandable through public traditions or individual predispositions, but rather one that must be addressed as creatively and uniquely constituted in partners' interlaced actions. Following from Bateson's (1972) work, many refer to this as "the relational level of meaning." Its purview is broad, encompassing private meaning systems (Baxter, 1987; Montgomery, 1988), unique relational cultures (Montgomery, 1992; Wood,

1982), communicator style (Norton, 1983), and implicit assertions about the relationship between interactants (Rogers & Millar, 1988). Bakhtin (1981, 1984, 1986) builds his dialogic ideas on a similar notion: The self exists only in relation with others, and communication constitutes that relationship.

If communication is the bridge between partners, then their relationship is at the gap. Relationships exist in time–space between people, in the "world in between consciousness" (Clark & Holquist, 1984, p. 9). In more intimate relationships, the gap undoubtedly narrows and can even approach merger from time to time, but merger is never quite accomplished. Multivocality is inherent in social existence and so interpersonal voices are always unmerged. Even when partners appear to hold the same view, they do so from different perspectives. Moments of complete or pure joint action, of merger, cannot exist. Rather, close relationships, like all social systems, are always and simultaneously comprised of both fusion with and differentiation from, both centripetal and centrifugal forces, both interdependence and independence. In each is the seed for the other. From a relational dialectics perspective, bonding occurs when both interdependence with the other and independence from the other promote relational well-being. Perhaps Bakhtin's greatest contribution to our thinking about personal relationships is his celebration of this assumption.

Bakhtin also enriched the notion of dialectical praxis, which posits that relationship parties communicatively react to dialectical exigencies that have been produced from their past interactions and, in so doing, they recreate the dialectical circumstances that they will face in the future. From Bakhtin's dialogic perspective, interaction between relationship parties is laced with a broader variety of praxical reverberations: a dialogue of the distant already-spoken with the expressed utterance of the present; a dialogue of the immediately prior utterances with the present utterance; a dialogue of the present utterance with the anticipated response of the listener, and a dialogue of the present utterance with the anticipated response of a generalized other, whom Bakhtin (1986) refers to as the *superaddressee*.

In this quartet of givens that are inherent in any utterance, relationship parties create new dialogic realities in their praxical, communicative choices of the moment. Much like jazz improvisations, these praxical improvisations are both creative and reflective of established patterns. Over the years, we (Baxter, 1988, 1990; Baxter & Montgomery, 1996; Montgomery, 1992, 1993) have described and illustrated some of the more frequently recurring patterns. For instance, *denial* patterns represent an effort to subvert, obscure, or deny the presence of a contradiction by legitimating only one dialectical force to the exclusion of countervailing ones. The couple that tries to "tell each other everything," to be completely open, denies the legitimacy of keeping some things secret, excluding some details, retaining some privacy, and so on. *Disorientation* involves a fatalistic attitude in which contradictions are regarded as inevitable, negative, and unresponsive to praxical change. Much like the animals in the classic learned helplessness studies (Seligman, 1975), some couples facing the continual contradictions of social existence seem to resign themselves to a frustrating, debilitating relational life that they cannot understand much less change, but that they continue to recreate in their interaction (Bateson, 1972; Cronen, Pearce & Snavely, 1979). *Spiraling inversion* describes alternation between and among contradictory forces over time, as when a couple establishes a rhythm between being autonomous and being connected over a week's agenda of activities. *Segmentation* describes alternation over topic or activity domains; for example, a couple may typically spend vacation time together to go hiking, but he takes additional time away from her to climb mountains and she takes time away from him to ski. *Balance* is typified by compromise in which the parties dilute oppositions by fulfilling them only in part, as when a couple tries to achieve and maintain a middle point between openness and closedness—a style of communication that is not wholly one or the other, but somewhere in between. *Integration* is a response by which the parties fully respond to all opposing forces at once. A family that comes together at dinner time to celebrate each individual's autonomy through serial reports of the day's happenings has established a praxical ritual that integrates the forces of connection and autonomy. *Recalibration* reframes a contradiction such that the polarities are encompassed in one another, thereby transcending the form of an opposition without resolving it. For instance, a couple in a long-distance marriage would likely experience quite vividly the contradictory forces of connection and autonomy. If they responded by frequently sending each other love letters, presents, and daily e-mail messages, they might come to perceive that they are closer while they remain separated. Finally, *reaffirmation* involves an acceptance of the inevitability of contradiction, but in contrast to disorientation patterns that lament this fact, reaffirmation celebrates contradiction as the essence of social existence. This positive, reaffirming approach is evident in couples who see the dialectical challenges of relating as signs that their relationship "is real," "is interesting," or "is alive."

Descriptions of these recurring patterns, however, are insufficient for understanding praxis without also attending to the creativity of the interactive moment. Our scholarly attention, therefore, is turning more and more toward consideration of the unintended consequences, emergent possibilities, and trial-and-error nature of social interaction.

Totality

Volosinov/Bakhtin (1973)[1] eloquently remind us that "meaning is context bound, but that context is boundless" (pp. 218–219). Communication is al-

---

[1]In recognition of the uncertainty of authorship associated with this work, we choose to use both authors' names in the citation.

ways situated in historical, environmental, cultural, relational, and individual contexts. According to Bakhtin, the *chronotopic* nature of communication obligates researchers to take both sociospatial and temporal contexts into account. Most social scholarship tends to privilege only the sociospatial context to the relative neglect of the temporal context (Werner & Baxter, 1994). Temporality is addressed by attending not only to processes in and through time, but also to processes by which actors jointly construct meaningful continuities and discontinuities among the past, present, and future. Like Bakhtin, we are suspicious of teleological approaches that privilege dialectical synthesis; instead, we view relationship change as fundamentally indeterminant. Relationship parties act within the context of constant interplay between stability and change and they do so in emergent ways that cannot be predetermined.

Heraclitus, through his river analogy, and Altman and his colleagues (1990; see Brown et al., chap. 7, this volume), through their transactional view, emphasize the integration of people in dialogue into the ongoing flow of the social context; people "act into" a context. They are, at once, going with the flow, but in doing so, they are affecting the flow and becoming part of the pattern. Persuaded by these notions, we have developed some uneasiness with perspectives that have people acting primarily out of, because of, or in reaction to the context. These views invest context with a directional, causal power foreign to the interactive tenets of relational dialectics. Thus, we are less inclined to presume the kinds of life-cycle forces espoused by Rawlins (1992) in his discussion of life stages or the progressive relationship phases espoused by Conville (1991).

Totality, as we envision it, encourages us to think about the world as a process of relations or interdependencies. A husband and wife in conversation, for instance, continually and simultaneously act as individuals, as a couple, and as members of their community and of their culture. A smile, a question, an argument, a celebration simultaneously express aspects of these different social relationships involving the couple. Furthermore, any particular action or set of actions may simultaneously address different dialectical forces in these different relational connections. Strolling arm in arm, oblivious to their neighbors, and closely attentive to each other, partners may express connection to each other, disconnection with their neighbors, and yet connection to the generalized others of their culture who subscribe to such behavior as normative for intimate couples. Multiple identities of selves, relationships, communities, and cultures emerge in the process of such interactions, and we are becoming increasingly intrigued with the interconnections among these processes.

Personal relationships, for instance, are, at once, both an ongoing product and producer of social dialogue. Relationships are created in the communicative interactions involving selves and societies, but also create selves and societies. That is, the interaction of partners, simultaneously defines their own relationship and relationships, in general, in their culture. We extend this notion by recognizing that there are multidirectional communicative pathways among selves, relationships, and cultures. Constructive repercussions flow in many directions at the same time. Cultural constructions, like the number one song on some chart, are appropriated to be unique relational constructions, like "our song" that, in turn, influence the cultural construction, in this example by perhaps extending the song's stay on the charts. In this kind of praxical pattern, the song becomes both "everyone's song" and "our song," and in each instance, it can have distinctive, even contradictory significance in the meanings constructed from its lyrics and melody. The point to be made is that these constructions do not exist in a social vacuum. Their influence flows throughout the social structure demarcated by selves, relationships, and cultures.

SOME IMPLICATIONS FOR UNDERSTANDING RELATIONAL INTERACTION

Adopting a relational dialectics perspective leads to a rethinking of established interpretations of interpersonal communication, which have mainly been monologic, sometimes dualistic, but rarely dialogic. Space constraints limit our discussion here to only a couple of the examples we have developed to illustrate the differences among monologic, dualistic, and dialogic ways of conceptualizing (see Baxter & Montgomery, 1996).

Rethinking Closeness

Perhaps the strongest presumption in the study of relationship quality is that closeness varies in sync with mutual dependence (e.g., Rusbult, Drigotas, & Verette, 1994), perceptual congruence (e.g., Byrne, 1992), and positive affect (e.g., Hatfield & Rapson, 1993). Essentially, this monologic view subscribes to the notion that the more interdependent, similar, and loving a couple is, the closer, more viable their relationship is. Some voices of counterpoint to this assumption can be identified if one listens carefully. Some argue that partners need to be differentiated from each other in order to develop healthy self-identities (Askam, 1976) and to expand their personal efficacy (Aron & Aron, 1986). A few others argue that personal privacy is an important need in relationships (Burgoon, 1982). Still others argue that conflict is normal and functional in close relationships (Hawes & Smith, 1973). These voices of counterpoint represent a dualistic view, one that recognizes that closeness is sometimes achieved with mutual independence, difference, and negative affect.

To move the analysis of closeness to a dialogic perspective, however, requires a sensitivity to the simultaneous interplay in relationships between centripetal and centrifugal forces of both unity and division. Bakhtin's (1984, 1986) notion of the social self, which shares some qualities with Mead's (1934) conceptualization of self, constitutes the best first lesson in thinking dialogically. A dialogic view of self rejects conceptions of self as unitary, autonomous, private, and separate; dialogism also rejects conceptions of self as fused, joined, blended and communed with the other. Instead, dialogism assumes that the forces of both separateness and togetherness are constantly engaged during a couple's interactions. As each force plays off the other over time, senses of self are created. Thus, the self is always becoming and is known only through the metaphors of mind, emotion, and spirit that emerge in the language of our interaction with others. As Clark and Holquist (1984) paraphrase Bakhtin:

> As a unique becoming, my I-for-myself is always invisible. In order to perceive that self, it must find expression in categories that can fix it, and these I can only get from the other. So that when I complete the other, or when the other completes me, she and I are actually exchanging the gift of a perceptible self. (p. 79)

This dialogic view holds salient both the self as distinctively realized and the self as reflected by the other. Such a multivocal view of self emerges only when scholars incorporate into their thinking the simultaneous interaction between the forces of autonomy and the forces of connection. In that ongoing, dynamic tension, selves are created and recreated.

Assuming this kind of interplay between the contradictory radiants of connectedness and the radiants of separateness as the basis for relational research produces a complicated view of closeness. Interviewed couples, for instance, describe a "Me–We Pull," a desire to be with the partner while at the same time to be separate from the partner "to be their own person and to do their own thing" (Baxter, 1990, p. 76). The salience of this Me–We Pull appears not to be associated with the overall level of satisfaction in a relationship. We suspect that this is because, first, most partners, at least in our culture, regard the autonomy–connection tension to be an inherent feature of being in a relationship, and second, satisfaction and dissatisfaction may be associated more with how the autonomy–connection contradiction is managed moment to moment (i.e., the praxical patterns) rather than its presence, per se. Both of these suspicions deserve concentrated scholarly investigation.

Understanding the Me–We Pull is further complicated by its multivocal character. It is expressed in different forms and emerges differently in different interactive circumstances. Goldsmith (1990), for instance, describes five different meanings that couples in a qualitative interview study associated with the tensions surrounding autonomy and connection. These included whether or not to enter into a romantic relationship, whether or not to be engaged in an exclusive relationship, how to apportion time and energy given competing demands of relating and the demands of other life activities, how to be fair and tolerant of partners' sometimes contradictory rights and obligations to each other, and whether or not the relationship would involve a long-term commitment. Reading the relationship literature with an eye to the multivocal meanings of autonomy and connection suggests that meanings change with changes in family structure like the birth of the first child (Stamp, 1994), movement toward relationship dissolution (Baxter, 1983; Masheter, 1991), maturation through the life cycle (Rawlins, 1992), and pervasive changes in couple dynamics, like negotiating dual careers (Hertz, 1986) or long-distance relationships (Gerstel & Gross, 1984). Researchers with a dialogic view of dialectics are likely to study the interactive dynamics of these relational moments. Their goal is to render a description of closeness and attendant centrifugal forces that is less tidy, more inconsistent, and less finished than descriptions rendered by those with monologic and dualistic perspectives, but in so being, reflects key qualities of the relational lives they are studying.

Rethinking Certainty

Considering the dialectical tensions among the many manifestations of certainty and uncertainty provides another extended example that illustrates how a dialogic perspective leads to a rethinking of established presumptions. The search for predictability and order is the scientific enterprise as it has been commonly understood. It is not surprising, then, that certainty occupies the monologic seat of privilege in the study of communication in personal relationships. Well-established research programs have equated relationship processes with efforts to reduce uncertainty (e.g., Berger & Bradac, 1982) and to develop stable cognitive knowledge structures like role definitions (e.g., Forgas, 1979), protypes (e.g., Fehr, 1993), plans and scripts (e.g., Berger & Bell, 1988), and more abstract memory organizing schemes (e.g., Honeycutt, 1993). Closely aligned with this body of research are efforts to describe stable sets of communication strategies by which relationship partners seek to accomplish goals such as affinity seeking, information seeking about the other and the status of the relationship, compliance gaining, social support, maintaining the relationship, and disengaging from the relationship (see Daly & Wiemann, 1994, for a review). The presumed link between mind and action that underpins these lines of inquiry precludes the dialogic notion of indeterminancy in social interaction. These monologic research efforts deemphasize the contingency of the interactive moment in favor of a rationalistic view of the person as goal directed.

Dualistic voices can be heard in this literature as well, and they tend to argue one of three positions. First, some critique the theories that privilege certainty by providing research data and interpretations that run counter to major theoretical predictions (e.g., Planalp & Honeycutt, 1985; VanLear & Trujillo, 1986). Second, some claim that uncertainty, excitement, spontaneity, unpredictability, and novelty are salient or important to the well-being of relationships (e.g., Aron & Aron, 1986; Cupach & Metts, 1986). Finally, others (e.g., Fitzpatrick, 1988; Mikulas & Vodanovich, 1993) report that there is great variability among individuals and among relationships in their demand thresholds for certainty and uncertainty. That is, some people and some couples possess a propensity for thrill seeking, ambiguity, and change, and others need stability, rigidity, and order.

Assuming a dialogic view leads to different patterns of thinking about relating, compared to these monologic and dualistic notions. Unlike much of the work just reviewed—in which certainty and uncertainty are conceptualized as individual-level phenomena residing in the self-contained mind of one person about the other—dialogic conceptualizations view certainty and uncertainty as jointly owned by both interactors. Individuals do not simply observe another's degree of consistency and predictability, but they help to construct it through dialogue. Also, dialogic views respect not only the givens from the past that others associate with plans, prototypes, and predispositions, but also the spontaneity of the present. Furthermore, they assume that the present can transform the past. One example is when couples undertake revisionist history by reconstructing their joint memory of their past (e.g., Duck, Pond, and Leatham, 1991). In addition, dialogic thinkers acknowledge the interaction between certainty and uncertainty, recognizing, for instance, that each is dependent on and interactively defined by the other. For instance, the existence of a choice, an uncertainty, gives couples the attributional evidence needed to reach a stable conclusion about themselves and their relationship. Similarly, the certainty associated with relational trust and security motivates couples to embrace new experiences, thereby preventing stagnation. A dialogic perspective also encourages exploration of the multivocal meanings associated with the certainty and uncertainty dialectic. For instance, a re-analysis of Baxter's (1990) couple interview data indicates that informants variously connected this dialectic with knowledge about individual partners, plans for getting together, the novelty versus routine of their interactions, the emotional excitement of romance, and the state of the relationship. Furthermore, these radiants of meaning appeared in a roughly chronological sequence across couples. However, earlier sense makings did not necessarily disappear with the emergence of a subsequent meaning; rather, the pattern that emerged in the informant discourse was that of increasingly complex layering of dialectical meanings. Finally, a dialogic rethinking encourages examination of praxis patterns by which couples behaviorally manage the certainty–uncertainty knot of contradictions.

Although dialectically oriented research in this vein is quite limited to date, evidence suggests that couples engage a number of the praxis patterns that are associated with other dialectical tensions. That is, partners have been observed to variously oscillate between moments of certainty and uncertainty in an effort to fulfill both necessities over time (Hause & Pearson, 1994), to segment the dialectic by privileging certainty when the issue is knowledge about the partner and the state of the relationship and by privileging uncertainty when the issue is romance and the immediate interaction episode (Baxter, 1990), and to integrate the two forces in spontaneously enacted, daily rituals, like teasing, that allow them to address needs for novelty and stimulation while meeting needs for predictability and certainty (e.g., Bruess, 1994).

The examples of dialogic rethinking that we have sketched here in short descriptive strokes are suggestive of the themes in a growing body of inquiry consistent with a relational dialectic perspective. These example also indicate that we are only beginning to realize the complex implications of revising our thinking about communication in personal relationships.

DIALOGIC INQUIRY

Just as we believe that social phenomena can be more richly understood as dialogue between and among multiple disparate meanings, we believe that inquiry can be similarly enriched with an infusion of dialogic thinking. Because inquiry is a kind of social interaction as is relational communication, to the extent that we recognize and encourage a dialogic view of communication in personal relationships, we must also do so with regard to inquiry.

To set the stage for a dialogic discussion of inquiry, examine the diagram in Fig. 8.1, which we slightly modified from Rosengren (1989). The diagram describes alternative conclusions about research findings, depending on whether researchers represent the same perspective and whether they find the same results. Considering the cells in order, Cell 1 includes those instances when different researchers adopt the same perspective and report similar results. This epitomizes the traditional notion of objectivity. Even if one takes this as evidence for an objective, singular reality, one must consider whether such findings reflect more how something is being studied than what is being studied. Cell 2 represents the ideal of triangulation: different perspectives leading to the same conclusions. Seemingly, such consensus occurs from time to time. Yet, Bakhtin (1986) cautions that even when people coming from different perspectives agree, they do so from different points of

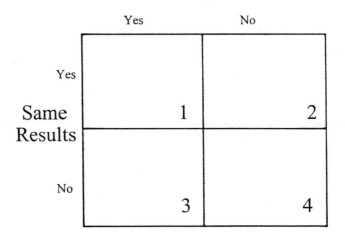

FIG. 8.1   Alternative conclusions about research findings. From "Paradigms Lost and Regained," by K. E. Rosengren, 1989, in B. Dervin,
L. Grossberg, B. J. O'Keefe, and E. Wartella (Eds.), *Rethinking Communication, Volume 1: Paradigm Issues,* Newbury Park, CA: Sage,
p. 33, copyright © 1989 by Sage. Adapted by permission of Sage.

reference, and so, are agreeing to something that is different for each of
them. We liken this to a scene in Woody Allen's *Annie Hall,* in which the
main characters, when asked how often they make love, give the same quantitative answer: "three or four times a week"; but he interprets this to mean,
"Almost never," and she interprets it to mean, "Constantly." Cell 3, depicting different conclusions from research conducted from the same perspective, is considered a problem, even a failure, by many social researchers.
However, dialogic scholars who do not subscribe to a stable, objective reality
but assume constant change, contradictory social factors, and socially constructed knowledge expect situations represented by this third cell and are
not disturbed by them.

Cell 4 especially captivates our scholarly interest because it represents different perspectives leading to different conclusions, which is the angst of a
pluralistic community of inquiry. Rather than trying to ferret out the cause of
such differences or using the differences to argue for the comparative worth
of one perspective over another, this situation should spur concerted dialogic
interaction. That interaction should address not the inadequacy of inquiry,
but the complexity of social existence. In our work, we are in search of a kind
of active, undefensive exchange between and among perspectives that is
foundational to dialogic approaches. We seek to explore the possibilities for
ironic and edifying inquiry hinted at by Rorty (1989), but by engaging (rather

than excluding) traditional perspectives. We seek to recognize the pluralistic scholarly community of incommensurate views described by Feyerabend (1993), but without adopting an "anything goes" mentality. We seek the invention of new alternatives that underpins Kuhn's (1970) scientific revolutions, but with a recognition that invention occurs all of the time and rarely results in an overthrow of the old. We seek ways to embody Bakhtin's (1986) dialogism in the inquiry process, assuming that understandings emerge from the active interchange among incommensurate views.

We believe that the value of engaging incommensurate perspectives is realized less in theoretical debates about abstract epistemological and methodological stances and more in substantive exchanges of descriptions, interpretations, and conclusions about personal relationships. Pearce (1989) alludes to this when he compares the notion of social eloquence to rhetorical eloquence. The purpose of dialogic inquiry is not to persuade or convert participants to one's theoretical position, nor is it to converge with others at a new theoretical position, both of which are rhetorical goals. Rather, the purpose is to elaborate the potential for coordination, a process Pearce describes as a kind of interaction that brings about a social event that participants interpret as meaningful from their own, particular perspectives. Coordination does not require consensus. It does, however, require recognition and appreciation of different viewpoints and their definitional interdependence. It requires a willingness to engage those viewpoints in interactive ways that respect, protect, and even celebrate their differences. It also requires a commitment to explore, imagine, and be receptive to possibilities that emerge in interaction. What we are proposing here is that researchers be more aware of the possibilities of joint action in the service of relational scholarship, with colleagues holding very different views.

In essence, we can envision scholars collaborating to produce research in much the same way that people meaning different things can collaborate to produce a conversation. Collaborators do not necessarily have to agree; they do have to forge a relationship to produce something that works. Collaborators in inquiry recognize that their world views are different, but that these are "only differences to be lived with, not issues to be resolved" (Bochner, 1994, p. 29). They acknowledge and appreciate the unique values of their different purposes—the traditionalists to predict and explain, the constructionists to understand and interpret, and the critical theorists to contest and change—as ways of "helping people cope with the mysteries, ambiguities, and strangeness of lived experiences" (Bochner, 1994, p. 24).

Not all dialectical writers take this collaborative view of inquiry. Some (e.g., Georgoudi, 1984; Conville, chap. 2, this volume) limit dialectical inquiry to interpretive approaches. Others appear to limit the dialectical approach to a focus on recursive causation through a traditionalist lens (e.g., Poole & McPhee, 1994). Indeed, some of the chapter authors in this text express some reluctance about inviting all perspectives to the table of inquiry (see, e.g., Bochner et al. and Rawlins, chaps. 2 and 4, this volume). In contrast, our dialogic view is necessarily multivocal, respecting the internal integrity of each individual perspective, including traditional, interpretive, and critical ones. Their copresence helps to create the kind of dialectical contradictions that moves inquiry in new, heretofore unimagined directions. Tensions between and among rigor and imagination, fact and value, precision and richness, elegance and applicability, and vivification and verification push researchers to try different methods and to see different things in their data. We believe these tensions will not be escaped or transcended, and so we argue that they should not be ignored.

Producing "Good" Inquiry: Epistemological and Ontological Considerations

How might scholars working from disparate perspectives produce meaningful, coordinated interchanges about communication in personal relationships rather than "loose and wooly ways of speaking," which some associate with dialectical pluralism (Popper, 1965, p. 316)? What differentiates good pluralistic dialogue from not good pluralistic dialogue? These kinds of questions compel us to consider criteria that distinguish valued pluralistic inquiry.

First, scholars should respect the evaluative boundaries of perspectival domains. Distinct boundaries, defined in part by different self-imposed, evaluative standards, separate the different perspectives in pluralistic inquiry. A dialogic view honors such boundaries, recognizing that to blur them is to obstruct the site for multivocal interaction. Guba (1990) warns against "the tendency displayed by adherents of all paradigms to set challenges for other paradigms in terms that cannot be meaningful to them (p. 373). Many who have offered critiques of pluralistic approaches for studying personal relationships (e.g., Bostrom & Donohew, 1992; Burelson, 1991; Fitzpatrick 1993) appear to expect all participants in the dialogue to adopt the same evaluative criteria. To criticize research situated in interpretive, social theory for attempting to vivify and dramatize theoretical tenets rather than attempting to verify through objective, inductive scientific practices is to ignore the integrity of a different perspective. In pluralistic dialogue, participants recognize that critical theorists are no more likely to adjudicate contrary conclusions emerging in one of their studies by referencing a neutral language of observation than traditionalists are likely to judge the worth of a finding by referencing emancipation. Pluralistic dialogue does not challenge the integrity of evaluative criteria unique to a particular perspective. Rather, it recognizes and respects diversity in viewpoints, acknowledging that universal credibility for an idea is not possible nor desirable in a complex social world.

Respect for perspectival boundaries should not lessen expectations for rigorous inquiry, but rigor is defined as conformity to the tenets of the particular adopted perspective (see Cappella, 1989). As Schwandt (1994) notes, lack of such conformity is likely to lead to charges of *solipsism* (the conclusion is based strictly on the whim of the author) or *relativism* (any conclusion will do equally as well). Simplistic, uninformed research practices that disregard a perspective's conventions are rarely judged positively even in a pluralistic community that expects innovation to be associated with some deviance. No matter the perspective, assumptions should be stated and methods should be explained in relation to the perspective's ideals of inquiry, and the reporting should be accessible to other scholars. The particulars of accomplishing these things, however, differ from perspective to perspective, from inquiry genre to inquiry genre. The expectations of any genre apply only to work done in that genre (Bakhtin, 1981). In short, the legitimacy of perspectives is "plural, local and context specific" (Lather, 1990, p. 321).

A second criterion for good dialogic inquiry is that it should have a both–and rather than an either–or orientation. Dialogic inquiry never asks which one perspective is true, right, or should triumph over the others. For instance, Fitzpatrick's (1993) criticism of Rawlins' (1992) work, although acknowledging and referencing at least two different perspectives on inquiry, is decidedly nondialogic by faulting Rawlins for applying a humanistic model, thereby "snatching defeat from the jaws of victory" for the scientific model (Fitzpatrick, 1993, p. 86). So too are many attacks of traditional inquiry that argue for replacing it with alternative perspectives. The evaluative issue in pluralistic dialogue is whether the integrity of different perspectives is preserved while recognizing each as viable.

Krippendorff (1989) speaks of an ethical imperative for dialogic inquiry, which incorporates respect and empathy for the identity of other perspectives. The ethical imperative expands beyond a "Do unto others as you would have them do unto you" theme by incorporating an active commitment to the dynamics of the dialogue itself. In accepting and respecting the viability of other perspectives, dialogic "participants . . . are committed to the process of dialoguing without assuming the authority to determine its direction. They possess the empathy that allows them to switch positions and see the world, including themselves, through someone else's constructions" (Krippendorff, 1990, p. 90). This emergent process, like any human process, could result in coercion and demagoguery (Cappella, 1989), but it is principled on the kinds of respect for difference and open exchange of ideas that are likely to deter such possibilities better than monologic approaches to inquiry do. The purpose of dialogue is not to merge voices, but to allow for the possibility of differences. The rigor of this dialectically oriented dialogue is not defined by its consistency and completeness, as in some other approaches, but rather by its ability to represent and coordinate multiple, incommensurate views (Pearce & Chen, 1989).

Third, scholars' contributions to the dialogue should keep the scholarly conversation going. The principles of communication are as implicated in the dialogue of inquiry as they are in the dialogue of the intimates whom we study. Conversation in both instances requires coordination built on responses and reactions that fit together in ways that are viewed by the participants as meaningful in their own, unique frames of reference. Participation must be active and responsive to sustain the conversation.

Beyond simple participation, however, dialogic inquiry should be framed by curiosity. Participants should be inclined to ask questions, eager to explore possibilities, unsettled with the answer of the day. Their conversational actions should perturb current understandings in ways that encourage the consideration—more likely, the creation—of new or different possibilities (McNamee, 1988). The conversation stopper of self-satisfying certainty should be avoided, as should the search for once-and-for-all solutions, resolutions, and finalized conclusions. In this way, the dialogue continues. Krippendorff (1989) has labeled this evaluative notion as the "social imperative," and he summarizes it for social scientific inquiry as well as for communication in general: "In communication with others, maintain or expand the range of choices possible" (p. 93).

Fourth, the dialogue should contribute to understanding. Dialogic inquiry does not aspire toward agreement or consensus about ideas, but it aspires toward complex, sophisticated perceptions of social existence. A significant challenge in this is finding ways to exchange information between incommensurate perspectives (Montgomery & Duck, 1991). One way is to translate research assumptions, concerns, and conclusions into the vocabularies of different perspectives. Such translations cannot be exact, nor can they result in the sharing of the same meanings for any particular concept. Furthermore, the accents of ontological origins make translations sound foreign to "natives," never quite "right." Nevertheless, translations can spur new and more complex ways of thinking as one contemplates something in a different vocabulary (Bochner, Cissna & Garko, 1991; Cappella, 1994). Thus, the concept of *social realities*, as it has been translated into the language of traditional views has encouraged new concerns for "representational validity" of behavioral coding schemes, "relational knowledge," social levels of analysis, and multiple perspectives on interaction (see Montgomery & Duck, 1991).

Extensive translations can transform information gained from one perspective into a form more useful for a different perspective. For instance, Altman, Vinsel, and Brown's (1981) transactional assumptions about the interplay of forces associated with openness and closedness, which Altman himself has explored with ethnographic methods (Altman & Ginat, 1989; Brown et al., chap. 7, this volume), have been transformed by VanLear (1991; chap.

6, this volume) into hypotheses, which he tested under traditional epistemo-logical assumptions and with traditional methods. As with any translation, there can never be a one-to-one, transformational correspondence between the information stemming from these different inquiry efforts. Yet, incom-mensurability does not mean that two perspectives are completely disassoci-ated; most often, some conceptual bridges, however subtle, imperfect, and limited, are possible (Feyerabend, 1981). These are often fruitful points at which dialogue can begin.

The scholarship that meets these criteria appears messy to most of us schooled under more traditional notions of inquiry. It seems messy because it is open-ended, uncertain, and inconclusive. This kind of scholarship is per-petually changing; new criteria develop as new positions provoke new ten-sions between and among perspectives.

Dialogic Methods

The discussion of otological and epistemological issues has set the stage for exploring a more pragmatic question: "How might the plurality of perspec-tives be actively engaged in a dialogue of inquiry that is useful for studying relational dialectics?" We believe that the potential for realizing the dialectic nature of communication in personal relationships is enhanced with atten-tion to different methodological points as sites of dialogic engagement.

Between and Among Multiple, Distinct Voices

The particular methods of choice are not as important as the fact that the methods acknowledge that the text of any communication event emerges from the interaction of multiple voices or perspectives and that these voices are not uniquely identified with individuals, but with the relationship be-tween individuals (McNamee, 1988). It is a misreading of dialectics that op-erationalizes contradictions experienced by a couple as interpersonal conflict in which only two voices are heard, each emanating from a self-contained in-dividual. Certainly, antagonistic contradictions occur from time to time in the form of interpersonal conflict, but this is not equivalent to the tensions of relational dialectics. Methods of study must distinguish many more than two voices expressing the tensions of relating and must link these voices to the re-lationship, not to separate individuals in the relationship. The methods must listen for a common voice as it emanates from different relational partners and also for different voices in the cracking, disjointed articulations of a sin-gle partner describing his or her contradictory experiences of the relationship.

The literature testifies to a seemingly infinite variety of data-gathering and data-analyzing methods that can capture this relationally dialectic quality of multivocality. Analyzing partners' personal accounts—their "views, theories, understanding, conceptions, knowledge, and so forth" (Burnett, 1987, p. xi)—is one way. These accounts may be reported by the researcher, as Rawlins (1992; chap. 4, this volume) does in his study of dialectical processes in friendships, or they may be performed, as Ellis and Bochner (1992; Bochner, Ellis & Tillman, chap. 3, this volume) do in recounting their personal experiences of dealing with the incommensurate, contradictory, and dilemmatic relational tensions surrounding life crises. Accounts can be gathered in the form of narratives, diary entries, interviews, responses to preordained descriptive terms, and retrospective self-reports (see explanations and examples in Burnett, McGhee & Clark, 1992; Conville, 1988, chap. 2, this volume; Denzin & Lincoln, 1994; Ellis & Flaherty, 1992).

Besides accounts, dialectical voices have been discerned in interaction analyses of ongoing communication events (e.g., VanLear, 1991; chap. 6, this volume), analyses of interview data (e.g., Baxter & Widenmann, 1993), discourse analyses of conversational texts (e.g., Masheter, 1994), participant observations (e.g., Altman & Ginat, 1989), and structured self-reports (e.g. VanLear, 1991). Cultural artifacts like films and novels and place markings like architecture and home decorations have been analyzed (e.g., Gauvain, Altman, & Fahim, 1983). The specific method of gathering and analyzing data is not the crucial issue. Whatever method is chosen, however, must capture the intrinsic dialectical quality of polyvocality.

Through Time

Attention to time is not an afterthought in dialogic inquiry; it cannot be added into the equation for inquiry after other aspects for study have been described (Shoter, 1993). The incorporation of time is not merely based on studying communication elements set in motion. Rather, the dialogic focus on time mandates the study of relational change—an inherent and constant quality that gives identity to those communication elements. Explicitly recognizing this perspective on time helps to guard against the problem of describing incomplete, unfinalized processes as if they were complete, whole, and conclusive. The anchoring temporal qualities for studies of relational dialectics should be of the sort that preserve the event's historicity and emphasize its ongoing, indeterminant nature, its moment-by-moment novelty.

Temporal qualities that can be referenced in studies of relational dialectics include amplitude, salience, scale, sequencing, pace, and rhythm (Werner & Baxter, 1994). The definitions of these vary, depending on whether linear or cyclical–spiraling conceptions of time are adopted. Linear views see communication in relationships moving forward, toward some end state, and are characteristic of determinant, teleological dialectical perspectives that assume efficient causation. Spiral views emphasize repetition of patterns and change leading to something different, but not toward some final end state.

This latter view is characteristic of indeterminant dialectical perspectives like relational dialectics. In this spiral context, *amplitude* refers to how intense the change is; *salience* describes the time orientation in terms of past, present, or future; *scale* refers to the duration of events and patterns of events; *sequencing* describes the order of a series of events; *pace* conveys how frequently events occur within some set time period; and *rhythm* combines amplitude, scale, sequence, and pace to describe how regular or irregular communication events are. Werner and her colleagues use these temporal qualities as reference points in ethnographic descriptions of dialectical tensions as expressed in rituals, ceremonies, and celebrations (Werner, Haggard, Altman, & Oxley, 1988), home environments (Werner, Altman, & Oxley, 1985), and social networks (Werner, Altman, Oxley, & Haggard, 1987).

Other examples are worthy of note as well. VanLear (1991) uses mathematical modeling techniques to investigate Altman, Vinsel, and Brown's (1981) expectations for cyclic and spiral change in relationships (see Van-Lear, chap. 6, this volume). With very different purposes and methods, Rawlins' (1992; chap. 4, this volume) interpretive analysis of interview data provides tracings of dialectical fluctuations in friendship over the life course, from childhood to old age, with stops to focus in detail on a number of developmental stages in between. Masheter (1994) uses episode analysis, an interview-based procedure, to describe changes in dialectical features of relationships before and after divorce. These examples only hint at the variety of methods potentially sensitive to time.

Between and Among Different Data Sets

A third methodological point for potential dialogue is between and among different sets of data, created at different places, under different circumstances, and with different participants. By picking up the strands from discrete studies, researchers can braid dialectical struggle between and among forces into an understanding of communication in close relationships. The strands in this braid might rely on a host of data-analysis techniques, from examining narrative accounts to examining the findings of experimental studies. Explication of dialectical views often have proceeded in this way. Early articulations of the centrifugal forces countering centripetal inclinations toward openness emerged from viewing contradictory research results as substantive information rather than evidence of research failings (see, e.g., Altman, Vinsel, & Brown, 1981; Bochner, 1982).

A more strategic version of this interweaving can be accomplished by planning a research program that accesses relationships at different places, different times, or different circumstances. Rawlins' (1992; chap. 4, this volume) extensive study of friendship from a dialectical perspective exemplifies this approach. He intermixes the voices of fiction writers, traditional social scientists, and relational partners representing a variety of life stages, thereby painting a complex, dialectical picture of friendship.

Involving the Researcher

A fourth methodological encounter point for dialogue involves the researcher. As this chapter emphasizes, inquiry is, itself, a dialogic, interpersonal process that necessarily juxtaposes the researcher's perspective with those of the people who participate in his or her studies, who collaborate in the research, and who serve as disciplinary and interdisciplinary colleagues. The conventions of different research genres allow, in different ways, the dynamic, creative, and dialogic qualities of these interactions to be reflected and reflected on as part of the research. Constructionists view research as self-reflexive, relationally situated activity (Gergen & Gergen, 1991; McNamee, 1994) and so, explicitly engage research participants and research colleagues in efforts to create interpretations that could not have been created without such dialogic interaction (see, e.g., Ellis & Bochner, 1992). Perspectives that are less likely to entertain dialogue with research participants on such an egalitarian plane of interaction and interpretation still have epistemological room for viewing the researcher as an active participant in dialogic research. In traditional views, for instance, where information from participants is often treated like concrete cinderblocks, researchers can be more open to building architecturally complex, perhaps even Escherian structures by assuming that the nature of reality is, itself, contradictory. Van-Lear (1991) takes this track when he hypothesizes complex cycles of openness and closedness in personal relationships. Acknowledgment of alternatives, potentials, and opposite voices, then, becomes an integral part of the substance of knowledge.

McNamee (1994) extends these notions by framing the researcher as an active participant in the social community of scholars, engaged in ongoing, active interchanges with other researchers. She encourages researchers to ask of their projects such questions as: "Who is this research for?" "Who *could* it be for?" "How many different stories could be told?" "How might others frame the research questions?" "How might others design the research procedures?" (p. 16). With these and similar questions, researchers position themselves to entertain alternative perspectives.

We are encouraged by successful efforts to implement this approach to research as they are emerging across the social sciences. In the field of cultural anthropology, for example, Tedlock and Mannheim (1995) provide us with a rich collection of research exemplars, including dialogues among informants, between researchers and informants, and among researchers and the contrasting voices enacted in the uninterrupted discourse of single informants. The dialogic turn in cultural anthropology supplants the monologic works of a decade ago, which privileged the unitary authorial voice of the field researcher as he or she rendered a given culture internally consistent and consensual. Much of the research we have cited in this chapter hints that a similar dialogic turn can take place in the study of personal relationships.

CONCLUSION

To commit to a relational dialectics view is to accept that communication events, relationships, and life itself are ongoing and unfinalizable, always becoming, never being. There are no ideal goals, no ultimate endings, no elegant end states of balance, and no ultimate truth. There is only an indeterminate flow, full of unforeseeable potential that is realized in interaction. This view, which is admittedly unmethodical and indefinite, necessarily follows from accepting the integrity of multiple, valid, and contradictory perspectives engaged in dialogue. The challenge that engages us is to represent this perspective in a reconsideration of the ways we understand close relationships (see Baxter & Montgomery, 1996). We have been able only to hint here at the understandings that are emerging from this work.

REFERENCES

Altman, I. (1990). Toward a transactional perspective: A personal journey. In I. Altman & K. Christensen (Eds.), *Environment and behavior studies: Emergence of intellectual traditions* (pp. 225–255). New York: Plenum.

Altman, I., & Ginat, J. (May, 1989). *Social relationships in polygamous families.* Invited address presented at the annual meeting of the American Psychological Association, Boston.

Altman, I., Vinsel, A., & Brown, B. (1981). Dialectic conceptions in social psychology: An application to social penetration and privacy regulation. In L. Berkowitz (Ed.), *Advances in experimental psychology: Volume 14* (pp. 107–160). New York: Academic Press.

Aron, A., & Aron, E. N. (1986). *Love as the expansion of self: Understanding attraction and satisfaction.* New York: Hemisphere.

Askham, J. (1976). Identity and stability within the marriage relationship. *Journal of Marriage and the Family, 38,* 535–547.

Bakhtin, M. (1986). *Speech genres and other late essays.* (C. Emerson & M. Holquist, Eds., V. McGee, Trans.). Austin: University of Texas Press.

Bakhtin, M. M. (1981). *The dialogic imagination: Four essays by M. M. Bakhtin* (M. Holquist, Ed., C. Emerson & M. Holquist, Trans.). Austin: University of Texas Press.

Bakhtin, M. M. (1984). *Problems of Dostoevsky's poetics* (C. Emerson, Ed., Trans.). Minneapolis: University of Minnesota Press.

Bateson, G. (1972). *Steps to an ecology of mind.* New York: Ballantine.

Baxter, L. A. (1983). Relationship disengagement: An examination of the reversal hypothesis. *Western Journal of Speech Communication, 47,* 85–98.

Baxter, L. A. (1987). Symbols of relationship identity in relationship cultures. *Journal of Social and Personal Relationships, 4,* 261–280.

Baxter, L. A. (1988). A dialectical perspective on communication strategies in relationship development. In S. Duck (Ed.), *Handbook of personal relationships* (pp. 257–273). New York: Wiley.

Baxter, L. A. (1990). Dialectical contradictions in relationship development. *Journal of Social and Personal Relationships, 7,* 69–88.

Baxter, L. A., & Montgomery, B. M. (1996). *Relating: Dialogues and dialectics.* New York: Guilford.

Baxter, L. A., & Widenmann, S. (1993). Revealing and not revealing the status of romantic relationships to social networks. *Journal of Social and Personal Relationships, 10,* 321–338.

Berger, C. R., & Bell, R. A. (1988). Plans and the initiation of social relationships. *Human Communication Research, 15,* 217–235.

Berger, C. R., & Bradac, J. J. (1982). *Language and social knowledge: Uncertainty in interpersonal relations.* London: Edward Arnold.

Billig, M. (1987). *Arguing and thinking: A rhetorical approach to social psychology.* New York: Cambridge University Press.

Bochner, A. P. (1982). On the efficacy of openness in close relationships. In M. Burgoon (Ed.), *Communication Yearbook 5* (pp. 49–78). New Brunswick, NJ: Transaction Press.

Bochner, A. P. (1994). Perspectives on inquiry II: Theories and stories. In M. Knapp & G. Miller (Eds.), *Handbook of interpersonal communication* (2nd ed., pp. 21–41). Thousand Oaks, CA: Sage.

Bochner, A. P., Cissna, K. N., & Garko, M. G. (1991). Optional metaphors for studying interaction. In B. M. Montgomery & S. Duck (Eds.), *Studying interpersonal interaction* (pp. 16–34). New York: Guilford.

Bopp, M. J., & Weeks, G. R. (1984). Dialectical metatheory in family therapy. *Family Process, 23,* 49–61.

Bostrom, R., & Donohew, L. (1992). The case for empiricism: Clarifying fundamental issues in communication theory. *Communication Monographs, 59,* 109–129.

Bruess, C. J. (1994). *"Bare-chested hugs" and "tough-guys night": Examining the form and function of interpersonal rituals in marriage and friendship.* Unpublished doctoral dissertation, Ohio University, Athens, OH.

Burgoon, J. K. (1982). Privacy and Communication. *Communication Yearbook, 6,* 206–249.

Burnett, R. (1987). Reflection in personal relationships. In R. Burnett, P. McGhee, & D. D. Clarke (Eds.), *Accounting for relationships: Explanation, representation and knowledge* (pp. 74–93). London: Methuen.

Burnett, R., McGhee, P., & Clarke, D. D. (Eds.). (1987). *Accounting for relationships: Explanation, representation and knowledge.* London: Methuen.

Burleson, B. R. (1990). Comforting as social support: Relational consequences of supportive behaviors. In S. Duck, with R. Silver (Eds.), *Personal Relationships and Social Support* (pp. 66–82). London: Sage.

Byrne, D. (1992). The transition from controlled laboratory experimentation to less controlled settings: Surprise! Additional variables are operative. *Communication Monographs, 59,* 190–198.

Cappella, J. (1984). The relevance of the microstructure of interaction to relationship change. *Journal of Social and Personal Relationships, 1,* 239–264.

Capella, J. N. (1989). Remaking communication inquiry. In B. Dervin, L. Grossberg, B. O'Keefe, & E. Wartella (Eds.), *Rethinking communication, volume 1: Paradigm issues* (pp. 139–143). Newbury Park, CA: Sage.

Clark, K., & Hoquist, M. (1984). *Mikhail Bakhtin.* Cambridge, MA: Harvard University Press.

Conville, R. L. (1991). *Relational transitions: The evolution of personal relationships.* New York: Praeger.

Cronen, V., Pearce, W. B., & Snavely, L. (1979). A theory of rule-structure and types of episodes, and a study of perceived enmeshment in undesired repetitive patterns (urps). In D. Nimmo (Ed.), *Communication yearbook III* (pp. 225–240). New Brunswick, NJ: Transaction.

Cupach, W., & Metts, S. (1986). Accounts of relational dissolution: A comparison of marital and non-marital relationships. *Communication Monographs, 53*, 311–334.

Daly, J., & Wiemann, J. (Eds.). (1994). *Communicating strategically.* Hillsdale, NJ: Lawrence Erlbaum Associates.

Denzin, N. K., & Lincoln, Y. S. (Eds.). (1994). *Handbook of qualitative research.* Thousand Oaks, CA: Sage.

Duck, S., Pond, K., & Leatham, G. (1991, May). *Remembering as a context for being in relationships: Different perspectives on the same interaction.* Paper presented at the conference of the International Network on Personal Relationships, Normal, IL.

Ellis, C., & Bochner, A. P. (1992). Telling and performing personal stories: The constraints of choice in abortion. In C. Ellis & M. Flaherty (Eds.). *Investigating subjectivity* (pp. 97–101). Newbury Park, CA: Sage.

Ellis, C., & Flaherty, M. G. (Eds.). (1992). *Investigating subjectivity: Research on lived experience.* Newbury Park, CA: Sage.

Fehr, B. (1993). How do I love thee? Let me consult my prototype. In S. Duck (Ed.), *Individuals in relationships* (pp. 87–120). Newbury Park, CA: Sage.

Feyerabend, P. K. (1981). *Problems of empiricism: Philosophical papers, volume 2.* Cambridge, England: Cambridge University Press.

Feyerabend, P. K. (1993). *Against method* (3rd ed.). London: Verso.

Fitch, K. L. (1994). Culture, ideology, and interpersonal communication research. In S. A. Deetz (Ed.), *Communication yearbook 17* (pp. 104–135). Thousand Oaks, CA: Sage.

Fitzpatrick, M. A. (1988). *Between husbands and wives: Communication in marriage.* Newbury Park, CA: Sage.

Fitzpatrick, M. A. (1993). Review of *Friendship matters: Communication, dialectics, and the life course. Communication Theory, 3*, 83–85.

Forgas, J. P. (1979). *Social episodes: The study of interaction routines.* New York: Academic Press.

Gauvain, M., Altman, I., & Fahim, H. (1983). Home and social change: A cross-cultural analysis. In N. Reimer & E. S. Geller (Eds.), *Environmental psychology: Directions and perspectives* (pp. 180–218). New York: Praeger.

Georgoudi, M. (1984). Modern dialectics in social psychology. In K. Gergen & M. Gergen (Eds.), *Historical social psychology* (pp. 83–101). Hillsdale, NJ: Lawrence Erlbaum Associates.

Gergen, K., & Gergen, M. (1987). Narratives of relationship. In R. Burnett, P. McGhee, & D. D. Clarke (Eds.), *Accounting for relationships: Explanation, representation and knowledge* (pp. 269–288). London: Methuen.

Gerstel, N. & Gross, H. (1984). *Commuter marriage: A study of work and family.* London: Guilford.

Goldsmith, D. (1990). A dialectical perspective on the expression of autonomy and connection in romantic relationships. *Western Journal of Speech Communication, 54*, 537–556.

Guba, E. G. (1990). Carrying on the dialog. In E. G. Guba (Ed.), *The paradigm dialog* (pp. 368–378). Newbury Park, CA: Sage.

Hatfield, E., & Rapson, R. L. (1993). *Love, sex, and intimacy: Their psychology, biology, and history.* New York: HarperCollins.

Hause, K., & Pearson, J. (1994, November). *The warmth without the sting: Relational dialectics over the family life cycle.* Paper presented at the Speech Communication Association, New Orleans, LA.

Hawes, L. C., & Smith, D. (1973). A critique of assumptions underlying the study of communication in conflict. *Quarterly Journal of Speech, 59*, 423–435.

Hertz, R. (1986). *More equal than others: Women and men in dual-career marriages.* Berkeley: University of California Press.

Honeycutt, J. M. (1993). Memory structures for the rise and fall of personal relationships. In S. Duck (Ed.), *Individuals in relationships* (pp. 60–86). Newbury Park, CA: Sage.

Krippendorff, K. (1989). On the ethics of constructing communication. In B. Dervin, L. Grossberg, B. O'Keefe, & E. Wartella (Eds.), *Rethinking communication, volume 1: Paradigm issues* (pp. 66–96). Newbury Park, CA: Sage.

Kuhn, T. (1970). *The structure of scientific revolutions.* Chicago: The University of Chicago Press.

Lather, P. (1990). Reinscribing otherwise: The play of values in the practices of the human sciences. In E. G. Guba (Ed.), *The paradigm dialog* (pp. 315–332). Newbury Park, CA: Sage.

Masheter, C. (1991). Postdivorce relationships between ex-spouses: The roles of attachment and interpersonal conflict. *Journal of Marriage and the Family, 53,* 103–110.

Masheter, C. (1994). Dialogues between ex-spouses: Evidence of dialectic relationship development. In R. Conville (Ed.), *Structure in communication study* (pp. 83–102). New York: Praeger.

McNamee, S. (1988). Accepting research as social intervention: Implications of a systemic epistemology. *Communication Quarterly, 36,* 56–68.

McNamee, S. (1994). Research as relationally situated activity: Ethical implications. *Journal of Feminist Family Therapy, 6,* 69–83.

Mead, G. H. (1934). *Mind, self and society.* Chicago: University of Chicago Press.

Mikulas, W. L., & Vodanovich, S. J. (1993). The essence of boredom. *Psychological Record, 43,* 3–12.

Montgomery, B. M. (1988). Quality communication in personal relationships. In S. Duck (Ed.), *Handbook of personal relationships* (pp. 343–359). New York: Wiley.

Montgomery, B. M. (1992). Communication as the interface between couples and culture. In S. Deetz (Ed.), *Communication yearbook 15* (pp. 475–507). Newbury Park, CA: Sage.

Montgomery, B. M. (1993). Relationship maintenance versus relationship change: A dialectical dilemma. *Journal of Social and Personal Relationships, 10,* 205–224.

Montgomery, B. M., & Duck, S. (1991). Methodology and open dialogue. In B. M. Montgomery & S. Duck (Eds.), *Studying interpersonal interaction* (pp. 323–336). New York: Guilford.

Norton, R. (1983). *Communicator style: Theory, applications, and measures.* Beverly Hills, CA: Sage.

Oldfather, P., & West, J. (1994). Qualitative research as jazz. *Educational Researcher, 23,* 22–26.

Pearce, W. B. (1989). *Communication and the human condition.* Carbondale: Southern Illinois University Press.

Pearce, W. B., & Chen, V. (1989). Ethnography as sermonic: The rhetorics of Clifford Geertz and James Clifford. In H. W. Simons (Ed.), *Rhetoric in the human sciences* (pp. 119–132). Newbury Park, CA: Sage.

Planalp, S., & Honeycutt, J. M. (1985). Events that increase uncertainty in personal relationships. *Human Communication Research, 11,* 593–604.

Poole, M. S., & McPhee, R. D. (1994). Methodology in interpersonal communication research. In M. Knapp & G. Miller (Eds.), *Handbook of interpersonal communication* (2nd ed., pp. 42–100). Thousand Oaks, CA: Sage.

Popper, K. (1965). *Conjectures and refutations: The growth of scientific knowledge.* New York: HarperCollins.

Rawlins, W. K. (1992). *Friendship matters: Communication, dialectics and the life course.* New York: de Gruyter.

Rogers, L. E., & Millar, F. E. (1988). Relational communication. In S. Duck (Ed.), *Handbook of personal relationships* (pp. 289–306). New York: Wiley.

Rorty, R. (1989). *Contingency, irony, and solidarity.* Cambridge, England: Cambridge University Press.

Rosengren, K. E. (1989). Paradigms lost and regained. In B. Dervin, L. Grossberg, B. J. O'Keefe, & E. Wartella (Eds.), *Rethinking communication, volume 1: Paradigm issues* (pp. 21–39). Newbury Park, CA: Sage.

Rusbult, C. E., Drigotas, S. M., & Verette, J. (1994). The investment model: an interdependence analysis of commitment processes and relationship maintenance phenomena. In D. J. Canary & L. Stafford (Eds.), *Communication and relational maintenance* (pp. 115–140). New York: Academic Press.

Schwandt, T. R. (1990). Paths to inquiry in the social disciplines. In E. G. Guba (Ed.), *The paradigm dialog* (pp. 258–276). Newbury Park, CA: Sage.

Schwandt, T. R. (1994). Constructivist, interpretivist approaches to human inquiry. In N. Denzin & Y. S. Lincoln (Eds.), *Handbook of qualitative research* (pp. 118–137). Thousand Oaks, CA: Sage.

Seligman, M. (1975). *Helplessness.* New York: Freeman.

Shotter, J. (1993). *Cultural politics of everyday life.* Toronto: University of Toronto Press.

Stamp, G. H. (1994). The appropriation of the parental role through communication during the transition to parenthood. *Communication Monographs, 61,* 89–112.

Tedlock, D., & Mannheim, B. (1995). *The dialogic emergence of culture.* Chicago: University of Illinois Press.

VanLear, C. A. (1991). Testing a cyclical model of communicative openness in relationship development: Two longitudinal studies. *Communication Monographs, 58,* 337–361.

VanLear, C. A., & Trujillo, N. (1986). On becoming acquainted: A longitudinal study of social judgment processes. *Journal of Social and Personal Relationships, 3,* 375–392.

Volosinov, V. N./Bakhtin, M. M. (1973). *Marxism and the philosophy of language* (L. Matejks & I. R. Titunik, Trans.). Cambridge, MA: Harvard University Press.

Werner, C. M., Altman, I., & Oxley, D. (1985). Temporal aspects of homes: A transactional perspective. In I. Altman & C. M. Werner (Eds.), *Human behavior and environment: Advances in theory and research* (pp. 1–32). Beverly Hills, CA: Sage.

Werner, C. M., Altman, I., Oxley, D., & Haggard, L. M. (1987). People, place and time: A transactional analysis of neighborhoods. In W. Jones & D. Perlman (Eds.), *Advances in personal relationships: A research annual* (vol. 1, pp. 243–275). Greenwich, CT: JAI.

Werner, C. M., & Baxter, L. A. (1994). Temporal qualities of relationships: Organismic, transactional and dialectical views. In M. L. Knapp & G. R. Miller (Eds.), *Handbook of interpersonal communication* (2nd ed., pp. 323–379). Newbury Park, CA: Sage.

Werner, C., Haggard, L., Altman, I., & Oxley, D. (1988). Temporal qualities of rituals and celebrations: A comparison of Christmas Street and Zuni Shalako. In J. E. McGrath (Ed.), *The social psychology of time: New perspectives* (pp. 203–231). Newbury Park, CA: Sage.

Wood, J. T. (1982). Communication and relational culture: Bases for the study of human relationships. *Communication Quarterly, 30,* 75–84.

Author Index

A

Allan, G., 145, *152*
Alliger, G. M., 25, *38*
Altman, I., 3, *15*, 47, *59*, 64, *80*, 84, 89, 90, 92, *105*, 116, 121, 123, 125, 126, 127, 130, *134*, 137, 138, 139, 140, 143, 144, 146, 149, 150, *152*, *153*, *154*, 164, 174, 176, 177, *179*, *183*
Anderson, J. A., 109, *134*
Arluke, A., 96, *105*
Aron, A., 165, 168, *179*
Aron, E. N., 165, 168, *179*
Askham, J., 141, *152*, 165, 179

B

Bagarozzi, D. A., 121, 122, 127, *135*
Baker, G. L., 116, *134*
Bakhtin, M. M., 2, 14, *15*, 43, 53, *59*, 66, 67, 71, 75, 76, 78, *80*, 156, 158, 159, 161, 162, 163, 166, 169, 171, *179*, *183*
Bales, R. F., 143, 145, 146, *152*
Banski, M. A., 48, *62*
Barthes, R., 22, *36*
Bates, E., 140, *152*
Bateson, G., 71, *80*, 110, 119, 122, *134*, 161, *179*
Bavelas, J. H., 28, *38*
Baxter, L., 3, 4, 10, *15*, 20, 23, 25, 29, 30, 35, 36, *36*, *37*, 43, 47, 48, 49, 51, 52, 54, *59*, 64, *80*, 84, 85, 86, 88, 90, 91, 94, 98, 99, 100, *105*, *106*, 116, 117, 120, 123, 124, 128, *134*, 138, 141, 142, 146, 147, 150, *152*, 157, 161, 162, 164, 165, 166, 167, 168, 169, 176, 179, *179*, *183*
Beavin, J. H., 115, 116, 121, 122, *136*
Bell, R. A., 167, *180*
Benjamin, L. S., 143, 147, *152*
Benson, J. K., 3, *15*
Benson, P., 42, *60*
Berger, C. R., 115, *134*, 167, *180*
Berger, J., 44, *60*
Berger, P. L., 111, *134*
Berger, R., 102, *106*
Berzon, B., 102, 103, *106*
Billig, M., 158, 161, *180*
Bochner, A. P., 23, *37*, 42, 43, 45, 47, 50, 51, 52, 54, *60*, 64, 71, *80*, *81*, 84, *106*, 171, 174, 176, 177, 178, *180*
Bolton, C. D., 19, *37*
Booth, W. C., 63, 68, *81*
Bopp, M. J., 65, *81*, 159, *180*
Bostrum, R., 172, *180*
Bradac, J. J., 167, *180*
Brady, I., 42, *60*
Braithwaite, D. O., 83, *106*
Bridge, K., 25, 35, *37*
Brown, B. B., 3, *15*, 47, *59*, 64, *80*, 84, 89, 90, *105*, 116, 121, 126, 127, 130, *134*, 137, 138, 140, 143, 146, 147, 149, 150, *152*, *154*, 174, 177, *179*
Brown, M. A., 86, 95, 96, 100, *107*
Bruess, C. J., 169, *180*
Bruner, J., 42, 44, 46, 53, *60*
Buck, R., 117, 118, 119, *134*
Bullis, C., 30, *37*

Bundek, N., 85, 93, 98, *105*

Burgoon, J. K., 145, *153*, 165, *180*
Burke, K., 74, *81*
Burleson, B. R., 172, *180*
Burnett, R., 176, *180*
Buss, A., 3, 14, *15*
Butler, S., 54, *60*
Byrne, D., 165, *180*

C

Cain, R., 85, 87, 88, 89, 102, 103, *106*
Campbell, D. T., 110, *134*
Cappella, J. N., 115, 116, 129, *135*,
    173, 174, *180*
Cass, V. C., 102, *106*
Chaikin, A., 92, *106*
Chan, C., 25, *37*
Chemers, M. M., 140, *152*
Chen, V., 174, *182*
Cline, R., 103, *106*
Cissna, K. N., 23, *37*, 174, *180*
Clark, K., 162, 166, *180*
Clarke, D. D., 176, *180*
Cohen, S. P., 146, *152*
Coleman, E., 102, 103, *106*
Coles, R., 43, 46, *60*
Conville, R. L., 19, 20, 21, 23, 26, 28,
    32, 35, *37*, 47, 48, *60*, 141, *153*,
    159, 164, 171, 176, *180*
Cooley, C. H., 142, *152*
Cornforth, M., 3, *15*
Cox, D. E., 23, *37*
Crites, S., 42, *60*
Crohan, S. E., 148, *153*
Cronen, V., 163, *180*
Cupach, W., 168, *181*

D

Daly, J., 167, *181*
Dedo, J. Y., 143, 147, *153*
Deetz, S, 111, *135*
Denzin, N. K., 147, *153*, 176, *181*
Derlega, V. J., 92, 97, 98, 102, *106*
Dickson, K. L., 143, 147, *153*
Dindia, K., 85, 86, 87, 89, 90, 93, 94,
    95, 96, 97, 98, 99, 100, 101,
    102, 103, 104, *106*
Donahew, L., 172, *180*
Drecksel, G. L., 126, *135*
Drigotas, S. M., 165, *183*

Duck, S., 3, *15*, 20, *37*, 88, *106*, 143,
    144, *153*, 168, 174, *181*
Duxbury, L. E., 25, *37*

E

Edgar, T., 93, 95, 104, *107*
Ellis, C., 43, 44, 47, 48, 50, 51, 52, 54,
    56, 57, 58, *60*, *61*, 176, 178, *180*

F

Fahim, H., 138, *153*, 176, *181*
Fehr, B., 167, *181*
Felmlee, D. H., 144, *154*
Feyerbend, P.K., 110, *135*, 171, 175,
    181
Fisher, B. A., 118, 119, 121, 126, *135*
Fitch, K. L., 158, 173, *181*
Fitzpatrick, M. A., 125, 126, *136*, 168,
    172, *181*
Flaherty, M., 43, *61*, 176, *181*
Fogel, A., 143, 147, *153*
Forgas, J. P., 167, *181*
Frank, A .W., 43, 58, *61*
Franck, D., 54, *61*

G

Gard, L., 85, *106*
Garfinkle, H., 114, *135*
Garko, M. G., 174, *180*
Gauvain, M., 138, *152*, *153*, 176, *181*
Geertz, C., 23, *37*, 43, *61*, 114, *135*
Georgoudi, M., 150, *153*, 171, *181*
Gergen, K., 178, *181*
Gergen, M., 178, *181*
Gershman, H., 85, *106*
Gerstel, N., 167, *181*
Ginat, J., 138, *152*, 154, 174, 176, *179*
Glaser, B. G., 72, *81*
Goldsmith, D., 166, *181*
Goffman, E., 83, 84, 93, 101, 102, 104,
    106, 119, *135*
Gollub, J. D., 116, *134*
Gottman, J. M., 116, 127, *135*, 148,
    153
Gourd, W., 47, *62*
Gross, H., 167, *181*
Guba, E. G., 172, *181*

H

Haggard, L. M., 139, 140, 149, *153,* *154*, 177, *183*
Hale, J. L., 145, *152*
Haley, T., 115, *135*
Hamill, D., 43, *61*
Harris, L., 141, *153*
Hatfield, E., 165, *181*
Hause, K., 169, *181*
Hawes, L. C., 165, *181*
Hawking, S., 109, *135*
Hecht, M. L., 94, 97, 101, *107*
Heisenberg, W., 110, *135*
Henry, J., 79, *81*
Henderson-King, D. H., 144, *153*
Herman, N. J., 87, 93, 95, 97, *106*
Hertz, R., 167, *181*
Higgins, C. A., 25, *37*
Holl, M., 72, *81*, 143, *154*
Holquist, M., 66, 67, 73, *81*, 162, 166, *180*
Holt, S. A., 143, 147, *153*
Honeycutt, J. M., 19, 30, *37*, 167, 168, *182*

I

Irwin, J., 88, 93, 94, 97, 101, *107*

J

Jackson, D. D., 28, *37*, 115, 116, 121, 122, *135*
Jackson, M., 43, 45, 47, 49, 51, 58, *61*
Jourard, S. M., 88, *106*

K

Kaplan, A., 110, *135*
Kiesinger, C. E., 43, 54, *61*
Kitayama, S. A., 143, *153*
Kline, W. B., 85, 88, 93, 103, 104, *106*
Knapp, M., 20, *37*, 123, 127, *135*
Krauss, B. J., 93, 97, *107*
Krebs, S., 90, 94, *106*
Krieger, S., 50, *61*
Krippendorff, K., 173, 174, *182*
Kuhn, T., 141, *153*, 171, *182*

L

LaRossa, R., 21, 22, *37*
Lather, P., 173, *182*
Leary, T., 143, 147, *153*
Leatham, G., 168, *181*
Levinger, G., 19, 20, *37*
Levi-Strauss, A. J., 21, 22, *37*
Limandri, B., 84, 87,88, 90, 96, 97, 101, 102, 104, *106*
Lincoln, Y. S.,176, *181*
Lofland, J., 72, *81*, 114, *135*
Luckman, T., 11, *134*

M

McCall, G. J., 119, *135*
McDonald, G., 103, *106*
McGhee, R., 176, *181*
McNamee, S., 174, 175, 178, *182*
McPhee, R. D., 171, *182*
MacFarlane, I., 90, 94,*106*
Maldonado, N., 85, 93, 98, *106*
Mannheim, B., 178, *183*
Maranhaos, T., 46, *61*
Marks, G., 85, 93, 98, *106*
Markus, H. R., 143, *153*
Marquit, E., 77, *81*
Margolin, G., 25, *37*
Marx, K., 9, *15*
Masheter, C., 141, *153*, 167, 176, 177, *182*
Mason, J., 85, 93, 98, *107*
Matusov, E., 143, 147, *153*
Mazanec, M. J., 102, *107*
Mead, G. H., 142, *153*, 166, *182*
Mecke, J., 68, *81*
Messinger, D., 143, 147, *153*
Metts, S., 168, *181*
Mikulas, W. L., 168, *182*
Millar, F. E., 145, *153*, 162, *182*
Miller, D. T., 143, *153*
Montgomery, B., 3, 4, *15*, 23, 29, *37*, 49, *59*, 84, 85, 86, 88, 90, 91, 99, 100, *105*, 116, 117, 120, 123, 124, *134*, *135*, 138, 141, 142, 146, 147, 150, *152*, *153*, 157, 158, 161, 162, 165, 174, 179, *181*, *182*
Mon't Ross-Mendoza, T., 94, 97, 101, *107*

Morgan, H. J., 118, *135*
Murphy, R., 3, *15*
Murphy, S., 88, 93, 94, 97, 101, *107*

N

Norton, R., 162, *182*
Nussbaum, J. F., 102, *107*
Nwokah, E., 143, 147, *153*

O

Ochberg, R. L., 43, *61*
Oldfather, P., 156, *182*
O' Neil, J., 23, *37*
Oxley, D., 139, 140, 149, *153, 154,*
177, *183*

P

Pachanowsky, M., 34, *37*
Paradis, B. A., 102, *107*
Perks, M., 88, *107*
Patterson, M. L., 147, *153*
Pearce, W. B., 86, *107*, 163, 171, 174,
180
Pearson, J., 169, *181*
Pennebacker, J. W., 89, *107*
Perkins, D. D., 149, *152*
Perlman, D., 143, 144, *153*
Pertonio, S., 92, 94, 97, 100, 101, *107*
Planalp, S., 19, 30, *37*, 168, *182*
Plummer, K., 102, *107*
Polkinghorne, D., 42, *61*
Pond, K., 168, *181*
Ponse, B., 93, 95, *107*
Poole, M. S., 171, *182*
Popper, K., 172, *182*
Powell-Cope, G. M., 86, 89, 95, 96,
100, *107*
Prager, K. J., 88, *107*
Prentice, D. A., 143, *153*

R

Rapson, R. L., 165, *181*
Rawlins, W. K., 3, 12, *15*, 20, 23, *37,*
38, 47, 48, 49, 54, *61*, 63, 64,
65, 72, 73, 74, *81*, 84, 89, 121,

125, *135*, 143, 144, 150, *154,*
164, 167, 173, 176, 177, *182*
Reeder, H. M., 94, 97, 101, *107*
Richardson, J., 85, 93, 98, *107*
Richardson, L., 42, 43, 50, 53, 58, *61*
Ricoeur, P., 75, *81*
Rogers, L. E., 115, 120, 121, 122, 123,
127, *135*, 145, *153*, 162, *182*
Rogoff, B., 139, *152*
Rorty, R., 23, *38*, 45, 47, 52, 58, *61,*
63, 71, *81*, 170, *182*
Rose, D., 50, 59, *61*
Rosenblum, B., 54, *61*
Rosengren, K. E., 169, 170, *183*
Rosenwald, G. C., 42, *61*
Roth, P., 54, *61*
Ruiz, M., 85, 93, 98, *106*
Rusbult, C. E., 165, *183*
Rutherford, P. K., 19, 30, *37*
Rychlak, J. F., 3, *15*

S

Sarbin, T., 43, *61*
Schafer, R., 43, *62*
Schutz, W. C., 142, 145, 147, *154*
Schwandt, T. R., 173, *183*
Seligman, M., 163, *183*
Sexton, L. G., 41, 42, 43, 44, 45, 50, *62*
Sharp, S. M., 86, *107*
Shaver, P. R., 118, *135*
Shotter, J., 52, *62*, 161, 176, *183*
Siegel, K., 93, 97, *107*
Simmel, G., 147, *154*
Simmons, J. L., 119, *135*
Smith, D., 165, *181*
Snavely, L., 163, *180*
Snow, B., 91, 104, *107*
Sorenson, T., 91, 104, *107*
Spencer, T., 97, 98, 101, 102, 103, 104,
107
Stamp, G. H., 48, *62*, 167, *183*
Staples, B. A., 47, *59*, 138, 143, 150,
152
Steil, J. M., 145, *154*
Stewart, J., 58, *62*
Strauss, A. J., 72, *81*
Sullivan, H. S., 143, 145, 147, *154*
Summit, R. C., 90, *108*
Suppe, F., 110, *135*

T

Tannen, D., 31, *38*
Taylor, D. A., 89, *105*, 123, 125, 130, *134*
Tedlock, B., 43, 53, 62,178, *181*
Tieu, T., 85, 87, 89, 90, 93, 94, 95, 96, 97, 98, 99, 100, 101, 102, 104, *106*
Tillman-Healy, L. M., 43, 53, 54, 58, *62*
Todorov, T., 66, 67, 71, 76, *81*
Trujillo, N., 116, 123, *136*, 168, *183*
Turner, E., 48, *62*
Turner, J. H., 2, *15*
Tyler, S., 45, *62*

V

VanLear, C. A., 104, *108*, 115, 116, 122, 123, 124, 125, 126, 127, 128, 129, 130, 132, *135*, *136*, 168, 174, 176, 177, 178, *183*
Verette, J., 165, *183*
Veroff, J., 144, *153*
Vinsel, A., 3, *15*, 64, *80*, 84, 90, *105*, 116, 121, 126, 127, 130, *134*, 137, 138, 146, 149, 150, *152*, *154*, 174, 177, *179*
Vodanovich, S. J., 168, *182*
Volosinov, V. N., 163, *182*

W

Waugh, J., 43, 45, *60*

Warner, R. M., 126, *136*,
Watt, J., 129, 132, *136*
Watzlawick, P., 28, *38*, 115, 116, 119, 121, 122, *136*
Weeks, G. R., 65, *81*, 159, *180*
Weinstein, A., 44, 52, 53, *62*
Wells, J. W., 85, 88, 93, 95, 103, 104, *108*
Weltman, K., 145, *154*
Werner, C. M., 47, 48, 51, 52, 54, *62*, 138, 139, 140, 141, 142, 143, 147, 149, 150, *152*, *153*, *154*, 164, 176, 177, *183*
West, J., 156, *182*
Whitehead, A. N., 123, *136*
Widenmann, S., 176, *180*
Wiemann, J. M., 144, 145, *154*, 167, *181*
Williams, K. J., 25, *38*
Williamson, R. N., 125, 126, *136*
Wilmot, W., 98, *106*
Wood, J. T., 24, *38*, 161, *183*
Wu, S., 118, *135*

Y

Yeats, W. B., 28, 29, *38*
Yerby, J., 47, 49, *62*

Z

Zebrowitz, L. A., 143, *154*
Zeitlow, P. H., 116, 122, 124, 125, 127, *136*

Subject Index

A

Abuse, sexual, 83, 84, 87, 90–91, 94, 96, 97, 102
Adolescence, 63, 73
Adulthood, 63
AIDS, *see* HIV
Affect, 143–144, 146, 147, 149, 151
Alienation, 6, 19, 33
Apathy/engagement, 27, 28, 29, 30, 31, 32, 33, 35–36
Attachment/loss, 42, 56, 148
Autonomy/connection, 6, 19, 20, 29, 30, 31, 33, 100, 101, 120, 138, 141, 142, 147, 157, 166–167

B

Both/and, 160, 173
and either/or, 78, 159–160, 173

C

Causes, 139
Centripetal/centrifugal, 14, 141, 157–158, 160–162, 166, 167, 177
Certainty/uncertainty, 7, 8, 18, 20, 26–27, 28, 29, 30, 31, 33, 35, 167–169
Change (*see also* Cycles), 3, 7–8, 12, 84, 103, 105, 156, 158–161
evolutionary, 18–19
facets of, 7–8, 86–91
linear and spiraling, 89–91
process and event, 87–88
and stability, 6

teleological and indeterminate, 88–89
trajectories of, 7, 129–133, 134
Childhood, 63, 72
Closeness, 165–167
and separation, 8
Coming out, 85, 87–91, 95–99, 100, 101, 102–103, 105
Communication, meaning of, 161
Communication boundary management theory, 92, 99
Contradiction, 3–6, 10–11, 12, 18–21, 48, 64–65, 72, 84–86, 99–103, 104, 105, 113, 120, 124, 156, 157, 158, 172
binary vs. multivocal, 4, 157, 159
facets of, 4–7
primary and secondary, 157–158
Culture, 138, 145–146, 164–165
professional and relational, 24–25, 27, 30–31, 33, 34
Cycles, 122, 123, 124, 125, 126, 127, 129, 130

D

Dialectics
contextual, 72
diological writings, 68–80
diologism and, 66, 84
fundamental, 142–146, 157–158
individual, 117–119, 120–121, 158
interpretive, 79

indigenous, 29, 30, 31, 33–36
meaning of, 2, 14, 23, 46–48,
    51–53, 64–65
metadialectics, 31–34
and narrative, 50–54
relational, 25, 34, 49, 57–59,
    78, 116, 117–123, 133,
    155, 158–61, 165, 176, 179
and transactionalism, 139–141
Dialogic complexity, 160–161
Disclosure
    and concealment, 83–105
    don't ask/ don't tell, 98–99
    self-disclosure, 9, 83, 86–105
    spiraling disclosure, 89–91,
        104
    strategies of, 93–99
Disintegration, 6, 7, 18, 20, 32, 33, 35
Dualism, 158–161, 165, 167–168

E

Eclecticism, principled, 14
Emotion, 118–121
Engagement, 59, 142–143, 146, 147,
    148, 149, 151
Encapsulation, 79
Evolutionary 18, 19
Expressive, 84, 85
Expression/restraint, 42, 120, 121, 122,
    124, 126

F

Family, 44
Friendship, 63–65, 68–74, 76–80

H

Helical model, 18, 20, 28, 31–33
Heteroglossia, 66–67
HIV and AIDS, 83, 84, 85, 87, 93, 94,
    96, 97, 98, 105
Homosexuality, 83–90, 93, 95–96, 97,
    98–104, 105

I

Independence and dependance, 5, 120

Information, control and management
    of, 92–94
Inquiry (*see also* Methods, Social Sci-
    ence)
    construction/discovery
        dialectic, 111–113
    dialectic, 141
    dialectical empiricism, 109
    dialogic, 14, 169–179
    logical positivism, 109, 110,
        113
    and metaphor, 113–114, 133
    pluralistic, 169–179
    radical empiricism, 51
    traditional, 110–111
    writing practices and
        narrative, 45, 49–50
Intertextuality, 2–3, 13–14, 67, 70,
    76–77

J

Jazz, 155–156, 162
Joint action, 53, 161

M

Metaphor, 113–117, 133, 156, 166
Methods (*see also* Inquiry, Social Sci-
    ence), 12–14, 103–104, 113–117
    dialogic, 175–179
    quantitative, 13, 110,
        114–117, 133
Monologism, 67, 158–161, 165,
    167–168, 173
Motion, 64, 65
Multivocality, 4, 71, 85–86, 120, 156,
    160, 162–163, 166, 168, 172

N

Narrative, personal, 9, 13, 17, 21–22,
    29, 35, 42–59, 63, 73–74, 77,
    104, 126, 176
    relationship, 25, 36
    exemplars, 54–57
    facets of, 43–45

O

Openness, 4, 6, 29, 30, 31, 33

and closedness, 11, 30, 31, 84,
    85, 86, 89, 90, 124, 126,
    130, 137, 138, 139, 146,
    149, 157, 160, 163, 174
Oblique/direct, 27, 28, 29, 31, 35

P

Praxis, 3, 9–10, 12, 64, 84, 91–99, 105,
    123, 156, 165
    patterns of, 123–126, 162–163
    and disclosure of stigma,
        93–99
Predictability/novelty, 29, 30, 31, 116,
    126–128, 129, 148, 157, 162–163
Privacy regulation, 42

R

Recursive, 18
Reflexivity, 43, 59
Regulation, 144–146, 149, 151
Relationship
    change, 148–149
    development, 8, 160–161
    emergence, 128–133
Resynthesis, 6, 7, 8, 18, 20, 32, 33, 34,
    35

S

Schismogenetic, 122

Security/alienation, 6, 7, 8, 28, 19–20,
    31, 35
Self-reflexivity, 43, 59
Simulacrum, 22
Social science (*see also* Inquiry, Methods), 42, 43, 44, 45–49, 49–54,
    58–59, 80,
Stability/change, 116, 127–128, 130,
    138, 148–149, 151, 164
Stigma, 83–99
Stories, *see* Narrative
Structural analysis, 22–23, 35
Subjectivity, 43, 54
Superaddressee, 162–163

T

Temporality (*see also* Change), 9–10,
    18, 47, 53, 129–133, 149,
    176–177
Totality, 3, 10–12, 64, 84, 99–103, 105,
    146–149, 150–151, 156, 163–165
Transactionalism, 139–141, 142, 144,
    146, 150, 151, 164

U

Uncertainty principle, 110
Utterance, 3, 9, 52, 66–67, 71–72, 76,
    104, 162